# Rose's
# Melting Pot

# ROSE'S MELTING POT

## A Cooking Tour of America's Ethnic Celebrations

### ROSE LEVY BERANBAUM

William Morrow and Company, Inc.
New York

Library of Congress Cataloging-in-Publication Data

Beranbaum, Rose Levy.
    Rose's melting pot / Rose Levy Beranbaum.
        p.      cm.
    ISBN 0-688-12261-2
    1. Cookery, International.    I. Title.
TX725.A1B377        1993
641.59—dc20                                      93-34110
                                                    CIP

Printed in the United States of America

First Edition

1  2  3  4  5  6  7  8  9  10

BOOK DESIGN BY CHARLOTTE STAUB

*To my brother, Michael,*
*my first and ever most appreciative*
*culinary audience*

# ACKNOWLEDGMENTS

The photographs for this book were produced in a joyful creative atmosphere, thanks to the creative genius and gentle spirit of its photographer, Amos Chan, and the unique abilities and dedication of a wonderful team:
Food Stylists: Rick Ellis, William Smith and Brett Kurzweil, Kevin Pavlina
Prop Stylists: Lanie Strahler

Special appreciation to:
Judith Sutton, copy editor
Terry Frishman and Gary Gluck of Creative Marketing, for heirloom props that add so much to enhance the beauty of food
Sachie Oba for her exquisite sushi accoutrements
Also to Rick Rodgers, who cheerfully tested all the recipes innumerable times, giving so much of himself to each one

And, as always, special love to Maria D. Guarnaschelli, who brought so many individual talents together to make this book what it is.

# CONTENTS

# INTRODUCTION

Food is my window on the world. While many people's first thoughts when traveling abroad are of museums and monuments, mine are of restaurants, food markets and kitchen supply stores. And the memories of my travels that I hold most dear are of special meals shared: Tandoori Chicken at Moti Mahal (Chicken Palace) in Delhi, bright green abalone liver at a sushi bar in Tokyo, goose with chestnuts at a mountaintop inn overlooking Limousin in the Corrèzes mountains, fresh black and white truffles presented on an antique scale in Bern, lamb chops with home-made current jelly at a friend's home in London, fresh porcini salad at another friend's home in Florence. These are a few among many culinary moments that have shaped my sensory awareness and appreciation for the diversity of flavors, textures and aromas. At times I am quite sure I remember every meal I've ever eaten and I am convinced that every bite I take is part of my continuing education. If this sounds like an excuse for gluttony, it is not (not entirely). It is, however, a passion and curiosity that gives both intellectual and physical pleasure and offers a splendid way in which to view and connect with the many cultures of the world.

Growing up in New York City (the ultimate melting pot) also enabled me to experience many different cuisines, to purchase ingredients necessary to re-create favorite ethnic recipes at home and to make them my own. After a while, I stopped viewing these recipes as "ethnic." They have simply become part of my repertoire. And, fortunately, most of the ingredients required to achieve the authentic flavor of the recipes in this book are now available in supermarkets throughout the country.

There is no feeling more rewarding than the process of providing delicious, nourishing home-cooked meals for family and friends and at the same time introducing them to new flavors and perhaps a glimpse of another culture. It is a tradition and a joy that I feel privileged to be able to cast back on the waters of this wonderful world.

# NOTE REGARDING WEIGHTS AND MEASURES

As per my usual style, I have offered both volume measure and ounces and grams for ingredients where weighing would be desirable or in any way helpful. When buying produce or canned goods, for example, it is helpful to know the weight as this is how it is sold. Although most people, including myself, will not weigh 3 grams of parsley, the weight is useful for caterers who may want to make large multiples of the recipe.

I have rounded off the ounces to the nearest third of an ounce and the grams usually to the nearest whole number; therefore, *do not expect the mathematics of the avoirdupois system to correlate exactly with the metric system.* If you have a scale that does not have a digital readout, simply round off the ounces and grams to the nearest readable number. Although the weights are as precise as I could make them, in most instances, when cooking, they can be interpreted with far more flexibility than when measuring or weighing ingredients for baking.

## NOTE REGARDING PLASTIC WRAP

My preferred plastic wrap for rolling pie dough and for wrapping things when they need to be airtight is Saran Wrap because it is very smooth (lies flat and does not get caught up in the dough) and is absolutely airtight. Many other wraps intentionally have microscopic "breathing" holes, designed to protect food items such as fruits and vegetables, which would mold if stored airtight.

NOTE REGARDING
SALT

I find that people's taste for salt varies widely and that mine falls in the middle range. Because salt flavors food more evenly when it is added early in the cooking process rather than added all at once at the very end, I offer a suggested amount rather than specify "season to taste." After trying one of my recipes, you will gain a sense of how my middle-range taste compares with yours and you can adjust all the other recipes accordingly if you like.

I prefer to use unsalted broth and butter because doing so enables me to use as much of the ingredient as I want without adding more salt. A cup of salted canned broth, for example, contains almost a teaspoon of salt.

I usually use kosher salt rather than table salt to sprinkle on roasts because it distributes more evenly. There is no difference in flavor because kosher and table salt both come from exactly the same source. The only difference in flavor occurs in instances where the salt does not dissolve fully as, for example, in salads. The kosher salt, which is coarser, will remain in granules and therefore be perceived differently on the tongue.

If you would like to use kosher salt for these recipes, use the same amount *if using Morton brand. If using Diamond brand,* you will need 1¾ times the volume amount. (The weight is the same.)

Fine sea salt has a purer, almost "sweeter" flavor and can be used interchangeably by weight (or to taste). The volume, however, will vary from brand to brand.

 GENERAL POINTERS
FOR SUCCESS

- Whenever possible, taste as you cook and adjust the seasonings as necessary toward the end of cooking.
- Start checking roasts as soon as they appear cooked, well before the anticipated time, to gauge their progress and avoid overcooking.
- Choose the freshest seasonal ingredients.
- Cook recipes with love.

NOTE REGARDING WEIGHTS AND MEASURES

# SOUPS AND APPETIZERS

# FRESH SHIITAKE MUSHROOM SOUP

Many years ago, when I worked at *Ladies' Home Journal*, one of the first recipes I developed was a mushroom soup very similar to this one. It is probably the best remembered of all my recipes from that time. I still love it, but I am now offering this improved version using fresh shiitakes. They offer a deep, earthy flavor.

This soup is a perfect cool-weather first course to be followed by a hearty roast of beef, pork or chicken. It is also lovely as part of a casual ski weekend supper of soup and sandwiches.

| INGREDIENTS | MEASURE | WEIGHT | |
| --- | --- | --- | --- |
| | *volume* | *ounces* | *grams* |
| dried porcini mushrooms | | 1 ounce | 28 grams |
| dry vermouth, heated | ¼ liquid cup | | |
| fresh shiitake mushrooms, stemmed | | 20 ounces | 567 grams |
| unsalted butter | 6 tablespoons | 3 ounces | 85 grams |
| 2 medium onions, chopped | 2 cups | 9 ounces | 255 grams |
| sugar | ½ teaspoon | | |
| all-purpose flour | ¼ cup (measured by dip and sweep method) | 1.25 ounces | 36 grams |
| water | 1 liquid cup | | |
| low-salt chicken broth, preferably College Inn, *or* 4 cubes Glace de Volaille (page 209), dissolved in 2¾ cups of boiling water with ¾ teaspoon of salt | 2¾ liquid cups (1 ½ 13.75-ounce cans) | 21.5 ounces | 612 grams |
| salt | 1 teaspoon | | 6.7 grams |
| black pepper, freshly ground | ¼ teaspoon | | |

MAKES: about 7 cups as an
  appetizer
SERVES: 6

Quickly rinse the dried porcini mushrooms under cold water to remove any grit. Place them in the hot vermouth and allow them to stand, covered, for at least 30 minutes, until softened. Lift out the mushrooms and chop them. Strain the vermouth through a cheesecloth-lined strainer and set both the mushrooms and vermouth aside, covered.

*(continued)*

Slice one third of the shiitakes and finely chop the rest.

In a large saucepot, melt the butter. Add the onions and sugar and sauté over medium heat, stirring often, for about 15 minutes or until golden. Add all the mushrooms and sauté for 5 minutes, stirring often. Stir in the flour until smooth and cook for 2 minutes, stirring constantly. Pour in the water and the reserved vermouth and stir until smooth. Add the broth, salt and pepper and heat to boiling, stirring constantly. Reduce the heat and simmer, uncovered, 10 minutes.

To serve, ladle into cups.

KEEPS: 3 days refrigerated, 3 months frozen. If planning to store, cool as quickly as possible by placing the saucepot in a sink, surrounding it with ice water and stirring until cool.

TO REHEAT: Bring the soup to a boil and simmer, uncovered, for 10 minutes. If the soup has thickened, add water until the desired consistency is reached.

# THE TRELLIS FRENCH ROASTED GARLIC SOUP

When I first met Marcel Desaulniers, chef/owner of The Trellis Restaurant in Williamsburg, Virginia, I was researching an article for *The New York Times* on foraging. While every other restaurateur I had called throughout the country had immediately testified as to how he did indeed use wild edibles, Marcel's off-the-wall response was, "What do you think—because I'm down here in Williamsburg I'm digging in the dirt for my food?" It was love at first cryptic remark. Since that time, we have shared many more laughs in addition to many memorable meals. Though I am not a big soup eater, I make an exception at The Trellis because Marcel's soups are masterfully robust, complex and deeply satisfying. He suggests serving this soup as a main course with a grilled herbed chicken breast sliced and placed on the top, but as an appetizer, it is splendid on its own.

4

| INGREDIENTS | MEASURE | WEIGHT | |
| --- | --- | --- | --- |
| | volume | ounces/pounds | grams |
| heavy cream | 4 liquid cups | | |
| 1 head of garlic, separated into cloves (about 8 to 10) | | 2.66 ounces | 75 grams |
| olive oil | a sprinkling | | |
| salt | a sprinkling + ¼ teaspoon | | |
| black pepper, freshly ground | a few grindings | | |
| unsalted butter | 1 tablespoon | 0.50 ounce | 14 grams |
| water | 2 tablespoons | | |
| 4 stalks celery, chopped | 2 cups | 8 ounces | 227 grams |
| 2 medium leeks (white part only), chopped | 1 cup | 4 ounces | 113 grams |
| 1 medium onion, chopped | 1 cup | 4.5 ounces | 128 grams |
| white pepper | ⅛ teaspoon | | |
| low-salt chicken broth, preferably College Inn, or 4 cubes Glace de Volaille (page 209), dissolved in 4 cups of boiling water with 1 teaspoon of salt | 4 liquid cups (2⅓ 13.75-ounce cans) | 32 ounces | 907 grams |
| russet potatoes, peeled, cut into 1-inch cubes and soaked in cold water | 4 cups | 2 pounds | 907 grams |

PREHEAT THE OVEN TO: 250°F.
BAKING TIME: 1 hour
SERVES: 8 as an appetizer, 4 as a main course

*Preheat the oven to 250°F.*

In a 2½-quart saucepan over medium heat, bring the heavy cream to a simmer. Keep a metal ladle in the saucepan and occasionally stir the cream so that it does not foam over the sides of the pot. Lower the heat if necessary so that the cream is barely simmering. Simmer until reduced by half, about 1½ hours.

Meanwhile, place the garlic cloves on a baking sheet. Sprinkle them with olive oil and season with a sprinkling of salt and the black pepper. Place the baking sheet in the preheated oven and roast the garlic until the cloves are soft, about 1 hour. Remove the baking sheet from the oven and cool slightly. Trim and peel the cloves. Set aside.

In a large saucepan, over medium-high heat, heat the butter and water. When hot, add the chopped celery, leeks

*(continued)*

and onion. Sprinkle with the ¼ teaspoon of salt and the white pepper and cook, stirring often to prevent browning, for 6 minutes. Add the peeled roasted garlic cloves and cook for about 4 minutes, until the vegetables are very soft but not browned. Add the chicken stock, then drain the potatoes, rinse with cold water and add to the stock. Bring to a boil, and lower the heat. Cover partially and simmer for 30 minutes or until the potatoes are very soft.

Remove the soup from the heat and purée it in batches in a food processor fitted with a metal blade. Strain it through a coarse sieve or wire strainer into the rinsed-out saucepan. Add the reduced cream and turn on the heat to low. Bring the soup to a simmer and allow it to simmer for 10 minutes, stirring occasionally. Adjust the seasonings.

To serve, ladle into cups.

# AVOCADO WITH SOY WASABI

This simple recipe, from my friend Hiroko, is an inspired combination of East and West. Wasabi is Japanese horseradish powder, which is made into a paste and served in sushi bars to dissolve in soy sauce as a pungent dipping sauce. If you want to add a little complexity, add chunks of cooked crabmeat and sprinkle it with roasted sesame seeds and you will have the makings of the famous California hand roll, without the rice.

I adore wasabi and am always especially thrilled when I discover a restaurant that has the freshly grated wasabi available. This is fairly commonplace in Japan but a rare event in America. The powder also makes a deliciously potent sauce. A little goes a long way as too much can cause an unpleasant burning, so start with just a small amount and add more as desired.

This is the perfect first course for a Japanese Chirashi Sushi dinner (page 101).

| INGREDIENTS | MEASURE | WEIGHT | |
| --- | --- | --- | --- |
| | *volume* | *ounces* | *grams* |
| 2 ripe avocados (preferably Haas from California) | | 6.75 ounces | 190 grams |
| lemon juice, freshly squeezed | 1 tablespoon | | |
| wasabi powder* | 1 tablespoon | | 6.5 grams |
| warm water | 2 teaspoons | | |
| soy sauce | ¾ liquid cup | | |

SERVES: 6 as an appetizer

Shortly before serving, to avoid discoloration, cut the avocados in half and remove the pit from each one by whacking the pit with the sharp blade of a chef's knife and lifting it out. Remove the avocados from the skin (specialty stores have an inexpensive little device that is ideal for this purpose). Place the avocado halves cut side down on a cutting board and slice crosswise. Drizzle with the

*Available at Eastern food stores or by mail order from Katagiri & Company, 224 East 59th Street, New York, New York 10022 (212-755-3566). The powder does not keep indefinitely, as it loses pungency if stored too long.

lemon juice. Arrange the avocado slices in a fan on serving plates and provide small saucers in which to pour the soy sauce.

Make the wasabi soy sauce as close to serving time as possible, as it loses flavor rapidly. Place the wasabi powder in a small bowl and stir in the warm water. The wasabi will be transformed into a soft smooth paste, best described (by Elizabeth Andoh in *At Home with Japanese Cooking*) as earlobe texture. (You will have 2¼ teaspoons of the paste.) Mold it with your fingers into 6 small balls. Pour 2 tablespoons of soy sauce into each small saucer and float a wasabi ball in each saucer. The wasabi should be stirred into the soy sauce with chopsticks before dipping the avocado slices.

# CAVIAR PESTO SHELLS

These delectable pasta shells filled with creamy Italian pesto and adorned by a Japanese-inspired sushi-like gleam of salmon eggs are the creation of Carlo Middione of Vivande in San Francisco. I first tasted this recipe when Carlo prepared it for a New York pasta press party. I made them for him and his wife, Elizabeth, when his book *The Cooking of Southern Italy* won the award for best cookbook in the international category of the Seagrams/International Association of Cooking Professionals. I had planned the celebration party even before I knew for sure that Carlo had won. This recipe makes a great party appetizer because it has visual appeal, elegance and can be prepared ahead.

*(continued)*

| INGREDIENTS | MEASURE<br>*volume* | WEIGHT<br>*ounces* | *grams* |
|---|---|---|---|
| fresh basil leaves | ½ cup, packed<br>(+ extra for garnish,<br>optional) | 1 ounce | 28 grams |
| Parmesan cheese, freshly grated | 2 tablespoons | 0.25 ounce | 7 grams |
| pignoli (pine nuts) | 1 tablespoon | 0.5 ounce | 11 grams |
| cream cheese, softened | 1 8-ounce package | 8 ounces | 227 grams |
| salt | 1 teaspoon | | 6.7 grams |
| boiling water | 1 quart | | |
| large macaroni shells* | 1½ cups | 3 ounces | 85 grams |
| red salmon caviar | 2 tablespoons | 1 ounce | 28 grams |

MAKES: about 36 shells
SERVES: 8 as an appetizer

EQUIPMENT: Pastry bag and
   number 5 star tip or a small
   spoon

In a food processor or blender, process the basil, Parmesan cheese and nuts until very finely chopped, stopping and scraping the container several times with a rubber spatula if necessary. Add the cream cheese to the pesto mixture. Process until well mixed, scraping the container with the spatula several times.

Add the salt to the boiling water and then slowly add the pasta so that the water continues to boil. Cook, uncovered, stirring occasionally, until just tender. Drain in a colander. Rinse under cold water and drain again. Pat dry.

Spoon the cheese mixture into a pastry bag (or heavy-duty zip-seal bag with one corner cut off) fitted with a large star tip (number 5, almost ½-inch diameter). Using your fingers to spread open the shells, pipe about 1 teaspoon of the mixture into each shell. Alternatively, you may spoon the mixture into each shell.

Arrange the shells on a serving plate, and spoon a few grains of caviar on top of the pesto-cheese mixture in each shell to garnish. Garnish the plate with fresh basil leaves if desired. Serve at once, or refrigerate for up to 30 minutes before serving.

*Do not use jumbo: The uncooked shells should measure ¾ inch in diameter.

# GRILLED PORTOBELLO MUSHROOMS

Restaurateur Richard Perry has been a respected member of the food community for many years. His newest restaurant, Orchids, in Cincinnati, Ohio, is spectacular and reflects his vast experience and expertise. The atmosphere offers both the charm of a small romantic place and, at the same time, the elegance and grandeur of a large one. I have eaten grilled portobellos in many restaurants, but never ones like these. The dark, meaty mushrooms are exceptionally moist and flavorful. Richard says the secrets are the small amount of anchovy paste and the Madeira in the marinade. This Italian-inspired marinade would also be great for lamb.

Serve this flavorful dish as the first course of a hearty meal with Rare Prime Ribs of Beef (page 158) or Pork Loin with Prunes and Apples (page 149). It is ideal because though full-flavored, it is also light.

| INGREDIENTS | MEASURE _volume_ | WEIGHT _ounces/pounds_ | _grams_ |
|---|---|---|---|
| 6 4-inch portobello mushrooms or 12 2¾-inch shiitake mushrooms* | | ¾ to 1 pound | 340 to 425 grams |
| extra virgin olive oil | 1 liquid cup | | |
| fresh rosemary, chopped | ¼ cup | 0.50 ounce | 12 grams |
| balsamic vinegar | ¼ liquid cup | | |
| 2 large cloves of garlic, minced | 1 tablespoon | 0.35 ounce | 10 grams |
| shallot, minced | 1 teaspoon | | 3 grams |
| Madeira wine | ¼ liquid cup | | |
| salt | 1 tablespoon | 0.75 ounce | 20 grams |
| black pepper, freshly ground | 1 teaspoon | | |
| unsalted butter, softened | 2 tablespoons | 1 ounce | 28 grams |
| anchovy paste | ¾ teaspoon | | |
| 6 slices of Italian bread (preferably from a round country loaf), toasted | | | |
| 1 large clove of garlic, halved | | | 6 grams |
| 6 large leaves fresh basil | | | |

*Portobellos are thicker and meatier with a deeper flavor, but shiitakes are also excellent.

SERVES: 6 as an appetizer

Run the tops of the mushrooms under cold water to remove any dirt. Rinse the gill sides quickly, as they will absorb water. With a small sharp knife, trim off the stems and discard them. Set the caps on paper towels to drain well.

In a large shallow nonreactive bowl, place the oil, rosemary, vinegar, minced garlic, shallot, Madeira, salt and pepper and stir to combine. Add the mushrooms, gill sides down, and allow them to marinate for 30 minutes, turning once to bathe them well in the marinade.

In the meantime, whisk together the softened butter and anchovy paste and set aside in a warm spot. Rub each piece of toast with the cut side of the garlic. Set them on serving plates. Stack the basil leaves on top of each other and slice them into chiffonade (long thin strips). Sprinkle the basil evenly over the toast.

Remove the mushrooms from the marinade, reserving the marinade. Grill or broil them for 5 to 10 minutes, turning once, or until tender when pierced with a skewer, brushing once or twice with the marinade. Portobellos are thicker than shiitakes and will take longer to cook through.

Arrange the mushrooms on top of the toast and spoon a little of the marinade over the mushrooms to moisten them. Brush or dab with the anchovy butter.

# FRIED SICILIAN ARTICHOKES

This recipe comes from a dear friend who grew up in Sicily. Angelica Pulverenti Hirshout is a professional chef and one of those rare people who is an instinctive and spontaneous cook. You could give her three ingredients and she would turn them into something magical. She also serves up her dishes with a disposition so sweet and loving it somehow becomes part of the recipe.

These deep-fried baby artichokes are encased in an aromatic, flavorful batter that forms a completely crisp, fine coating, keeping the artichokes moist within. They make a delicious appetizer either warm or at room temperature, or serve them as part of a larger antipasto, which could include Caviar Pesto Shells (page 9) and Grilled Portobello Mushrooms (page 12). I also enjoy them as a first course preceding Classic Chicken Cacciatore Piccante (page 135) and fried Polenta (page 173).

| INGREDIENTS | MEASURE | WEIGHT | |
| --- | --- | --- | --- |
| | *volume* | *ounces* | *grams* |
| 12 baby artichokes (about 1¾ inches across at the base) | | 2 to 3 ounces each | 56 to 85 grams each |
| salt | 1¼ teaspoons, divided | | |
| water | 1 liquid cup | | |
| all-purpose flour | 1 cup (measured by dip and sweep method) | 5 ounces | 144 grams |
| 2 medium cloves of garlic, finely minced | 1 tablespoon | 0.35 ounce | 10 grams |
| black pepper, freshly ground | a few grindings | | |
| sugar | a pinch | | |
| fresh rosemary, minced* | ½ teaspoon | | |
| fresh thyme, minced† | 1 teaspoon | | |
| pure olive oil for frying or a combination of olive oil and vegetable oil | 1 quart | | |
| 1 lemon, quartered | | | |

*Or ¼ teaspoon dried.
†Or ½ teaspoon dried.

Place the artichokes in a large saucepan, and add enough boiling water to cover them by about 2 inches. Sprinkle them with ¼ teaspoon of the salt and cover them with a clean wet towel to keep them submerged. Set the pan over high heat and boil rapidly for 7 to 10 minutes or until almost tender when pierced with a skewer. Remove the smaller ones as soon as they test done (the chokes will continue cooking in the oil so must be tender/firm and not at all overcooked). Drain immediately and rinse under cold water.

When the artichokes are cool enough to handle, remove the tough outer leaves until you reach the tender pale green leaves that are not fibrous. Trim a little from the bottom of the stems and trim off the pointed ends. Cut each artichoke lengthwise into halves (quarters if using larger ones). Remove any hairy chokes if necessary.

Place the water in a small bowl. Whisk in the flour, adding water if necessary to obtain a smooth paste the consistency of sour cream. Whisk in the garlic, the remaining 1 teaspoon of salt, the pepper, sugar, rosemary and thyme.

Twenty minutes before cooking, start heating the oil on a low flame until it reaches 375°F.

Dip each artichoke piece into the batter, holding it by the end of the stem, and coat it well. Carefully place it in the hot oil and fry for about 2 minutes or until golden brown. If the oil is not deep enough to cover the chokes, turn them to brown them evenly. Drain on paper towels and serve warm or at room temperature, lightly sprinkled with fresh lemon juice.

UNDERSTANDING

Olive oil has the most delicious flavor for frying the chokes. Do not use extra virgin oil, however, as its smoking point is too low and it could catch fire.

# DOLMADAKIA (Stuffed Grape Leaves)

Grape leaves are one of my favorite Greek dishes. Stuffed with firm rice, flavored with garlic, dill, lemon and olive oil, sweetened with the unusual addition of currants and pistachio nuts, they are irresistible. They are often served with plain yogurt as an accompaniment, but I so adore them I prefer to eat them "neat."

This savory appetizer is easy to make but a little time-consuming due to the wrapping process. It is well worth making, however, because the grape leaves contribute a delicious, slightly briny taste—but if you don't wish to roll little bundles, simply use the filling as a fabulous stuffing for chicken or cornish game hens.

| INGREDIENTS *Filling* | MEASURE *volume* | WEIGHT *ounces* | *grams* |
|---|---|---|---|
| grape leaves | 1 16-ounce jar (about 40 leaves) | 16 ounces | 454 grams |
| dry white vermouth | ¼ liquid cup | | |
| dried currants | ¼ cup | 1.5 ounces | 43 grams |
| extra virgin olive oil | 2 tablespoons | | |
| 1 bunch (about 7) green onions (white part only), finely chopped | ½ cup | 1.75 ounces | 50 grams |
| garlic, minced | 1 teaspoon | | 3 grams |
| fresh parsley, preferably flat-leafed, finely chopped | 1 tablespoon | | 4 grams |
| long-grain rice (preferably Uncle Ben's) | 1 cup | 6.75 ounces | 192 grams |
| fresh dill, finely chopped | 1 tablespoon | | 4 grams |
| pistachio nuts, shelled and coarsely chopped | ½ cup | 2 ounces | 57 grams |
| salt | 1 teaspoon | 0.25 ounce | 6.7 grams |
| sugar | 1 teaspoon | | 4 grams |
| black pepper, freshly ground | ½ teaspoon | | |
| boiling water | 1 liquid cup | | |
| 2 large cloves of garlic, slivered | 1 tablespoon | 0.25 ounce | 7 grams |

## BROTH

| | | | |
|---|---|---|---|
| beef broth, preferably College Inn, or Glace de Viande (page 205)* | 1 ¾ liquid cups (1 14.5-ounce can) | 14.5 ounces | 411 grams |
| sugar | 2 teaspoons | 0.25 ounce | 8 grams |
| olive oil | ¾ liquid cup | | |
| lemon juice, freshly squeezed | ¼ liquid cup | | |
| salt | ½ teaspoon† | 0.25 ounce | 6.7 grams |

| | |
|---|---|
| black pepper, freshly ground | a few grindings |
| thin lemon half-slices, for garnish | |
| OPTIONAL: plain yogurt, garnished with a few sprigs of fresh dill, for accompaniment | |

MAKES: 30–36 grape leaves
SERVES: 8 as an appetizer

EQUIPMENT: large casserole with a tight-fitting lid

Drain the grape leaves, unroll them and place them in a saucepan with boiling water to cover. Simmer for 2 minutes and drain. Rinse under cold water and carefully separate the leaves. There are usually about 30 perfect leaves and 10 torn ones in a jar; set aside the torn leaves to line the casserole. Pat the leaves dry and place on paper towels in a single layer to drain.

Heat the vermouth until very hot but not boiling and pour it over the currants. Cover with plastic wrap and allow to sit for at least 30 minutes.

In a medium saucepan, heat the olive oil and sauté the green onions over low heat for 2 minutes, stirring often, or until wilted. Add the minced garlic and parsley and sauté 30 seconds. Add the rice, dill, pistachio nuts, currants with the vermouth, salt, sugar, pepper and the 1 cup of boiling water. Simmer over low heat, covered, about 10 minutes or until the liquid is absorbed. Remove from the heat, uncover and allow to cool.‡

TO STUFF THE LEAVES: Place each leaf shiny side down (raised veins up) and put 1 tablespoon of filling in the center. Fold the base of the leaf over the stuffing, then

*If using homemade Glace de Viande (page 205), use 1 cube, dissolved in the 1 cup of boiling water. If necessary, simmer, stirring often, to dissolve the glace; if some of the water boils away during this process, add enough to equal 1 cup.
†If using the unsalted homemade broth, add only ⅛ teaspoon salt.
‡This is enough filling for 40 grape leaves. Any leftover may be frozen.

(continued)

fold the sides over, tucking the edges in snugly. Roll up each leaf, and leave the tip of the leaf beneath to prevent unrolling.

Line the casserole with some of the reserved torn leaves, saving 2 or 3 for the top. Place the filled grape leaves snugly in the casserole. Scatter the slivered garlic on top.

PREPARE THE BROTH: If using canned broth, bring it to a boil and reduce it to 1 cup. In a 4-cup heat-proof measure or bowl, combine the broth ingredients and stir well to blend them. Pour the broth over the grape leaves in the casserole and cover with the reserved leaves. Place a small heavy plate or pot lid (such as the glass lid from a double boiler) directly on top of the leaves to weight them down and prevent them from bobbing about and losing their filling as they simmer.

Cover the casserole and simmer over low heat for 45 minutes. Remove the casserole from the heat and allow the grape leaves to cool in the broth, covered. (Most of the broth will be absorbed into the grape leaves.)

To serve, drain well and arrange in a bowl with thin half-slices of lemon for garnish. If desired, accompany with a bowl of yogurt garnished with a few sprigs of dill.

STORE: Refrigerated (tightly covered) or frozen. Flavor improves on standing. To freeze, place filled uncooked or cooked grape leaves on a cookie sheet and freeze until frozen. Transfer to an airtight container.

KEEPS: 1 week refrigerated, 3 months frozen.

 POINTERS FOR SUCCESS

• These stuffed grape leaves are more "sweet" than the usual because I enjoy the contrast of the brininess against the sweet. If you prefer less sweetness, try reducing the sugar in the broth to 1 teaspoon.
• The stuffed grape leaves dry out if not kept well covered.

# COLD GARLICKY MEDITERRANEAN MUSSELS

This heady combination of sea and land with its briny mussels and herby, garlicky vinaigrette is Francine Pascal's signature hors d'oeuvre. In fact, she makes dozens of these for her annual Christmas party. Francine has a home on the French Riviera, which I'm sure is where the inspiration came from for this marvelous dish. The mussels need to be cooked a day or two ahead and marinated for the flavors to blend and the garlic and shallots to lose some of their sharp edge.

| INGREDIENTS | MEASURE volume | WEIGHT ounces/pounds | grams |
|---|---|---|---|
| mussels | | 2 pounds | 907 grams |
| unsalted butter | 1 tablespoon | 0.5 ounce | 14 grams |
| white onion, minced | ⅓ cup | 1.5 ounces | 40 grams |
| 1 medium clove of garlic, minced | 1 teaspoon, divided | | 3 grams |
| dry white vermouth | ½ liquid cup | | |
| fresh parsley, preferably flat-leafed | ¼ cup, tightly packed, divided | | 10 grams |
| fresh dill, stems removed | ¼ cup, loosely packed | | 8 grams |
| ½ shallot, minced | 1 teaspoon | | 3 grams |
| salt | a pinch | | |
| herbes de Provence* | ¼ teaspoon | | |
| Dijon mustard | 1 teaspoon | | 6 grams |
| red wine vinegar | 1 teaspoon | | |
| balsamic vinegar | ½ teaspoon | | |
| (reserved mussel broth) | (1 teaspoon) | | |
| Tabasco sauce | a splash | | |
| black pepper, freshly ground | 4 grindings | | |
| sugar | 2 pinches | | |
| extra virgin olive oil, at room temperature | 3 tablespoons | | |
| heavy cream, at room temperature | 2 tablespoons | | |

*A combination of regional herbs such as thyme, sage, rosemary and lavender, available in specialty food stores and some supermarkets.

*(continued)*

MAKE AHEAD: at least 1 or up to
   2 days
MAKES: about 30 hors d'oeuvres
SERVES: 6 as an appetizer

Rinse and scrub the mussels, but don't beard them until right before cooking.

In a large noncorrosive saucepan, over medium heat, melt the butter. When bubbling, sauté the onion and ½ teaspoon of the garlic until translucent, about 2 minutes. Add the vermouth and about 1 tablespoon of the parsley, and then the mussels. Steam, covered, about 5 minutes or just until the mussels open, stirring once or twice and removing them to a large bowl one at a time as they open, using tongs to drain any liquid back into the pot. Reserve 1 teaspoon of the broth.

When the mussels are cool enough to handle, remove the upper shells and pull the mussels out of the shells. Save the most attractive half of each shell and, if necessary, remove the connective muscle attached to the shell. Cover the mussels so that they stay moist and plump.

On a chopping board, combine the remaining garlic and the shallot, sprinkle with the salt and mince as finely as possible. If desired, chop the remaining parsley and the dill in a food processor. Alternatively, add it to the garlic and shallot and chop until finely minced.

In a medium bowl, place the garlic, and parsley mixture. Add the herbes de Provence, mustard, vinegars, reserved mussel broth, Tabasco, pepper and sugar. Whisk to combine. Gradually whisk in the oil and then the cream. Stir this mixture into the mussels, and cover tightly, preferably with Saran brand plastic wrap, which is absolutely airtight. Refrigerate for at least 1 or up to 2 days.

Place a mussel, coated with the herb mixture, in each shell and arrange on serving platters. Cover tightly with plastic wrap and refrigerate until 30 minutes before serving.

POINTERS
FOR SUCCESS

• Make the vinaigrette with very fresh garlic and mince it by hand.

In the past, it was necessary to soak mussels in salt water or in water with a little cornmeal sprinkled on the top to rid them of their sand. Although this technique was successful, it also resulted in some loss of flavor. Fortunately, mussels these days are cultivated in less sandy areas, so presoaking them is not usually necessary.

Mincing the garlic and shallot by hand results in the purest flavor. Definitive studies have proved that the oil in garlic changes flavor according to the manner in which it is smashed or cut. Adding salt when you mince the garlic and shallot causes them to soften, making it easier to mince them finely.

Having the oil at room temperature helps it to emulsify. The cream stabilizes the emulsion, keeping it from separating.

# PERFECT PITCHA (pehCHA) (Calf's Foot Jelly)

These translucent jellied rectangles contain small morsels of meat and tender cartilage brightened with little flecks of fresh parsley and a liberal scattering of fresh garlic, blanched briefly to tame its sharp bite. The gelatin is entirely natural, produced from the calf's foot itself during the slow simmering.

The only tedious part of this recipe for me used to be removing and chopping the sticky meat from the bones. The Cuisinart, however, reduces the chopping part of this process to mere seconds. And it also makes grating the tangy fresh horseradish accompaniment a tearless task!

The quality of jellied stickiness that certain foods have is something that people either adore or abhor. But I have never understood why some people who find *oeuf en gelée* (egg in aspic) perfectly acceptable, in fact elegant, turn up their noses at calf's foot jelly. Perhaps if it were named *pied de veau en gelée*. . . . But in a Jewish deli, this classic appetizer is called plain *pitcha*. To my ear, it is an endearing name for a truly ethnic delicacy, a sort of Slavic/Jewish soul food, and I am including this recipe because for those like myself and Elliott who adore it, a refined homemade version with crystal-clear jelly and gently cooked garlic is

*(continued)*

a rare treat. In fact, I am sure I will have several converts among the garlic lovers, not to mention health food eaters! This is the first recipe I made for Elliott that he pronounced "perfect," thus its name.

I enjoy serving *pitcha* as part of a large ethnic buffet that includes Authentic Russian Pumpernickel Bread (page 51), No-Compromise Old-Country Chopped Liver (page 28), Jewish Deli Smoked Tongue (page 156) and The Very Best Luchshon Kugel (page 184).

| INGREDIENTS | MEASURE *volume* | WEIGHT *ounces/pounds* | *grams/kilograms* |
|---|---|---|---|
| 2 to 3 calf's feet, each cut into 6 pieces | | 3 pounds | 1 kilogram/ 360 grams |
| water | 3 quarts | | |
| 2 large onions, unpeeled, cut into eighths | | 1 pound | 454 grams |
| 3 large cloves of garlic unpeeled, cut in half | | 0.75 ounce | 21 grams |
| salt (uniodized) | 1 tablespoon | 0.75 ounce | 20 grams |
| black pepper, freshly ground fine | 1 ½ teaspoons, divided | | 4 grams |
| 2 egg whites and the crushed eggshells | | | |
| 1 large head of garlic (about 8 to 10 cloves), finely minced | ½ cup | 3 ounces | 85 grams |
| fresh parsley, preferably curly, finely chopped | ½ cup | 1 ounce | 32 grams |
| dried thyme | 1 teaspoon | | |
| OPTIONAL: freshly grated horseradish, for accompaniment | | | |

MAKE AHEAD: several hours
MAKES: about 64 2-inch by 1-inch cubes
SERVES: 16 as an appetizer (recipe can be halved)

EQUIPMENT: large stockpot (10 quarts), large fine strainer, cheesecloth, 2 medium rectangular Pyrex baking dishes (11 inches by 7 inches by 2 inches) or 1 large one (15 inches by 10 inches by 2 inches)

Place the calf's feet in a colander and slowly pour boiling water over them, turning to scald all the pieces. Using the back of a paring knife, scrape them well to remove any surface debris, then scrub them with a stiff brush.

Place the cleaned calf's feet in the stockpot and add the water. Turn on the heat to high and bring the water to a boil. Reduce the heat to medium and simmer for 15 minutes, skimming off any scum that rises to the surface two or three times. Add the onions, halved garlic cloves, salt and ½ teaspoon of the pepper, reduce the heat to low and simmer, covered, for about 4 hours, or until the meat easily separates from the bone.

Use a slotted skimmer or spoon to remove the bones and vegetables to a cheesecloth-lined strainer suspended over a large bowl. Press them to remove as much liquid as possible. Discard the vegetables and set the bones and meat aside to cool.

Pour all the cooking liquid through the strainer. Let stand 5 minutes, then skim the fat off the top. Wash the stockpot and return the strained, skimmed liquid to it. Add the egg whites and crushed eggshells and whisk until foaming. Bring to a simmer, then simmer for about 3 minutes, carefully ladling the broth through the coagulated egg white to clarify it, without breaking up the egg white. Strain the broth through clean cheesecloth into a large bowl and measure it. If you have less than 8 cups, add water as necessary, return the liquid to the rinsed stockpot and bring it to a boil. If you have more, return it to the rinsed stockpot and, over high heat, reduce the liquid to 8 cups. Taste for salt. The broth should be a little overly salty as on chilling the saltiness will diminish. Add the garlic and boil for 3 minutes. Remove the stockpot from the heat.

Remove as much meat and soft gristle from the bones as possible. Chop it coarsely, using a food processor or a large chef's knife sprayed with nonstick vegetable spray. Sprinkle evenly with the remaining 1 teaspoon of pepper, the chopped parsley and thyme. Mix well so the seasonings are very evenly distributed through the meat.

Spread the meat evenly over the bottom of the 2 rectangular dishes or 1 large dish. Pour the broth over. Cover tightly with plastic wrap (preferably Saran brand) and chill for several hours, until set. Cut into cubes about 2 inches by 1 inch.

SERVE: Chilled. Pass freshly grated horseradish if desired.

KEEPS: Up to 1 week refrigerated. *Pitcha* can be frozen for up to 2 months but needs to be reheated and allowed to refirm, or the texture of the jelly will not be smooth.

*(continued)*

• Use calf's feet. Larger cow's feet will not have sufficient gelatin to set the mixture.

Uniodized salt is used for *clarity* of the aspic. Iodized salt would make it cloudy.

# GRIBONYES (GRIBonyehz)

When I was a child, I preferred these crunchy flavorful fried bits of chicken skin to candy. My grandmother made them every Friday night from the neck skin and other pieces of skin from the chicken. But I was never allowed more than two as Grandma thought them difficult for a child to digest. The rest of the gribonyes went to my father, who, she claimed, had an iron stomach.

One of the first things I cooked when I began living on my own was gribonyes. My intention was that for once I would have the whole batch all to myself with no admonishing finger crooked in my direction. The problem was that all those years I assumed that the gribonyes were made from chicken fat because I couldn't see why skin would be considered hard to digest. After all, my grandmother did not skin the chicken before roasting it.

So I cut the chicken fat into small pieces, placed them in a frying pan set on low heat and impatiently waited for them to turn golden and crunchy. Instead, the pieces of fat became smaller and smaller until finally, when all the fat had rendered, they were reduced to the size of pin heads. I had inadvertently made schmaltz (chicken fat), not gribonyes! Next try I used the chicken skin and achieved authentic gribonyes: the ideal Slavic/gourmand garnish for chopped liver, salad and just plain noshing (Yiddish for snacking with faint overtones of pigging out).

| INGREDIENTS | MEASURE | WEIGHT | |
| --- | --- | --- | --- |
| | *volume* | *ounces* | *grams* |
| chicken skin | ½ cup | 4 ounces | 113 grams |
| 1 large clove of garlic, cut in half | | | 6 grams |
| salt | ⅛ teaspoon | | |
| black pepper, freshly ground | a few grindings | | |

MAKES: scant ½ cup (1¼ ounces/ 35 grams)

EQUIPMENT: heavy skillet, preferably cast iron, large enough to hold the chicken skin in one layer (about 11 inches)

Cut the chicken skin into 1-inch by 1-inch pieces. Place them in a single layer in the frying pan. Add one of the garlic halves and turn the heat to low. Sprinkle with salt and pepper and cook very slowly for about 1 hour, stirring every 10 or 15 minutes. When the garlic begins to color, remove and discard it. Then, impale the second garlic clove half on a fork, cut side down, and use it to continue to stir the chicken skin. This imparts a lovely garlic flavor without browning the garlic, which would make it bitter.

Cook until the chicken skin has rendered all its fat and turns golden and crisp. Drain on paper towels. Gribonyes are delicious warm or at room temperature and a great garnish for chopped liver.

POINTERS FOR SUCCESS

• Do not attempt to cook the skin in one flat sheet; it needs to be in small pieces and curl up as it's frying to have the best, most succulent texture.

UNDERSTANDING

Allowing the skin to cook in its own fat without draining removes the maximum amount of fat from the skin.

# No-Compromise Old-Country Chopped Liver

I couldn't do a book on ethnic food and not include what is perhaps the most beloved of all dishes from my own ethnic group. The truth is, however, I didn't grow up liking chopped liver. My grandmother made it every Friday night, but it just didn't strike me as something I would be interested in eating. All this changed when I started cooking myself and discovered that if the livers are not overcooked, they are moist and soft instead of leathery and that chopping them coarsely as opposed to reducing them to a paste results in a much more appealing texture. My best secret, however, for fabulous chopped liver is frying the onions until they caramelize. Their tart sweetness against the lush richness of the liver is utterly pleasing.

These days my mother uses mayonnaise instead of schmaltz (chicken fat) in a stab toward health, but my feeling is I'd rather have just a little chopped liver once in a while made with goose or chicken fat and be damned.

Chopped liver is always a welcomed addition to any buffet but it is traditional as a holiday appetizer and as a first-course spread on challah for a Shabbus (Friday night) roast chicken dinner (page 123).

| INGREDIENTS | MEASURE | WEIGHT | |
| --- | --- | --- | --- |
| | *volume* | *ounces/pound* | *grams* |
| 2 hard-cooked large eggs* | | 4 ounces | 113 grams |
| goose or chicken fat | ¼ cup + 2 teaspoons, divided | | |
| 12 chicken livers, trimmed and dried on paper towels | | 1 pound | 454 grams |
| salt | 1 teaspoon | | |
| 2 small onions, chopped | 1½ cups | 6.5 ounces | 182 grams |
| black pepper, freshly ground | a few grindings | | |
| sugar | a pinch | | |

*To hard-cook: Place 2 large eggs in a pan of cold water. Bring to a simmer and cook at a simmer for 20 minutes. Do not allow the water to boil. With a slotted spoon, remove the eggs and place them under cold running water for about 15 seconds. When cool, roll the eggs on the counter, using light pressure to crush the shells evenly for ease in removal.

*Chopped liver has the best texture and flavor soon after preparation. Extended chilling affects its moist creaminess and dulls its flavor. I like to prepare it a few hours before serving and set it near a cold window.*

On a wooden board or in a wooden chopping bowl, coarsely chop the eggs. Set aside.

In a medium frying pan over medium heat, heat ¼ cup of the fat until hot. Sauté the livers, turning them until browned on all sides, and just cooked through, about 7 to 10 minutes. Remove them with tongs to the chopping board or bowl. Sprinkle with ½ teaspoon of the salt.

Lower the heat under the frying pan and add the onions. Sprinkle with the remaining ½ teaspoon of salt, the pepper and sugar and sauté, stirring often, until deep golden brown, about 7 minutes. Spoon the onions on top of the liver, along with the cooking fat.

With a large knife, coarsely chop together the eggs, liver and onions just until blended. Do not make a smooth purée. If the mixture seems a little dry, add the remaining 2 teaspoons of fat and mash it lightly with a fork, just so that it holds together. Taste and adjust the salt and pepper. Spoon the chopped liver into a serving bowl without packing it.

# CHINESE-STYLE HONEY MUSTARD LAMB RIBLETS

These little morsels are delectable—easy to eat as finger food and lovely with cocktails. They are a great favorite and economical as well as simple to prepare. The flavorings are based on the memory my husband had of his favorite chicken wing dish in a Chinese restaurant in Toronto, where he was raised.

This recipe together with the Filipino-Inspired Chicken Shrimp (page 33) and Plum Sauce (page 35), Peking version of Perfect Crisp Roast Duck (page 140) and Authentic Chinese Zingy Red Shrimp (page 98) are the makings of a great Chinese banquet.

| INGREDIENTS | MEASURE<br>*volume* | WEIGHT<br>*ounces/pounds* | *grams/kilograms* |
|---|---|---|---|
| 1 lamb breast, well trimmed of fat, cut in half crosswise, then cracked between each rib | | 3 pounds | 1 kilogram/<br>360 grams |
| honey | ½ liquid cup | 6 ounces | 168 grams |
| Dijon mustard | ½ liquid cup | 4.5 ounces | 130 grams |
| curry powder | 2 tablespoons | | |
| soy sauce | 1 tablespoon | | |
| 1 medium clove of garlic, minced | 1 teaspoon | | 3 grams |
| salt | 1 teaspoon | | |
| fresh ginger, peeled and minced* | 1 teaspoon | | 3.5 grams |

(PARBOILING TIME: 30 minutes)
PREHEAT THE OVEN TO: 325°F.
BAKING TIME: 1 hour
SERVES: 6 as an appetizer

UP TO 3 DAYS AHEAD: Cut the lamb into individual riblets and remove as much fat as possible from them. Place the riblets in a large saucepot, and cover with water. Bring to a boil and boil 30 minutes, skimming often, to remove the fat. Drain the riblets and place them in a single layer in a 9-inch by 13-inch baking pan. Set aside at room temperature or refrigerate, covered, until ready to cook.

*Preheat the oven to 325°F.*

*Or ½ teaspoon ground.

(continued)

In a small bowl, mix the remaining ingredients. Spoon half the mixture over the riblets, and bake for 30 minutes. Turn the riblets and spoon on the remaining honey mixture. Bake 30 minutes more or until the riblets are tender and browned. Serve hot or at room temperature.

NOTE: These riblets will reheat successfully.

VARIATION: These riblets are also delicious barbecued. If barbecuing, there is no need to remove the fat or to precook the ribs, as the heat of the barbecue fire melts it. Do not add the sauce until the very end of barbecuing, or after removing the riblets from the grill, as it burns easily. Grill the riblets about 20 minutes, turning often.

# FILIPINO-INSPIRED CHICKEN SHRIMP

I first encountered the Filipino technique of boning chicken wings as a college student in a course in international foods. It amazed me how much the boned wings looked like shrimp. It was such a perfect trompe l'oeil I decided to stuff the wings with what they resembled. The moist fried chicken wings with their crispy skin make perfectly harmonious containers for the succulent morsels of coriander-flavored shrimp.

This dish works well as an hors d'oeuvre served with drinks or as a first course for a fish dinner, such as the Salmon Steak with Dijon Mustard and Black Mustard Grains (page 108).

| INGREDIENTS | MEASURE | WEIGHT | |
|---|---|---|---|
| | *volume* | *ounces/pounds* | *grams* |
| FILLING | | | |
| 8 ounces, shrimp shelled and coarsely chopped | | 7 ounces (peeled) | 200 grams |
| green onions (white parts only), minced | 2 tablespoons | 0.50 ounce | 14 grams |
| water chestnuts, finely chopped | 2 tablespoons | 0.75 ounce | 20 grams |
| fresh coriander, chopped | 2 tablespoons | 0.50 ounce | 10 grams |
| peanut oil | 1 ½ teaspoons | | |
| soy sauce | 1 teaspoon | | |
| salt | ¼ teaspoon | | |
| white pepper, freshly ground | a few grindings | | |
| 16 chicken wings, first joint with wing tip attached* | | 1 ½ pounds | 680 grams |
| BATTER | | | |
| cornstarch | ¼ cup | 1 ounce | 30 grams |
| all-purpose flour | 3 tablespoons | 1 ounce | 28 grams |
| salt | ½ teaspoon | | |
| 2 large eggs, well beaten | 3 fluid ounces | 7 ounces | 100 grams |
| water | 2 tablespoons | | |
| vegetable oil for deep-fat frying | | | |
| Plum Sauce (page 35) | 1 recipe | | |

*The second joints (miniature drumsticks) can be frozen and used to make Tandoori Chicken (page 126).

*(continued)*

In a medium nonreactive bowl, combine all the ingredients for the filling. Mix well. Cover and refrigerate until well chilled.

Using a small sharp knife, carefully debone the chicken wings, leaving the skin intact: Starting at the joint end, cut through the joint. Insert the tip of the knife straight in and cut all around between the skin and the bone, cutting the tendons. Use your fingers to scrape the flesh back from the outside edges of the 2 bones. As you work down toward the wing tip, the wing will turn inside out (like removing a glove). Wiggle the bones and spread them sharply apart until they snap off at the wing tip joint. (Do not use a knife for this, as it will risk making a hole in the skin.) Smooth out the flesh and skin so that the skin is right side out again. Stuff each wing with filling, but do not pack it in.* The fastest, easiest way to stuff the wings is to place the filling in a 1-quart heavy-duty zip-seal bag, cut a ½-inch opening in one corner and pipe the filling into each wing.

Using a small skewer or a toothpick, close the opening in each wing. Chill until ready to fry.

In a small deep bowl, combine the cornstarch, flour and salt. Stir in the beaten eggs. Mix until smooth. Add the water and stir until well blended. Allow the batter to sit for at least 10 minutes.

Twenty minutes before cooking, start heating the oil, poured 2 inches deep into the skillet or deep-fat fryer, over low heat until it reaches 375°F.†

Meanwhile, dip the chicken wings in the batter and place on a cookie sheet or flat plate. Cover the wings with plastic wrap and refrigerate for at least 10 minutes.

Deep-fry the wings, in batches, for 4 to 5 minutes, turning once, or until golden brown. Drain on paper towels. Be sure to remove all of the toothpicks or skewers. Serve warm with Plum Sauce.

*Any leftover filling can be shaped into balls, dipped in batter and fried.
†The wings can also be baked, at 400°F. for 40 minutes. Omit the batter and place the wings on a rack in a baking pan. Deep-frying is preferable, however, as the shrimp filling stays more tender and the wings crisper.

ROSE'S MELTING POT

# PLUM SAUCE

This savory plum sauce, similar to the one served in Chinese restaurants, is a perfect accompaniment for both the Filipino-Inspired Chicken Shrimp (page 33) and the Peking Duck version of Perfect Crisp Roast Duck (page 140).

| INGREDIENTS | MEASURE | WEIGHT | |
| --- | --- | --- | --- |
| | *volume* | *ounces* | *grams* |
| 2 1-pound cans purple plums, drained (reserve ¾ cup of juice) | | 21.75 ounces (drained weights) | 618 grams |
| apricot preserves | ½ cup | 6 ounces | 170 grams |
| 2 medium cloves of garlic, minced* | 1 tablespoon | 0.50 ounce | 10 grams |
| fresh ginger, grated | 2 teaspoons | 0.50 ounce | 12 grams |
| red rice vinegar or cider vinegar | 1 tablespoon | | |
| brown sugar | 1 teaspoon | | |
| soy sauce | ½ teaspoon | | |
| salt | ¼ teaspoon | | |
| black pepper, freshly ground | ¼ teaspoon | | |
| cayenne pepper | a pinch | | |

MAKES: 1 cup

Remove and discard the pits and skins from the plums. Purée the plums in a food processor until smooth. Place the purée in a small heavy saucepan, and add the remaining ingredients.† Add enough of the reserved juice to make the mixture the consistency of applesauce.

Bring the mixture to a boil and simmer for 15 minutes, stirring often. Remove the garlic. If a silky smooth sauce is desired, strain. Serve at room temperature.

KEEPS: Refrigerated, indefinitely.

UNDERSTANDING

For the best flavor, it is preferable to mince the garlic instead of using a press. Pressed garlic develops an acrid flavor.

*It is preferable to put the minced garlic in a tea strainer for ease in removal.
†Available in Chinese food stores.

# BREAD

# RAISIN PECAN BREAD

This is my favorite new bread. Raisin/nut loaves have been very popular over the last few years, appearing in bakeries throughout New York City. The secret for the special texture of my version is the ground pecans added to the dough. The resulting bread is dense, chewy but fine-textured and studded with sweet moist raisins and the soft crunch of broken pecans. It is so delicious it could be eaten for dessert, spread with a thin layer of softened sweet butter or cream cheese, or just plain (which in this instance is probably a contradiction in terms) as an appetizer with white wine or drinks.

| INGREDIENTS room temperature | MEASURE volume | WEIGHT ounces | grams |
|---|---|---|---|
| raisins | ¾ cup | 3.75 ounces | 108 grams |
| water | 1 liquid cup, divided | | |
| fresh yeast* *or/* | 1 packed teaspoon | 0.25 ounce | 5.6 grams |
| dry yeast (*not* rapid-rise) | 1 scant teaspoon | | 2.3 grams |
| sugar | ⅛ teaspoon | | |
| bread flour | 2 cups (measured by dip and sweep method), divided, + about ½ cup for kneading | 11 ounces | 312 grams |
| honey | 1 tablespoon | | |
| whole wheat flour | ⅓ cup | 1.75 ounces | 50 grams |
| pecans, finely ground | ½ cup | 1.5 ounces | 42.7 grams |
| salt | 1 ¼ teaspoons | | 8.5 grams |
| vegetable oil | 2 teaspoons | | |
| pecan halves, coarsely broken | 1 ½ cups | 5.25 ounces | 150 grams |
| cornmeal | about 1 teaspoon | | |

*Fresh yeast causes dough to rise faster than dry.

*(continued)*

SPONGE AND RISING TIME: 8½ to
  10 hours
PREHEAT THE OVEN TO: 425°F.
BAKING TIME: about 1 hour
INTERNAL TEMPERATURE: 190°F.
MAKES: one 2¼-pound
  (1-kilogram) loaf, 10 inches by
  6½ inches by 4 inches high

*First thing in the morning or the night before:*

SOAK THE RAISINS: Place the raisins and ¼ cup of the water heated until hot in a small bowl. Cover with plastic wrap and allow to sit until softened, stirring once, for at least 1 hour or until ready to start the bread. Drain the raisins, reserving the liquid in a 1-cup liquid measure. Add enough of the remaining water to equal 1 cup.

PROOF THE YEAST: Place the yeast in a small bowl, crumbling the fresh yeast. Add the sugar and 1 tablespoon of the raisin water, warmed to a tepid 100°F., if using fresh yeast; if using dry yeast, increase the temperature slightly to 110°F. Stir until the yeast is dissolved. Set it aside in a draft-free spot for 10 to 20 minutes. By this time the mixture should be full of bubbles. If not, the yeast is too old to be useful. Discard the mixture and start over with fresher yeast.

MAKE THE SPONGE: In a large bowl, combine the yeast mixture, 1 cup of the bread flour, the remaining scant cup of raisin water and the honey. Whisk until very smooth, about 100 strokes. Cover with plastic wrap and allow to stand for 4 to 5 hours, or refrigerate overnight. If refrigerating, allow the sponge to sit at room temperature for 1 hour before proceeding. The batter will be very bubbly and spongy in texture.

In a medium bowl, combine the remaining 1 cup of bread flour, the whole wheat flour, ground pecans and salt. Stir this mixture into the sponge. Stir in the oil, broken pecans and the raisins and knead to distribute them throughout the dough, adding extra bread flour as needed to keep the dough from sticking. Turn out the dough onto a lightly floured surface and knead about 10 minutes, adding flour as necessary to keep the dough from sticking. It should be very elastic, smooth and cool to the touch and jump back when pressed with a fingertip. (The dough will weigh about 2¼ pounds/1041 grams.)

Form the dough into a ball. Place it in a large oiled bowl, turn the dough to coat it with the oil and cover it tightly with plastic wrap, preferably Saran brand, or a damp towel. Set it in a warm spot (80°F.) and allow it to rise for 1½ to 2 hours or until doubled in bulk. Punch down the dough, knead it lightly and allow to rise a second time. (The second rising takes about 1½ hours.) If time allows, repeat for a third rising of about 1¼ hours.

Punch down the dough and shape it into a 10-inch-long football-shaped loaf. Place the dough either on the cornmeal-sprinkled La Cloche bottom or a cornmeal-sprinkled rimless baking sheet. Cover it with a large bowl or plastic wrap sprayed with nonstick vegetable shortening. Let the dough rise until doubled in bulk, about 1 hour.

*At least 30 minutes before baking, soak the top of La Cloche if using it. Preheat the oven to 425°F. If not using La Cloche, preheat a baking stone or cookie sheet on a rack positioned toward the bottom of the oven.*

Slash the top of the dough with a sharp knife or straight-edged razor blade. (I like to make about 5 short cross-wise slashes to resemble an armadillo.) Place the soaked La Cloche top on top of the base or slide the dough directly onto the preheated baking stone or sheet.

If using La Cloche, bake at 425°F. for 15 minutes, then lower the temperature to 375°F. and continue baking for 40 to 45 minutes. If not using La Cloche, immediately lower the temperature to 375°F., and bake for 35 to 40 minutes. The bread is done when a skewer inserted in the middle comes out clean and an instant-read thermometer registers 190°F. Cool the bread, uncovered, on a rack. (The baked bread will stay warm for 2 hours.)

NOTE: Do not use parchment on the bottom of La Cloche unless it is greased or it will stick to the bread.

TECHNIQUE FOR MAKING DOUGH IN AN ELECTRIC MIXER, USING A 5-QUART OR LARGER ELECTRIC MIXER WITH DOUGH HOOK ATTACHMENT

To make the sponge, place the ingredients in the mixer bowl and, with the whisk attachment, beat about 1 minute or until very smooth. Remove the whisk attachment, cover the bowl tightly with plastic wrap and let it stand at room temperature for 4 to 5 hours, or refrigerate overnight. If refrigerating, allow it to sit at room temperature for 1 hour.

*(continued)*

Using the paddle attachment, add the flour/pecan mixture and mix just until smooth. Mix in the oil, raisins and broken pecans and add additional bread flour if necessary to form a soft, rough dough. Change to the dough hook, scraping off any dough that clings to the paddle, and mix on medium speed until the dough is smooth and elastic, about 10 minutes. After the first 3 minutes, if the dough still appears sticky and does not begin to clean the bowl, add additional bread flour a tablespoon at a time. If it seems dry, add water 1 tablespoon at a time. Form the dough into a ball and proceed as above.

POINTERS
FOR SUCCESS

• Store the baked bread at room temperature or freeze and defrost to room temperature or heat it. Do not refrigerate it as the starch in the flour crystallizes when cold.

UNDERSTANDING

This bread takes a relatively long time to rise because of the extra weight of the whole wheat flour, raisins and nuts. Extra risings make the grain more even and lighter.

Preheating the baking stone or sheet causes the dough to hold its shape and start to rise immediately when placed directly on it, resulting in the highest rise.

ROSE'S MELTING POT

# WALNUT FOUGASSE

I had never heard of *fougasse*, the flat, chewy, lotus-shaped French bread, until Gerald Asher from 21 Brands decided to throw a press party with the theme of an "unpretentious little French picnic," hired me to make it and expressed a desire for this bread. He explained that Alice Waters of Chez Panisse in Berkeley made it for all his West Coast parties and that he was sure she would share the recipe. As luck would have it, my cousin Joan, who lives just up the hill from Chez Panisse, was coming to New York and was happy to pick up a fougasse for me from Alice. She had scrawled the recipe on its brown paper bag, but by the time it got to New York and the walnut oil from the bread seeped through the paper, it was all but indecipherable.

The bread, however, was magnificent, with chewy texture and deep walnuty flavor, so my assistant, Joan Barendes, and I set out to re-create it. This was no easy task. The special ingredient in Alice's fougasse is "gappe," the browned milk solids resulting from clarifying butter. But it takes a lot of clarified butter to get enough gappe for even one loaf; no problem for a restaurant and, in fact, a great use for what is usually discarded but not very practical for the home cook. So we used melted butter instead and the bread did not rise. "Oh yes," said Joan, who had also been Madeleine Kamman's assistant, "Madeleine always said too much fat kills yeast and that yeast thrives on protein, which would be the main component of gappe. Let's try skimmed milk." It was a beginning. The final result was spectacular. I baked giant breads using a full-size sheet pan. Gerald flew the leftover breads back to California and mounted them on his kitchen wall, where they stayed for several years. I, for my part, started a collection of gappe in the freezer. If I don't have the full one-third cup to replace the skimmed milk, I add a tablespoon to the dough along with the starter. It adds a special richness of flavor.

Fougasse is an excellent appetizer for a French-inspired dinner, with a main course such as Salmon Steak with Dijon Mustard and Black Mustard Grains (page 108) or roast leg of lamb. *(continued)*

*Fougasse.* Originally one of the oldest French pastries, it is also called "fouace" and "fouasse." Originally it was an unleavened pancake-like creation made of wheat and cooked under the cinders in the hearth. In his 1534 book *Gargantua*, Rabelais included a recipe for fougasse. Fougasses from the regions of Chinon and Touraine have been particularly popular for hundreds of years. Today these rustic dough cakes are baked in the oven, occasionally salted and usually served on Christmas or Twelfth Night. Fougasse used to be a popular dessert all over France, but today it is mainly made in the south. Najac, in Rouergue, has an annual fougasse festival to celebrate its love for this pastry. In Auvergne, fougasse is traditionally filled with candied fruits, while in Provence it is often basted with orange flower water. The "fougasette," a smaller version of this pastry, is made in Nice of brioche dough. It is usually shaped like a plaited loaf and seasoned with orange flower water and saffron.

| INGREDIENTS<br>*room temperature* | MEASURE<br>*volume* | WEIGHT<br>*ounces/pounds* | *grams* |
|---|---|---|---|
| unbleached all-purpose flour, such as Hecker's | 3 cups (measured by dip and sweep method), + extra for kneading | 1 pound | 454 grams |
| fresh yeast* *or* | 1 packed tablespoon | 0.75 ounce | 17 grams |
| dry yeast (*not* rapid-rise) | 2½ teaspoons | 0.25 ounce | 6.75 grams |
| salt | 1½ teaspoons | 0.3 ounce | 10 grams |
| walnuts, coarsely chopped | ¾ cup | 2.75 ounces | 75 grams |
| walnut oil | ½ liquid cup | | |
| skimmed milk† | 1¼ liquid cups, divided | | |

SPONGE AND RISING TIME: 3 to 4 hours
PREHEAT THE OVEN TO: 425°F.
BAKING TIME: 20 to 25 minutes
MAKES: One 1¾-pound (785-gram) loaf, 15 inches by 11½ inches by 1½ inches high

EQUIPMENT: jelly-roll pan or cookie sheet at least 15 inches long, lightly oiled with a little walnut oil. Use a piece of plastic wrap to apply it.

PROOF THE YEAST AND MAKE THE STARTER: In a small bowl, mix 1 cup (5.25 ounces/148 grams) of the flour with the yeast and stir in enough of the skimmed milk or water to form a soft ball of dough (6 to 8 tablespoons).

Use a sharp knife to cut a cross into the top of the dough. Drop the dough into a large bowl of lukewarm water (110°F.) and set it aside in a warm spot. If the yeast is alive and active, in about 35 minutes it will have grown and produced enough carbon dioxide to lighten the dough and enable it to rise to the surface of the water. If the dough does not rise to the surface, this is a sure indication that the yeast is no longer active and you must start again with a fresher batch.

While the yeast is proofing, in a large bowl, stir together the remaining 2¼ cups of flour and the nuts. Make a large well in the center and add 2 tablespoons of the walnut oil, the salt and ¾ cup of the skimmed milk (or water-gappe mixture). With a wooden spoon, mix to form a stiff dough.

When the starter has risen to the top of the bowl, use your hand to lift it from the water and add it (dripping) to the dough. With an electric mixer and dough hook, or by hand, knead the dough, adding flour as needed to keep the dough from sticking. Continue kneading until the

*Fresh yeast causes dough to rise faster than dry yeast.
†Or ¾ cup of water mixed with ⅓ cup of gappe plus 6 to 8 tablespoons of water for the starter.

*(continued)*

dough is very elastic, smooth and cool to the touch and jumps back when pressed with a fingertip (about 10 minutes by hand, less with an electric mixer).

Oil a large mixing bowl with 2 tablespoons of the walnut oil. Roll the dough in the bowl to coat all sides and cover the bowl tightly with plastic wrap, preferably Saran brand, or a damp towel. Allow the dough to rise for 1 hour or until doubled in bulk (it can take as long as 2 hours if the room is cold).

Punch down the dough and add 2 more tablespoons of walnut oil. Knead in the oil. Allow the dough to rise a second time until doubled in bulk (about 45 minutes).

Gently punch down the dough and allow it to rise a third time until doubled in bulk (about 30 minutes).

Gently punch down the dough. With your fingers, press it out on the greased jelly-roll pan or cookie sheet to about 11 inches by 15 inches by ½ inch thick.

*Preheat the oven to 425°F.*

Allow the dough to rise for about 15 minutes or until it is ¾ inch high. Brush with the remaining 2 tablespoons of walnut oil. With a sharp knife, cut 7 diagonal slashes (cut through to the bottom of the pan) about 3 inches long and 2 inches apart, 3 on either side and 1 at the top, radiating around the bread. With your fingers, push the slashes open. Bake until crisp and golden brown, 20 to 25 minutes.

Use a large pancake turner to loosen the bread and lift it from the pan. Allow it to cool on a rack, covered loosely with a clean dry towel. This bread is delicious warm or at room temperature.

POINTERS
FOR SUCCESS

• Be sure to use fresh walnut oil that is not at all rancid. Store the oil in the refrigerator and it will keep for many months.

# PORTUGUESE SWEET BREAD

I first encountered this unique bread over tea in my friend Anna Colaiace's cozy restored colonial kitchen in Providence, Rhode Island. The recipe was taught to her by her Portuguese housekeeper, Fatima. My modification of this ethnic classic was to substitute potato water for the water for extra lightness.

This is the moistest, lightest, softest bread I have ever experienced, lighter and less buttery than brioche. It is perfect for those who can't decide which they prefer, cake or bread. It is also great toasted, for breakfast, spread with a tangy gilding of lemon curd, or even as part of a bread basket selection for dinner.

| INGREDIENTS<br>*room temperature* | MEASURE<br>*volume* | WEIGHT<br>*ounces* | *grams* |
|---|---|---|---|
| 1 medium potato | | 8 ounces | 227 grams |
| fresh yeast* *or* | 1 ½ packed teaspoons | 0.5 ounce | 14 grams |
| dry yeast (*not* rapid-rise) | 1 ¾ teaspoons | | 5 grams |
| sugar | ¾ cup + 1 ½ teaspoons, divided | 5.5 ounces | 156 grams |
| (potato water) | (2 tablespoons) | | |
| unbleached all-purpose flour, such as Hecker's | 4 cups (measured by dip and sweep method) + about 2 tablespoons for kneading | 20.7 ounces | 592 grams |
| 4 eggs, lightly beaten | ⅔ cup + 2 tablespoons, divided | 7 ounces<br>(weighed without shells) | 200 grams |
| salt | ½ teaspoon | | |
| unsalted butter, melted | 8 tablespoons | 4 ounces | 113 grams |
| milk | ⅓ liquid cup | | |
| whiskey | 1 teaspoon | | |
| lemon zest, finely grated (yellow portion of peel only) | 1 ½ teaspoons | | 3 grams |
| water | 1 teaspoon | | |

*Fresh yeast causes dough to rise faster than dry yeast.

*(continued)*

SPONGE AND RISING TIME: 4 to 5
  hours
PREHEAT THE OVEN TO: 350°F.
BAKING TIME: 40 to 45 minutes
INTERNAL TEMPERATURE: 190°F.
MAKES: two 8-inch by 4-inch by
  3¾-inch high loaves
each loaf: 1 pound, 6 ounces/632
  grams

EQUIPMENT: 2 lightly greased
  bread pans (4-cup capacity,
  8 inches by 4 inches by
  2½ inches)

*First thing in the morning or the night before:*

Cut the potato in half and boil it in unsalted water for about 30 minutes or until it feels tender when pierced with a skewer. Remove the potato to a paper towel and reserve 2 tablespoons of the water. Allow the potato to cool completely. Then peel the potato and put it through a ricer or coarse strainer. You will need ¾ cup, packed (6 ounces/ 175 grams). Set it aside, covered.

PROOF THE YEAST: Place the fresh yeast in a small bowl, crumbling the fresh yeast. Add the 1½ teaspoons of sugar and the reserved 2 tablespoons of potato water, warmed to a tepid 100°F., if using fresh yeast; if using dry yeast, increase the temperature slightly to 110°F. Stir until the yeast is dissolved. Set it aside in a draft-free spot for 10 to 20 minutes. By this time the mixture should be full of bubbles. If not, the yeast is too old to be useful. Discard the mixture and start over with fresher yeast.

In a large bowl, combine the potato, 2 tablespoons of the flour, 2 tablespoons of the beaten egg and the yeast mixture. Pour another 2 tablespoons of the egg into a small bowl for the topping; cover it and the remaining beaten egg with plastic wrap and refrigerate. Stir the potato mixture until smooth. Cover tightly with plastic wrap and allow to rise for 1 to 2 hours or until double in bulk.

Add the remaining flour, the remaining ¾ cup of sugar, the salt, reserved egg (except that for the topping), melted butter, milk, whiskey and lemon zest. Using a greased wooden spoon or spatula, mix the dough just until it comes together. Flour your hands lightly, as needed, and continue mixing with your hands for about 2 minutes or until the dough becomes very stretchy. If it does not begin to clean the bowl, add another tablespoon of flour. The dough will be very soft and sticky. Cover the bowl tightly with plastic wrap or a damp towel, and allow the dough to rise for 2 hours or until doubled in bulk.

With a greased wooden spoon or spatula, stir down the dough. Scrape the dough onto a well-floured counter (use about 2 tablespoons). Flour your hands and knead the dough very lightly for about 30 seconds, just to deflate

48                                            ROSE'S MELTING POT

and shape it. Divide the dough into 2 pieces. Shape each into a smooth rectangle and press it into the prepared pans. They will be about half-full. Cover the pans lightly with plastic wrap sprayed with a little nonstick vegetable shortening. Allow the loaves to rise until doubled in bulk, about 1 hour. (If you have used 4-cup capacity pans, the top of the dough should reach the top of the pans.) *At least 15 minutes before baking, preheat the oven to 350°F., with a baking stone or cookie sheet set on a rack positioned toward the bottom of the oven.*

Add the 1 teaspoon of water to the 2 reserved tablespoons of egg and lightly whisk to combine. Remove the plastic wrap and brush the loaves all over with this glaze without letting it drip down the sides of the pans, which could impede rising. Slash the top of each loaf with a sharp knife or straight-edged razor blade to enable it to rise evenly. (I like to make 3 diagonal slashes, evenly spaced, across each loaf.)

Set the pans on the baking stone or cookie sheet and bake for 30 to 45 minutes. Check after 25 minutes, and if the top crust is golden brown, tent the loaves loosely with a large sheet of heavy-duty aluminum foil and continue baking until done. A skewer inserted in the middle should come out clean and an instant-read thermometer should register 190°F. Unmold the breads onto racks and cool, top side up, covered with a clean towel to keep the crust soft.

TECHNIQUE FOR MAKING DOUGH IN AN ELECTRIC MIXER, USING A 5-QUART OR LARGER ELECTRIC MIXER WITH DOUGH HOOK ATTACHMENT

When mixing and kneading the dough, use the paddle attachment, starting on low speed and raising the speed to medium after all the flour is moistened. Raise the speed to medium and mix until the dough is smooth and elastic, about 2 minutes. If the dough does not begin to clean the bowl, add a tablespoon or so of flour. Then proceed as above.

*(continued)*

*Portuguese Sweet Bread.* Sweet bread is the traditional festival bread of both the Azores and Portugal. On Easter, almonds are often added to it, while on Twelfth Night it is usually topped with candied fruits. Portuguese cooks make it incredibly sweet while others opt for a more buttery or eggy consistency. Often saffron is added to the dough before cooking to give it a more exotic flavor.

• Portuguese bakers traditionally use a round pan, such as an 8-inch springform, for this bread. I find the bread bakes more evenly with a finer, softer texture in smaller pans, but if you would like to make one large round loaf, you will need to bake it for 1 hour and 10 to 20 minutes.

• Store the baked bread at room temperature or freeze and defrost to room temperature or heat it. Do not refrigerate it, as the starch in the flour crystallizes when cold.

UNDERSTANDING

Preheating the baking stone or sheet causes the dough to hold its shape and start to rise immediately when placed directly on it, resulting in the highest rise.

The high amount of sugar makes the bread very tender. The potato, butter, milk and eggs make the bread exceptionally moist. Potato (and potato water) is one of yeast's favorite foods, helping it to grow and multiply actively.

Unbleached all-purpose flour is preferable to bread flour for this bread because although it has more gluten-forming protein than bleached all-purpose, it has less than bread flour, which would make a chewier bread.

# AUTHENTIC RUSSIAN
# PUMPERNICKEL BREAD

It's the same story every time I invite my parents for dinner and bake bread. No matter how perfect the loaf, the same comment from Dad: "Delicious . . . [barely a pause] but when are you going to create a recipe for a really good pumpernickel?" After much delay, and many variations, I finally came up with this recipe, which is slightly sour, fairly dense and chewy, with the characteristic mild molasses flavor of true pumpernickel. Elliott, my husband, also enjoys pumpernickel, and he made a valuable contribution. He tried to get the recipe for his favorite pumpernickel bagels he picks up at a bakery on the way to work, but with no success. Then, one night, he came home with the amazing news that one of the workers from the bakery happened to come into his office for an X-ray and willingly revealed the special secret: caraway seeds, not so much to make their presence known, but just enough to impart a mysteriously delicious flavor.

This bread is flavorful enough to stand up to smoked meats such as Jewish Deli Smoked Tongue (page 156) and garlicky/peppery foods such as Perfect Pitcha (page 23).

*(continued)*

---

*Russian Pumpernickel Bread.* Throughout Russia, peasants have survived for centuries on a simple diet of rye bread, pickled cabbage soup and groats. In her 1745 book, *A Voyage to Russia*, the English governess Elizabeth Justice said of Russian peasants: "They need not lay by much to provide for Food; for they can make an hearty Meal of a piece of black sour Bread, some Salt, an Onion, or Garlick." Pumpernickel is one such black bread. It originated in Westphalia. Because of its robust flavor, it is often eaten with smoked meats, marinated fish or cheese. There are several hypotheses regarding the etymology of the name of this bread. "Pumper" may be an onomatopoeic reference to the action of the yeast and "nickel" may be a diminutive form of the name Nikolaus which, in German, is a colloquial term for a halfwit. Another interpretation claims that the name developed in the 1450s. During a severe famine in Osnabrück, local leaders baked a *bonum panicum* or "good bread" to sustain the town's poor. This bread was so popular that people continued to make it after the famine subsided, calling it "bumonickel," which then became "pumpernickel." Both explanations clearly show that this bread has a long history of being associated with the lower classes.

---

| INGREDIENTS room temperature | MEASURE volume | WEIGHT ounces | grams |
|---|---|---|---|
| fresh yeast* or | 1 packed tablespoon | 0.75 ounce | 17 grams |
| dry yeast (*not* rapid-rise) | 2½ teaspoons | 0.25 ounce | 6.75 grams |
| sugar | 2 tablespoons, divided | 1 ounce | 25 grams |
| water | 2⅓ liquid cups, divided | | |
| bread flour | 2 cups (measured by dip and sweep method), divided, + about ¾ cup for kneading | 11 ounces | 314 grams |
| pumpernickel flour (very coarse dark rye)† | 2 cups (measured by dip and sweep method) | 12.3 ounces | 352 grams |
| cider vinegar | 2 tablespoons | | |
| unsulfured molasses (preferably Grandma's) | ⅓ liquid cup | 4 ounces | 117 grams |
| whole wheat flour | 3 cups (lightly spooned into the cup) | 14 ounces | 400 grams |
| caraway seeds | 1 tablespoon | 0.25 ounce | 7 grams |
| unsweetened cocoa, preferably Dutch-processed | ¼ cup | 0.75 ounce | 20.5 grams |
| Medaglio d'Oro instant espresso powder‡ | 4 teaspoons | | 5 grams |
| salt | 1 tablespoon | 0.70 ounce | 20 grams |
| vegetable oil | 1 tablespoon | | |
| cornmeal | about 2 teaspoons | | |

*First thing in the morning or the night ahead:*

PROOF THE YEAST: Place the fresh yeast in a small bowl, crumbling the fresh yeast. Add ½ teaspoon of the sugar and ⅓ cup of the water, warmed to a tepid 100°F., if using fresh

---

*Fresh yeast causes dough to rise faster than dry yeast.
†Tuthilltown pumpernickel flour is the only one I have found that has truly coarse bran mixed in. Available by mail order: Tuthilltown Grist Mill, Albany Post Road, Gardiner, NY 12525, 914-255-5695. Alternatively, you can purchase supermarket rye flour (which is medium rye). As it weighs less, you will need 2½ to 2¾ cups instead of 2. Then replace 1 cup of the whole wheat flour with 1 cup (2 ounces/56 grams) of all-bran cereal, lightly crushed, or 1 cup of cracked wheat (not bulgur, which is toasted) available in health food stores.
‡Available in many supermarkets; most will place a special order if it is not regularly stocked.

SPONGE AND RISING TIME: 7 to 9
    hours
PREHEAT THE OVEN TO: 450°F.
BAKING TIME: about 1½ hours
INTERNAL TEMPERATURE: 190°F.
MAKES: one 4-pound loaf, 4½
    inches high by 9 inches in
    diameter, or two 2-pound loaves,
    3½ inches high by 8 inches in
    diameter.

yeast; if using dry yeast, increase the temperature slightly to 110°F. Stir until the yeast is dissolved. Set it aside in a draft-free spot for 10 to 20 minutes. By this time the mixture should be full of bubbles. If not, the yeast is too old to be useful, and you must start over with a fresher batch.

MAKE THE SPONGE: In a large bowl, combine the yeast mixture, 1 cup of the bread flour, 1 cup of the pumpernickel flour, the remaining 2 cups of water, the vinegar and molasses. Whisk until very smooth, about 100 strokes. Cover with plastic wrap and allow to stand 3 to 4 hours, or refrigerate overnight. If refrigerating, allow it to sit at room temperature for 1 hour before proceeding. The batter will be very bubbly and spongy in texture.

In a medium bowl, combine 1 cup of the remaining bread flour, the remaining 1 cup of rye flour, the whole wheat flour, caraway seeds, cocoa, instant espresso, the remaining 5½ teaspoons of sugar and the salt. Whisk to combine well. Stir this into the sponge together with the oil, and mix until firm enough to dump it onto the counter. The dough will be very sticky.

Knead about 10 minutes, adding flour as necessary to keep the dough from sticking. The dough should be a little tacky. Adding too much flour will make it drier and heavier. Continue kneading the dough until it is very elastic and cool to the touch and jumps back when pressed with a fingertip. If the dough is too much for you to knead in one batch, you can divide it in half and knead one portion at a time until smooth, keeping the remaining dough covered. Then knead the 2 portions together. (The dough weighs about 4¼ pounds/1 kilogram 960 grams.)

Form the dough into a ball, place it in an oiled large bowl and turn to coat with oil. Cover tightly with plastic wrap, preferably Saran brand, or a damp towel and set in a warm spot to rise for 1½ to 2 hours or until doubled in bulk (longer if using dry yeast or if the room is cold).

*(continued)*

Punch down the dough, knead it lightly and allow to rise a second time (about 1½ hours).

Punch down the dough. Shape it into an 8-inch ball, or divide it into 2 equal parts and roll each piece of dough into a 5-inch ball. Place the dough either on a cornmeal-sprinkled La Cloche bottom or cornmeal-sprinkled rimless baking sheet(s). Cover with a large bowl or plastic wrap sprayed with nonstick vegetable shortening. Let the dough rise until doubled in bulk, about 1 hour and 15 minutes.

*At least 30 minutes before baking, soak the top of La Cloche if using it. Preheat the oven to 450°F. If not using La Cloche, be sure to preheat a baking stone or cookie sheet on a rack positioned toward the bottom of the oven.*

Slash the top of the dough with a sharp knife or straight-edged razor blade. (I like to make 2 slashes about 2½ inches apart in one direction and a third slash perpendicular to them.) Place the soaked La Cloche top on top of the base or slide the dough directly onto the preheated baking stone or sheet.

If using La Cloche, bake at 450°F. for 15 minutes, lower the temperature to 400°F. and continue baking for 1 hour and 10 minutes for 1 large loaf, 40 to 45 minutes for 1 small loaf (half the recipe). If not using La Cloche, immediately lower the oven temperature to 375°F. and bake for 1 hour and 15 minutes to 25 minutes for 1 large loaf, 35 to 40 minutes for 2 small loaves. The bread is done when a skewer inserted in the middle comes out clean and an instant-read thermometer registers 190°F. Cool the bread, uncovered, on rack(s). (The baked bread will stay warm for 2 hours after baking.)

NOTE: Do not use parchment on the bottom of La Cloche unless it is greased, or it will stick to the bread.

TECHNIQUE FOR MAKING DOUGH IN AN ELECTRIC MIXER, USING A 5-QUART OR LARGER ELECTRIC MIXER WITH DOUGH HOOK ATTACHMENT

To make the sponge, place the ingredients in the mixer bowl and, with the whisk attachment, beat about 1 minute or until very smooth. Remove the whisk attachment, cover the bowl tightly with plastic wrap and let it stand at room temperature for 3 to 4 hours, or refrigerate overnight. If refrigerating, allow it to sit at room temperature for 1 hour before proceeding.

Using the paddle attachment add the flour mixture, and mix just until smooth. Add some of the additional bread flour if necessary to form a soft rough dough. Change to the dough hook, scraping off any dough that clings to the paddle, and mix on medium speed until the dough is smooth and elastic, about 10 minutes. After the first 3 minutes if the dough still appears sticky and does not begin to clean the bowl, add some of the extra remaining bread flour a few tablespoons at a time. If it seems dry, add water 1 tablespoon at a time. Form the dough into a ball and proceed as above.

POINTERS FOR SUCCESS

- It's worth the effort to order the coarse pumpernickel flour. Store it refrigerated or in a cold spot to keep it from becoming rancid.
- Be sure to use unsulfured molasses as the sulfured variety has an undesirably bitter edge.
- Store the baked bread at room temperature or freeze and defrost to room temperature or heat it. Do not refrigerate it, as the starch in the flour crystallizes when cold.

UNDERSTANDING

Preheating the baking stone or sheet causes the dough to hold its shape and start to rise immediately when placed directly on it, resulting in the highest rise.

Pumpernickel flour is actually coarsely ground rye flour. Increasing the amount of pumpernickel flour would result in a bitter flavor and denser texture, as would increasing the amount of whole wheat flour.

Because of the density of this bread, it is cooled uncovered to prevent pastiness.

VARIATION: Light Pumpernickel
For those who like the taste of pumpernickel but not the coarse dense texture, decrease the whole wheat flour to 2 cups and increase the bread flour to 3 cups.

# CLASSIC CHALLAH

Challah is a Jewish celebration bread somewhat reminiscent of brioche, although it contains oil instead of butter and is less rich in both fat and eggs. It comes in many shapes but most often is braided and sprinkled with poppy seeds. In all the years I was growing up, I cannot remember a Friday night without the traditional challah sitting on the table and the long serrated bread knife by its side. That is because Shabbus is the most important of all Jewish celebrations.

Grandma didn't bake her own challah; she bought it from a neighborhood kosher bakery. I remember it with fondness because of its appealingly plump four-braid symmetry, but the eggy flavor and cottony texture were not for me. I ate one small slice drizzled with a little honey and never wanted more. Perhaps it was out of a sense of ceremony (I still remember the Hebrew prayer for bread, though it's rare that I say it). So when I set out to create my own challah recipe, at first it was only the appearance I was trying to duplicate. Here then is my idea of what a pareve (dairy-free) challah ought to be at its best: yeasty and light but firm to the chew.

Because challah stales quickly, I like to slice and freeze any leftover wrapped airtight. The defrosted slices make great open-faced sandwiches thickly spread with chopped liver (page 26) or lightly spread with mustard and then paved with thin slices of Jewish Deli Smoked Tongue (page 156). Of course, the bread is also delicious lightly toasted and spread with preserves for breakfast.

| INGREDIENTS *room temperature* | MEASURE *volume* | WEIGHT *ounces* | *grams* |
|---|---|---|---|
| fresh yeast* *or* | 4 packed teaspoons | 1 ounce | 22 grams |
| dry yeast (*not* rapid-rise) | 1 tablespoon | 0.3 ounce | 9 grams |
| sugar | ½ cup, divided | 3.5 ounces | 100 grams |
| water | ¾ liquid cup, divided | | |
| bread flour or unbleached all-purpose flour, such as Hecker's | 4⅓ cups bread flour or 4½ cups all-purpose (measured by dip and sweep method) + ⅓ to 1 cup for kneading | 24 ounces | 680 grams |
| 5 large eggs | 1 liquid cup | 8.75 (weighed without shells) | 250 |
| vegetable oil | ⅓ liquid cup | | |
| cider vinegar | 1 tablespoon | | |
| salt | 2¼ teaspoons | 0.50 ounce | 15 grams |

TOPPING

| | | | |
|---|---|---|---|
| 1 large egg yolk | 1 tablespoon | 0.63 ounce | 18 grams |
| water | 1 teaspoon | | |
| poppy seeds | 1 tablespoon + 1 teaspoon | 0.50 ounce | 12 grams |

SPONGE AND RISING TIME: 5 to 6 hours
PREHEAT THE OVEN TO: 375°F.
BAKING TIME: 40 minutes
INTERNAL TEMPERATURE: 190°F.
MAKES: one 3-pound (1369-gram) loaf, 17 inches by 7 inches by 4 inches high

EQUIPMENT: 18-inch rimless baking sheet or inverted jelly-roll pan, lightly greased (grease the bottom side of the jelly-roll pan); 18-inch-long white serving plate (optional)†

*First thing in the morning or the night before:*

PROOF THE YEAST: Place the yeast in a small bowl, crumbling the fresh yeast. Add 1 teaspoon of the sugar and ¼ cup of the water, warmed to a tepid 100°F., if using fresh yeast; if using dry yeast, increase the temperature slightly to 110°F. Stir until the yeast is dissolved. Set it aside in a draft-free spot for 10 to 20 minutes. By this time the mixture should be full of foam. If not, the yeast is too old to be useful; discard the mixture and start over with fresher yeast.

*Fresh yeast causes dough to rise faster than dry yeast.
†Available at Dean & DeLuca, 560 Broadway, New York, New York 10012 (212-431-1691; outside New York, 800-227-7714).

*(continued)*

MAKE THE SPONGE: In a large bowl, combine 1 cup of the flour, 3 of the eggs, the yeast mixture and the remaining ½ cup of water. Whisk for about a minute or until smooth and full of bubbles. Sprinkle the remaining 3½ cups of flour on top, cover tightly with plastic wrap and allow to sit for 1 to 2 hours.

Add the remaining ½ cup less 1 teaspoon of sugar, the remaining 2 eggs, the oil, vinegar and salt to the sponge. Using a wooden spoon or spatula, work the flour into the liquid. Add more flour if the dough is too sticky to handle. Turn out the dough onto a lightly floured surface and knead about 10 minutes, adding some of the additional flour as necessary to keep the dough from sticking. It should be very elastic, smooth and cool to the touch and jump back when pressed with a fingertip. (The dough will weigh about 51 ounces/1460 grams.)

Form the dough into a ball. Place it in a large oiled bowl, turn the dough to coat it with the oil and cover it tightly with plastic wrap or a damp towel. Set it in a warm spot (80°F.) and allow it to rise for 1 hour or until doubled in bulk (it can take as long as 2 hours if the room is cold).

Punch down the dough, knead it lightly and allow to rise a second time. (The second rising takes about 45 minutes to an hour.)

Flatten the dough gently, so as not to activate the gluten and make it stretchy. If desired, at this point the dough can be wrapped loosely in plastic wrap, placed in a plastic bag and refrigerated overnight.

To shape the bread, divide the dough into 3 or 4 equal pieces. Lift each piece of dough from one end with one hand while using the other hand to pull and stretch it gently downward to form a 15- to 16-inch-long rope (14- to 15-inch if using 4 pieces), flouring your hands lightly if the dough is sticky. If the dough is very stretchy and springs back, allow it to sit until it relaxes enough to roll, keeping it covered with plastic wrap so that it doesn't dry.

Pinch the 3 or 4 ropes together at the tops and braid, pulling and stretching the dough slightly as you go. Pinch

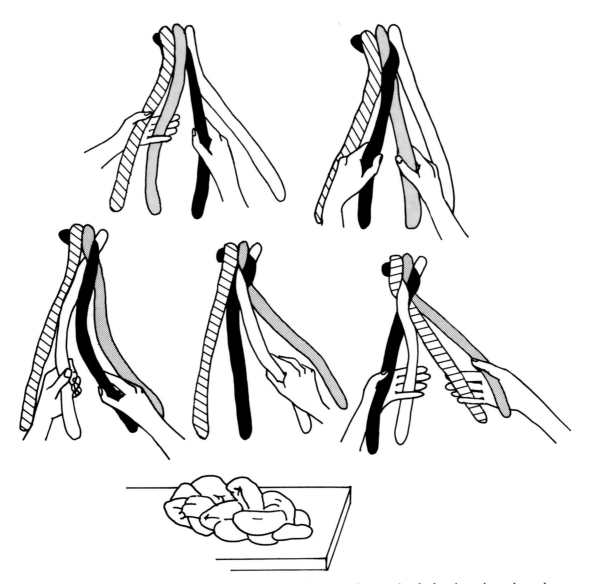

the strands together at the end of the braid and tuck it under a little at each end, pushing the ends together a little so that the loaf is about 15 inches long. Place the loaf on the prepared baking sheet. Spray or brush the dough lightly with water and cover it lightly with plastic wrap sprayed with a little nonstick vegetable shortening. Allow the loaf to rise until doubled in bulk, about 1 hour.

*At least 15 minutes before baking, preheat the oven to 375°F., with a baking stone or cookie sheet set on a rack positioned toward the bottom of the oven.*

(continued)

BREAD

In a small bowl, lightly whisk together the egg yolk and 1 teaspoon of water. Remove the plastic wrap and brush the challah all over with this glaze, going well into the crevices. Sprinkle the challah with the poppy seeds.

Set the baking sheet on top of the preheated baking stone or cookie sheet and bake 20 minutes. Tent loosely with a large sheet of heavy-duty aluminum foil and continue baking for 25 to 30 minutes. The bread should be deep golden brown. A skewer inserted in the middle should come out clean and an instant-read thermometer will register 190°F. Use 2 large pancake turners to remove the challah to a wire rack and, for a soft tender crust, cover the challah with a towel until cool.

TECHNIQUE FOR MAKING DOUGH IN AN ELECTRIC MIXER,
USING A 5-QUART OR LARGER ELECTRIC MIXER WITH
DOUGH HOOK ATTACHMENT

When mixing and kneading the dough, use the paddle
attachment to mix the dough, starting on low speed and
raising the speed to medium after all the flour is moistened. Change to the dough hook, scraping off any dough
that clings to the paddle, and mix on medium speed until
the dough is smooth and elastic, about 10 minutes. After
the first 3 minutes, if the dough still appears sticky and
does not begin to clean the bowl, add some of the additional flour a few tablespoons at a time. If it seems dry,
add water 1 tablespoon at a time. Form the dough into a
ball and proceed as above.

(continued)

**POINTERS FOR SUCCESS**

- Store the baked bread at room temperature or freeze and defrost to room temperature or heat it. Do not refrigerate it, as the starch in the flour crystallizes when cold.
- Both bread flour and unbleached all-purpose flour make excellent challah. The differences are minimal. It is interesting to note, however, that contrary to expectation, based on several trials, the bread flour resulted in a slightly denser, less chewy texture than did Hecker's unbleached flour. The bread flour challah was also slightly sweeter in flavor and slightly darker in color.
- Vinegar relaxes the gluten in the dough, making it easier to stretch into long strands. It also adds subtle depth of flavor.

NOTE: The challah can be baked as two 9-inch loaves but it will be easier to use a 3-strand braid, rolling each strand about 10 inches long.

Baking time will be 30 to 35 minutes. The baked bread will measure 13 inches by 5 inches by 3 inches.

**UNDERSTANDING**

Preheating the baking stone or sheet causes the dough to hold its shape and start to rise immediately when placed directly on it, resulting in the highest rise.

The deep color of this bread is because of the large amount of egg yolk and sugar in the dough.

# DAIRY DINNER CROWN CHALLAH

The softest, richest, most fabulous challah is actually a brioche, made with butter, but according to Kashruth laws, it cannot be served with a meat meal. This butter challah is at its very best eaten still warm or at least the same day it is baked.

| INGREDIENTS *room temperature* | MEASURE *volume* | WEIGHT *ounces* | *grams* |
|---|---|---|---|
| water | 1/3 liquid cup | | |
| sugar | 6 tablespoons, divided | 2.5 ounces | 80 grams |
| fresh yeast* *or/* | 4 packed teaspoons | 1 ounce | 22 grams |
| dry yeast (*not* rapid-rise) | 1 tablespoon | 0.33 ounce | 9 grams |
| bread flour | about 3 cups (measured by dip and sweep method), divided | 1 pound | 454 grams |
| 6 large eggs | | 12 ounces (weighed in the shells) | 340 grams |
| salt | 1 teaspoon | | 7 grams |
| unsalted butter (must be soft) | 16 tablespoons, divided | 8 ounces | 226 grams |
| Egg Glaze | | | |
| 1 egg, lightly beaten | 1 tablespoon | | |
| poppy seeds | 1 tablespoon | 0.33 ounce | 9 grams |

ADVANCE PREPARATION: at least 1 day or up to 2 days ahead
SPONGE AND RISING TIME: 4 to 5 hours
PREHEAT THE OVEN TO: 425°F.
BAKING TIME: 55 to 60 minutes
MAKES: one 2¼ pound (1047-gram) round loaf, 9 inches in diameter by 5 inches high

EQUIPMENT: heavy-duty mixer with paddle attachment and dough hook; 9-inch by 3-inch† round cake pan, well buttered

PROOF THE YEAST: In a small bowl, combine the water (a tepid 100°F. if using fresh yeast; a little warmer, 110°F., if using dry), 1 teaspoon of the sugar and the yeast (do not use hot water, or the yeast will die). If using fresh yeast, crumble it slightly while adding it. Set the mixture aside in a draft-free spot for 10 to 20 minutes. By this time, the mixture should be full of bubbles. If not, the yeast is too old to be useful and you must start again with newer yeast.

*Fresh yeast causes dough to rise faster than dry yeast.
†A 2-inch-high pan will also work, but the top decoration may spread apart a little without the additional support.

*(continued)*

MAKE THE SPONGE: Place ⅔ cup of the flour and 2 of the eggs in the large mixer bowl and whisk until mixed. Add the yeast mixture and whisk until smooth. Sprinkle the remaining flour over the mixture but do not mix it in. Cover tightly with plastic wrap (preferably Saran brand) and let it stand for 1½ to 2 hours.

In a medium-size heavy saucepan, over medium heat, melt 4 tablespoons (2 ounces/57 grams) of the butter, partially covered to prevent spattering. Do not stir. When the butter looks clear, continue to cook uncovered, watching carefully until the solids drop and turn dark brown. Watch carefully, as when the bubbling noise quiets, all the water has evaporated and the butter can burn easily. Remove immediately from the heat and pour the butter and brown solids into a medium bowl. When cool, stir in the remaining softened butter.

MAKE THE DOUGH: In a small bowl, whisk together the remaining sugar and the salt until well combined. Add this mixture together with the remaining 4 eggs to the sponge and beat on medium speed with the paddle attachment for about 5 minutes or until the dough is smooth, shiny and very elastic and begins to clean the bowl. If the dough starts to climb up the beater, change to the dough hook. Be sure to continue beating until the dough starts to mass together and come away from the sides.

Increase the speed to medium-high and add the butter by the tablespoon, beating until it is incorporated.

FIRST RISE: Scrape the dough into a lightly buttered bowl. It will be very soft and elastic. Sprinkle it lightly with flour to prevent a crust from forming. Cover the bowl tightly with plastic wrap (preferably Saran brand) and let it rise in a warm place (80°F., but not above or the yeast will develop a sour taste) until doubled in bulk, 1½ to 2 hours.

Refrigerate the dough for 1 hour to firm it so the butter will not separate. Then gently deflate the dough by stirring it with a rubber scraper and return it to the refrigerator for another hour so that it will be less sticky to handle.

REDISTRIBUTING THE YEAST AND FINAL RISE (6 HOURS TO 2 DAYS, CHILLED): Turn the dough onto a lightly floured surface and gently press it into a rectangle, flouring the surface and dough as needed to keep the dough from sticking to your hands. Fold the dough in thirds, brushing off any excess flour, and again press it out into a rectangle. Fold it again in thirds and dust it lightly on all sides with flour. Wrap it loosely but securely in plastic wrap and then place it in a large zip-seal bag or wrap it in foil, and refrigerate for at least 6 hours or up to 2 days to allow the dough to ripen and firm.

SHAPE THE CHALLAH: Gently knead the dough a few times to deflate it. For a braided top, divide the dough into 3 equal parts and roll each, on a lightly floured counter, into a rope about 26 inches long. If the dough is very elastic, allow it to rest, covered with plastic wrap, for 5 to 10 minutes. Braid the dough starting from the center and working toward each end, pinching it at the ends. Coil the braid into the pan, starting at the center and tucking the end underneath. Or, for an elegant snail shape, make 1 long thick rope and coil it in the same way. (The dough will not reach the sides of the pan until after rising.)

Cover the dough lightly with buttered plastic wrap and allow it to rise in a warm place until the top of the dough has reached the top of the pan, about 1½ to 2 hours. (Fresh yeast will work faster than dry.)

*Thirty minutes before baking, preheat the oven to 425°F. Lower an oven rack to the bottom shelf and place oven tiles or a baking sheet on it.*

Brush the challah with the egg glaze, going well into the crevices, being careful not to drip any down the sides of the pan, or it will impede rising. Sprinkle with poppy seeds.

Place the pan on the tiles or baking sheet and bake for 5 minutes. Lower the heat to 375°F. and continue baking 50 to 55 minutes or until a skewer inserted in the center comes out clean. An instant-read thermometer will register 190°F. After about 20 minutes at 375°F., or when the top crust is brown, tent it loosely with foil.

(*continued*)

Unmold the challah onto a wire rack and reinvert to cool top side up, covered with a clean towel to keep the crust soft.

POINTERS
FOR SUCCESS

- Use bread flour.
- Do *not* use rapid-rise yeast.
- Be sure the yeast is active, by proofing it.
- Do not place rising dough in an area warmer than 80°F. to 85°F.
- Do not allow the dough to rise more than recommended amounts or it will weaken the structure.
- Do not deflate the risen dough before chilling or the butter will leak out. If this should happen inadvertently, chill the dough for 1 hour and then knead the butter back into the dough.
- Unbaked dough can be frozen for up to 3 months.

UNDERSTANDING

Browning part of the butter gives the bread a richer flavor.

Unlike a cake, which is primarily a starch structure, bread depends on protein in the form of gluten to create its framework. The higher the protein content of the flour, the stronger the structure will be and the finer the grain of the bread (directly the opposite of cake). This dough is exceptionally wet. Just enough extra flour is added to handle it for shaping, resulting in a very light, soft bread.

I do not use rapid-rise yeast because the flavor development and texture are superior with slower rising.

# YORKSHIRE POPOVERS

Yorkshire pudding is the perfect, classic British accompaniment to Rare Prime Ribs of Beef (page 158). I have been working on perfecting this version for individual ones for fifteen years. My goal was a crisp, lofty, yet tender exterior, with a moist layer inside. It is only recently that I have finally accomplished my goal. There are two secrets: using a special popover pan,* with each cup

*My 6-cup popover pan is made by the Village Bakery division of Chicago Metallic (available through Maid of Scandinavia and Williams-Sonoma).

separated to allow air flow, which keeps the popovers from collapsing, and mixing some fat into the flour before adding the liquid (thank you, darling Shirley Corriher*) to prevent too much gluten development.

| INGREDIENTS | MEASURE | WEIGHT | |
| --- | --- | --- | --- |
| | *volume* | *ounces* | *grams* |
| bleached all-purpose flour | 1 cup (measured by dip and sweep method) | 5 ounces | 145 grams |
| salt | ½ teaspoon | | |
| sugar | ½ teaspoon | | |
| rendered beef fat† or melted unsalted butter | ¼ liquid cup, divided | 1.75 ounces | 52 grams |
| milk | 1 liquid cup | | |
| 2 large eggs | 3 fluid ounces | 3.5 ounces (weighed without shells) | 100 grams |

ADVANCE PREPARATION: at least 2 or up to 24 hours ahead
PREHEAT THE OVEN TO: 425°F.
BAKING TIME: 1 hour
MAKES: 6 large popovers or 12 small ones (muffin size)

EQUIPMENT: 6-cup popover tin (if using a black metal pan, reduce the initial 425°F. to 400°F.) or 12-cup muffin tin

In a large bowl, stir together the flour, salt and sugar. Add 2 tablespoons of the rendered beef suet or melted butter and, with a fork, mash and mix the fat into the flour until it resembles tiny peas. Slowly stir in the milk. Use a hand-held electric mixer or rotary beater to beat in the eggs one at a time, beating about 1 minute after each addition. Then beat until the batter is smooth. Cover and refrigerate for at least 2 or up to 24 hours. Beat lightly before using. (Small lumps of fat will remain visible.)

*Preheat the oven to 425°F.*

Place 1 teaspoon of the remaining rendered beef suet or melted butter in each of the 6 popover cups. (If using the smaller muffin pans, use ½ teaspoon in each of the 12 cups.) Use a small pastry feather or brush to coat the entire interior with the fat.

*Research biochemist, colleague and friend.
†To render beef fat, process 1 pound (454 grams) of beef suet into small pieces or chop it into small cubes, and place in a medium-size heavy saucepan. Add ¼ cup of water and cover tightly. Cook on the lowest possible heat for about 1 hour to 1 hour and 15 minutes, or until the fat is completely rendered, leaving only small golden bits. Stir a few times during the cooking to prevent overbrowning, which would give it an off flavor. You will get about 1¾ cups of melted fat, which will keep refrigerated for several months and frozen for several years.

(continued)

*Yorkshire Popover.* This light muffin puffs up when cooked so that it is nearly hollow, hence its name. The popover is almost identical to Yorkshire pudding, the most famous cuisine of the northern English province of Yorkshire. Here it is traditionally served as a first course accompanied by gravy or raspberry vinegar and followed by roast beef and potatoes. A typical Yorkshire meal such as this wouldn't be complete without a stew of dates and rhubarb, apple tarts or creamy, tangy Wensleydale cheese for dessert.

Ten minutes before baking time, place the popover or muffin tin in the oven to heat until the fat is almost smoking. (Place a large sheet of aluminum foil on the shelf under the tin to catch any bubbling fat.)

Pour the cold batter on top of the hot fat, filling the cups half-full. Bake for 15 minutes, then lower the heat to 350°F. and continue baking for 40 to 45 minutes for the 6 large popovers, 20 to 25 minutes for the 12 muffin-size ones. Ten minutes before the end of the baking time, open the oven door and quickly make a small slit in the side of each popover to release the steam and allow the centers to dry more.

With pot holders, lift the popovers out of the pans and serve immediately. Or place them on wire racks; they can be reheated in a 350°F. oven on a cookie sheet for 5 minutes.

NOTE: If you would like to make only half a batch, be sure to fill any empty popover or muffin cups with water. This will create steam, which will help the rising. If you leave them empty, the heat is drawn more to the empty cups than to the filled cups, slowing the baking and decreasing the rise.

UNDERSTANDING

Beef suet is the fat that surrounds the kidneys; it has the best flavor.

Allowing the batter to rest enables the flour to absorb the liquid evenly.

Pouring the cold batter onto the hot fat helps it to rise to its fullest height. Shirley Corriher tells me that in the South an esteemed trick for popovers is to put them in "a rising oven" (turning the heat up higher the moment the popovers enter the oven). This would also cause the batter to burst to its greatest advantage!

VARIATION: Herbed Yorkshire Popovers
Beat 3 tablespoons of minced fresh parsley, ¼ teaspoon of dry rosemary, and 1 medium clove of garlic, minced, into the batter.

# MAIN COURSES

# LATE-SUMMER PESTO

I adore pesto and never tire of it, despite the fact of its ever-present popularity. But I would never order it in a restaurant. For me it is home cooking—Sunday night comfort food.

My recipe for pesto, the fine balance of which evolved over the years, was originally influenced by Alfredo Viazzi. When he opened his first restaurant Trattoria da Alfredo in the West Village many years ago, I lived right across the street, and we quickly became friends. Pesto was a newly discovered culinary passion in America and Alfredo generously shared the secret for his special version. Instead of using pignoli, he used walnuts, which, to my taste, are far more interesting both in texture and flavor when combined with the basil, garlic and cheese. At the time, I was taking a college food course that required me to prepare a lunch for twenty people for a total of under $20. Pesto and pasta was the delicious answer, with enough money left over to spring for a huge bouquet of curly parsley as the centerpiece!

Pesto is named for the pestle in which the sauce was originally prepared. Every once in a while I enjoy making a small batch with my marble mortar and pestle. I love the coarse texture that results and toss my pasta portion right in the mortar, using it as my bowl. The marble is great for keeping the pasta hot!

Although nowadays fresh basil is available throughout the year, I still maintain a tradition of making pesto with the basil from my garden at the end of summer and freezing it in small foil packages to enjoy during the rest of the year. The food processor makes this an easy job.

(continued)

| INGREDIENTS | MEASURE | WEIGHT | |
| --- | --- | --- | --- |
| | *volume* | *ounces* | *grams* |
| walnut halves | 1 cup | 3.5 ounces | 100 grams |
| fresh basil leaves | 14 cups | 7 ounces | 200 grams |
| 3 large cloves of garlic, smashed | | 0.75 ounce | 21 grams |
| extra virgin olive oil | 1 liquid cup | | |
| salt | 1 teaspoon | | 6.7 grams |
| sugar | ½ teaspoon | | |
| black pepper, freshly ground | ½ teaspoon | | |
| cayenne pepper | scant ⅛ teaspoon | | |
| Parmesan cheese, freshly grated | 2⅓ cups (+ extra for serving) | 7 ounces | 200 grams |
| dried pasta | | (4 ounces per serving as a main course) | 113 grams |
| unsalted butter | (½ tablespoon per serving) | | |

MAKES: about 3½ cups pesto (enough for 26 to 28 main-course servings)

Place the walnuts in a food processor fitted with the metal blade. Pulse until coarsely chopped. Remove the nuts to a small bowl and set aside.

In batches, place the basil in the food processor and process until coarsely chopped, stirring down the leaves with a rubber spatula from time to time. Add the garlic cloves and process for a few seconds, until evenly mixed into the basil. Add the oil and seasonings and process just until mixed. Add the cheese and nuts and process for a few seconds, just until uniformly mixed. The texture should still be coarse.

For the freshest flavor, freeze any pesto you are not planning to serve within 3 days. Use squares of heavy-duty aluminum foil or individual plastic ice cube containers to make 2-tablespoon portions (a Number 40, 1¼-inch diameter ice-cream scoop works wonderfully for this), or make larger portions if desired. Store them in heavy-duty plastic freezer bags.

SERVE: Cook 4 ounces of pasta per person. If the pesto is in 2-tablespoon portions, it will defrost during the time it takes to cook the pasta. Toss the pasta with the pesto and

½ tablespoon of unsalted butter, or more olive oil, per serving. Add a few teaspoons of the pasta cooking water and about 1 tablespoon of freshly grated Parmesan cheese per serving if desired, saving a little cheese to sprinkle on top. (A dash of Cajun-style jalapeño sauce adds a sparkling dimension.)

KEEPS: 3 days refrigerated, 1 year frozen.

POINTERS FOR SUCCESS

- When growing basil, be sure to pinch off the flowers as soon as they appear to prevent bitterness in the leaves.
- Pesto can be stored in a crock or jar in the refrigerator by pouring an inch or two of oil on top to keep it fresh. I find it has the freshest taste, however, if frozen. Store the pesto in the heavy-duty freezer bags to contain the aroma of garlic and keep it from flavoring other stored foods.

VARIATION: Substitute fresh spinach for basil for a delicious winter pesto.

# SPAGHETTI WITH SUMMER GARDEN FRESH TOMATO SAUCE

I am always impatient waiting to make this simply delicious seasonal tomato sauce because the best plum tomatoes don't appear until the end of summer and the sauce doesn't work well with other juicier varieties. What makes it so special is that the tomatoes retain their incomparable fresh tomato essence but, unlike most recipes, are softened and integrated into the pasta by very brief cooking.

This recipe takes minutes to prepare and is a favorite family supper, but it is elegant and delicious enough to serve to company and can be increased easily to accommodate more people. Totally satisfying as a casual family supper with Italian bread, olive oil for dipping and an arugula salad. This pasta also is excellent as a first course to any grilled fare.

(continued)

| INGREDIENTS | MEASURE | WEIGHT | |
| --- | --- | --- | --- |
| | *volume* | *ounces/pounds* | *grams* |
| salt | 1 tablespoon + 1 teaspoon, divided | 1 ounce | 26 grams |
| ripe plum tomatoes | | 2 pounds | 908 grams |
| extra virgin olive oil | ¼ liquid cup | | |
| 2 small onions, chopped | 1½ cups | 7 ounces | 200 grams |
| 1 large clove of garlic, very thinly sliced | 1 tablespoon | 0.25 ounce | 7 grams |
| black pepper, freshly ground | a few grindings | | |
| fresh basil or flat-leafed parsley, finely chopped | ¼ cup | 1.5 ounces | 40 grams |
| spaghetti | | 1 pound | 454 grams |

SERVES: 4 as a main course, 8 as a first course

Fill a large pot with cold water and bring it to a boil to cook the pasta. Add the 1 tablespoon of salt.

Meanwhile, place the tomatoes in a large bowl and pour boiling water over them. Allow them to sit for 1 minute. Drain them in a colander and rinse them under cold water. Peel the tomatoes by inserting the tip of a sharp knife under the skin and using your fingers to slip off the skins.

Place a strainer over a medium bowl. Cut each tomato in half and, holding it over the strainer to catch all the juices, use your index finger to scoop out the seeds and discard them. Place the tomatoes and juice in a food processor and chop coarsely. Set aside.

In a large heavy frying pan, heat the oil over medium heat. Add the onions and fry, stirring often, for about 5 minutes or until translucent. Add the garlic and fry over low heat for about 30 seconds or until the garlic softens. Do not allow it to brown. Turn off the heat and add the tomatoes. Sprinkle them with the remaining 1 teaspoon of salt, the pepper and basil.

Boil the spaghetti just until no white appears in the center when a strand is cut. Do not allow it to overcook, or it will risk serious overcooking in the sauce. Drain the spaghetti, reserving a little of the water, and add it to the frying pan. Cook over medium heat, tossing constantly, for 2 to 3 minutes, until the spaghetti is well coated in the oil and tomatoes. Add a few tablespoons of the reserved pasta water if necessary to moisten it. Serve at once.

NOTE: If desired, pass freshly grated Parmesan cheese.

VARIATION: For marinara sauce, omit the onions and, after adding the tomatoes, simmer on low heat, stirring occasionally, until thickened, 20 to 30 minutes. Remove from the heat and add the basil.

POINTERS
FOR SUCCESS

• To facilitate tomato peeling, using a small sharp knife tip, make a small cross into the skin of each tomato before adding the boiling water. Some gadget stores or catalogs carry a small plastic device with tiny crossed metal blades that will accomplish this with one motion. If the tomatoes are not very ripe, place them in a pot of boiling water and boil them for about 30 seconds.

# PIG-OUT SPAGHETTI CARBONARA

There is carbonara and carbonara. Everyone's recipe is different because traditionally the dish included leftovers on hand. My version, however, is not based on leftovers and happens to be one of my all-time favorite recipes. It's obviously not for someone on a low-cholesterol diet, but rather a special once-in-a-great-while treat for those who dare. It is a hearty and satisfying dish, the sauce slightly creamy—just enough to coat the pasta nicely—and intensely flavorful with the sensuous blend of smoky bacon, fruity olive oil and mellow butter. The succulent, woodsy fresh porcini elevate the dish to a more fabulous height.

In addition to its great flavor, this recipe has special sentiment to me because it launched my food career in the test kitchens of *Ladies' Home Journal.* Each applicant for the job was required to take a practical exam that consisted of making an omelet, composing a fruit salad and boning a chicken. We were also asked to bring in a recipe that could be prepared using staples usually found in the home pantry. I had misunderstood and brought in a typed recipe rather than the intended cooked one. In a moment of inspiration I said, "Let me make it now; that will be case in point that it can be prepared using staples on hand and better still, in rapid-fire time." Even without the fresh porcini and using plain, unsmoked bacon, I got the job.

*(continued)*

| INGREDIENTS | MEASURE *volume* | WEIGHT *ounces/pounds* | *grams* |
|---|---|---|---|
| bacon, preferably corncob smoked* | | 8 ounces | 227 grams |
| OPTIONAL: fresh porcini mushrooms | | 8 ounces | 227 grams |
| extra virgin olive oil | ¼ liquid cup | | |
| unsalted butter | 4 tablespoons | 2 ounces | 56 grams |
| 1 large clove of garlic, very thinly sliced | 1 tablespoon | 0.25 ounce | 7 grams |
| 4 large egg yolks | ¼ cup + 2 teaspoons | 2.5 ounces | 74 grams |
| heavy cream | ¼ liquid cup | | |
| Parmigiano-Reggiano cheese, freshly grated | ¾ cup + extra for serving, if desired | 1 ounce | 32 grams |
| salt | ½ teaspoon + 2 tablespoons | 1.5 ounces | 44 grams |
| black pepper, freshly ground | ½ teaspoon | | |
| cayenne pepper | a sprinkling | | |
| spaghetti | | 1 pound | 454 grams |
| (water from the boiling pasta) | (¼ liquid cup) | | |
| fresh parsley, preferably flat-leafed, minced | ½ cup | 1 ounce | 28 grams |

SERVES: 4 as a main course

Place 4 large pasta bowls or dinner plates in the oven with a pilot light or heat set to very low. Fill a large pot with at least 4 quarts of cold water, cover it and bring the water to a boil.

Meanwhile, in a large wok or 12-inch Dutch oven, fry the bacon over medium-low heat until medium crisp. Drain it on paper towels, and break it into ½-inch pieces. Drain all but a thin film of the bacon fat from the pan.

If using the porcini, remove any dirt with a wet paper towel and cut off the very ends of the stems. Cut them into ¼-inch slices and then cut them into ½-inch squares.

Add the olive oil and butter to the pan with the bacon fat and heat over medium-low heat. If using the porcini, add them and cook, covered, for about 10 minutes or until tender, stirring once or twice. Add the garlic and sauté for about a minute or until softened, stirring constantly. Do

*Available through mail order from Harrington's, Main Street, Richmond, Vermont 05477 (802-434-4444).

not allow the garlic to brown, or it will be bitter. Remove from the heat and set aside.

In a small bowl, whisk the egg yolks lightly. In a small saucepan or the microwave oven, scald* the heavy cream. Add it gradually to the yolks, whisking constantly.

In another small bowl, stir together the cheese, the ½ teaspoon of salt and the black and cayenne peppers.

When the water for the pasta boils, add the 2 tablespoons of salt and the pasta. Cook it until al dente, about 15 minutes, or until no white appears in the center when a strand is cut. Shortly before the end of cooking, remove ¼ cup of the boiling water with a ladle and whisk it into the egg yolk mixture. Turn the heat on under the wok or Dutch oven to medium low.

Drain the cooked pasta and add it to the hot pan. Sauté, stirring with a large fork, until it is evenly coated with the butter-oil mixture. Add the reserved bacon, the cheese mixture and the parsley. Using 2 large forks, toss to blend. Empty the pasta into a large bowl. Add the egg yolk mixture and toss quickly to blend it in without scrambling the yolks. Transfer at once to the serving bowls. Pass extra grated cheese and a pepper mill.

UNDERSTANDING    My friend and colleague Faith Willinger, who lives in Tuscany, worked out this method of cooking the yolks with the hot pasta water to lessen the danger of bacteria that may be present in uncooked egg yolks.

*Bring it just to the boiling point; small bubbles will appear around the edge.

# SPICY LINGUINE AND CLAM SAUCE

This is probably on a par with spaghetti al pesto as our favorite, most often served, pasta dish. I never order it in a restaurant because it is so much more delicious home-made. My secrets for intense clam flavor and perfect texture are: steaming the small, tender clams just until they open (not continuing to cook them in the sauce); using part of the liquid from the clams for cooking the linguine and part of it for the sauce; and sautéing the linguine in the clam sauce. The latter technique coats the strands of linguine and causes the wonderful flavors to merge with the pasta. A touch of hot pepper is the perfect finishing touch.

| INGREDIENTS | MEASURE | WEIGHT | |
|---|---|---|---|
| | volume | ounces/pounds | grams |
| 4 dozen small (2-inch) littleneck clams* | | 1½ pounds | 680 grams |
| extra virgin olive oil | scant ¼ cup | | |
| 4 large cloves of garlic, very thinly sliced | ¼ cup | 1 ounce | 28 grams |
| OPTIONAL: hot pepper flakes | ½ teaspoon | | |
| black pepper, freshly ground | a few grindings | | |
| fresh basil or flat-leafed parsley, finely chopped | ¼ cup | 0.75 ounce | 20 grams |
| linguine (preferably #7 De Cecco) | | 1 pound | 454 grams |

SERVES: 4 as a main course

EQUIPMENT: wok or large frying pan

In a colander or steamer set over a large saucepot containing about 1 cup of boiling water, steam the clams until they pop open, about 15 to 20 minutes, removing them to a bowl as they open. Remove the colander or steamer and boil down the water and clam juices to about 2 cups.

While the liquid is reducing, remove the clams from the shells, reserving a few in the shells for garnish, and distribute them equally among 4 large soup dishes. Cover them with plastic wrap and place them in the oven with

*Or 6 dozen (2½ pounds/1 kilogram 134 grams) 1½-inch Manila clams, if available (left in their shells).

*(continued)*

a pilot light or heat set very low. Place the clams for garnish in a small bowl, cover and keep warm in the oven.

Pour ½ cup of the reduced broth into a small glass measuring cup and reserve. Add enough water to the liquid remaining in the saucepot to cook the linguine. (Do not salt, as the clam juice is very salty.)

In a wok or 12-inch frying pan, heat the oil. Add the garlic, optional hot pepper flakes and black pepper and fry on low heat for about 30 seconds or until the garlic softens. Do not allow it to brown. Add the reserved clam broth and basil or parsley and remove from the heat.

Boil the linguine until no white appears in the center when a strand is cut. Drain it and add it to the skillet. Cook over medium heat, tossing constantly until the linguine is well coated in the oil and juices and all but a few tablespoons of the liquid have been absorbed. Add the linguine to the serving bowls and toss to mix in the clams. Garnish with the reserved clams in the shell and serve at once.

NOTE: If desired, the clams can be added to the wok with the linguine. I find it easier to distribute the clams evenly by dividing them beforehand.

UNDERSTANDING The easiest way to open clams is to steam them. When they open, they are perfectly cooked. If the clams are small and tender, there is no reason to chop them.

# SHRIMP, SQUID AND CHIPOTLE PASTA

I adore the fiery-smoky flavor of the chipotle pepper, which is actually a smoked red jalapeño. When I first tasted this pasta, served as a side dish with lobster at Vincent's on Camelback in Scottsdale, Arizona, I was struck by the brilliant blending of Italian and Southwestern cuisines. When I came home I re-created the pasta recipe and added the shrimp, squid and coriander. The sweet, nutty flavor of the squid is perfect to balance the fire of the chipotle. This has since become my favorite Southwestern-style dish, ideal for entertaining as most of the preparation can be done hours ahead and the final cooking takes under fifteen minutes. This dish also happens to be delicious even with plain noodles—though I urge you to try the chipotle version.

| INGREDIENTS | MEASURE volume | WEIGHT ounces/pounds | grams |
|---|---|---|---|
| 2½ dozen small shrimp | | 1 pound | 454 grams |
| small squid, cleaned | | 1½ pounds | 680 grams |
| sauce from chipotles in adobo sauce* | 1 teaspoon | | |
| extra virgin olive oil | ⅓ liquid cup, divided | | |
| 3 large cloves of garlic, finely chopped | 2 tablespoons, divided | 0.75 ounce | 21 grams |
| 1 fresh green chili pepper, cored and sliced into very thin rounds, seeds poked out, divided† | about 6 inches long | 0.66 ounce | 18 grams |
| dry chicken base‡ | 2 teaspoons | | |
| salt | to taste | | |
| black pepper, freshly ground | to taste | | |
| fresh pasta, preferably chipotle (page 84) | ½ to ¾ recipe | 10 to 12 ounces | 280 to 340 grams |
| fresh coriander leaves, rinsed and dried | ½ cup | 0.5 ounces | 14 grams |

*Available in cans in Spanish markets (or through mail order from Coyote Cucina: 800-866-HOWL). It contains vinegar, tomato, onion, garlic, herbs and spices.
†Wash your hands after handling the chili to prevent irritation. If it seems exceptionally fiery, cut back the amount.
‡Available in 7-ounce jars in the spice section of supermarkets. Or substitute 2 bouillon cubes dissolved in a little hot water.

*(continued)*

SERVES: 4 as a main course
ADVANCE PREPARATION: Marinate the shrimp and squid for at least 1 hour or up to 10 hours

EQUIPMENT: wok or large skillet

*At least 1 or up to 10 hours before final preparation:*

Shell and devein the shrimp. Place them in a bowl large enough to hold them and the squid. Slice the squid crosswise into ⅜-inch rings and place them in the bowl. Add the adobo sauce, 1 tablespoon of the oil, 1 teaspoon of the garlic and 1 teaspoon of the green chili pepper. Cover tightly and refrigerate. Add the remaining garlic and green chili pepper to the remaining oil, cover and allow to sit at room temperature.

When ready to cook, bring a large pot of water to a boil for the pasta. Add ½ tablespoon of salt.

While the water is heating, separate the shrimp from the squid. Heat the wok or skillet and then turn the heat down to low. Add half of the oil-garlic-green chili mixture and sauté, stirring frequently, until the garlic has softened. Don't allow it to brown. Add half of the chicken base. Raise the heat to medium high and add the shrimp. Sprinkle them lightly with salt and pepper and cook, stirring constantly, until the shrimp turn pink, about 1 minute. With a slotted skimmer, remove them to a bowl.

ROSE'S MELTING POT

Turn the heat to low, add the remaining oil-garlic mixture and cook until the garlic has softened. Add the remaining chicken base, raise the heat to medium high and add the squid. Sprinkle it lightly with salt and pepper and cook just until the squid is opaque and tender (about 2 to 3 minutes but no longer or it will toughen). With a slotted skimmer, remove the squid to the bowl with the shrimp. If the squid has given off a lot of liquid, reduce the liquid to about ½ cup. Remove from the heat.

Boil the pasta for 3 minutes or until firm but tender. Drain it well and add it to the wok or skillet. Over medium heat, toss the pasta to coat it well with the juices. Add the coriander, shrimp and squid and continue tossing until well mixed. Serve at once.

UNDERSTANDING  Marinating the seafood is essential to blend the flavors. Without this process, the seafood does not blend with the pasta but rather seems to stand apart. The squid often exudes liquid as it cooks, making it necessary to reduce the juices.

# Fresh Chipotle Pasta

| INGREDIENTS<br>*room temperature* | MEASURE<br>*volume* | WEIGHT | |
|---|---|---|---|
| | | *ounces* | *grams* |
| chipotles in adobo* | ¼ cup (include 2 teaspoons of the sauce) | 1.75 ounces | 50 grams |
| unbleached all-purpose flour | 2 cups (measured by dip and sweep method) | 10.36 ounces | 296 grams |
| salt | 1 teaspoon | | 6.7 grams |
| 4 large eggs | 6½ fluid ounces | 7 ounces<br>(weighed without shells) | 200 grams |

MAKES: about 20 ounces of pasta
(enough for 6 to 8 servings)

Remove all the seeds from the chipotles as they will interfere with the smoothness of the pasta dough.

In a food processor with the metal blade, place the chipotles (with the sauce), the flour and salt. Process for a few minutes, until the chipotle is finely ground. With the motor running, add the eggs and process for a few seconds or until the egg is absorbed and the dough begins to clump and cleans the sides of the bowl. Do not allow it to form a ball. If the dough feels very sticky, add a tablespoon of flour and pulse in until absorbed. The dough should be very soft but not sticky.

Empty the dough onto a lightly floured counter and knead it for about 5 minutes or until it is silky smooth and no longer sticky. Add a little flour as needed to keep the dough from sticking.

Wrap the dough in plastic wrap, preferably Saran brand, and allow it to sit at room temperature for at least 30 minutes or up to 4 hours, or refrigerate it for up to 2 days before rolling and cutting.

*Available in cans in Spanish markets (or through mail order from Coyote Cucina: 800-866-HOWL).

Divide the dough into 6 parts. Using one piece at a time (keep the remainder covered), put the dough through the widest setting of a pasta machine 3 times, folding it in thirds after each rolling. Repeat rolling on progressively finer settings, finishing at the second finest. Flour the dough lightly between rollings if it seems at all sticky. Hang the dough on a drying rack or place it on a lightly floured cloth for about 5 to 10 minutes to dry slightly.

Run each strip of dough through the ¼-inch-wide fettuccine cutter to cut it into noodles. Then cook at once, or hang the noodles on a rack for about 10 minutes or until they are partially dry, or place them on a lightly floured towel and cover with a cloth until ready to cook. If you hang the noodles, be sure to remove them before they dry completely, or they will break at the point where they touch the rack. The uncooked noodles can be refrigerated for 1 to 2 days or frozen. If freezing, allow them to dry completely first to keep them from sticking together.

COOK: 3 minutes in a large pot of boiling salted water (1 tablespoon of salt). If frozen, add a few minutes to the cooking time, and cook until just tender.

NOTE: For 4 servings, use half to three-quarters the recipe.

# MUSSELS IN MUSTARD DILL CREAM

I spent the first five years of my life in Far Rockaway, three blocks from the ocean. My first smells were honeysuckle and the ever-present salty ocean air. My first memories were ocean ones; among them long jetties encrusted with tangles of bearded mussels, black and shiny with the foaming surf crashing against them. "We don't eat them," my mother explained, "but other people do." I accepted this at the time, but now I am happily among the "other people." For me, unadorned raw oysters and steamed mussels taste most like the way the ocean smells.

This special mussel dish was one Elliott and I both loved at a former neighborhood restaurant. I tried several times to re-create it but something was always missing. Finally, I remembered a trick that a French chef once shared with me: A whisper of curry powder, so little as not to be detectable, can add dimension and mystery to certain sauces.

Word of warning: Wash the mussel shells well before steaming them; this sauce is so good guests will want to lick the sauce from them!

| INGREDIENTS | MEASURE *volume* | WEIGHT *ounces/pounds* | *grams/kilograms* |
|---|---|---|---|
| mussels | | 4 pounds | 1 kilogram 814 grams |
| unsalted butter | 4 tablespoons, divided | 2 ounces | 56 grams |
| 2 shallots, minced | 2 rounded tablespoons | 0.75 ounce | 22 grams |
| white onion, minced | ⅔ cup | 3 ounces | 80 grams |
| dry white wine or dry white vermouth | 2 liquid cups | | |
| 2 bay leaves | | | |
| heavy cream | 1⅓ liquid cups | | |
| Dijon mustard | 2 teaspoons | 0.50 ounce | 12 grams |
| fresh dill, minced | ¼ cup | 0.50 ounce | 14 grams |
| black pepper, freshly ground | 4 grindings | | |
| curry powder | ⅛ teaspoon | | |

*(continued)*

Rinse and scrub the mussels, but don't beard them until right before cooking.

Cut 2 tablespoons of the butter into about ½-inch pieces and refrigerate.

In a large noncorrosive saucepan, over medium heat, melt the remaining 2 tablespoons of butter. When bubbling, sauté the shallots and onion until translucent, about 2 minutes. Add the wine and bay leaves, and then the mussels. Steam, covered, about 5 minutes or just until the mussels open, stirring them once or twice and removing them to serving bowls one at a time as they open, using tongs to drain any liquid back into the pot. Place them in the oven on the lowest possible setting to keep warm.

If the broth is sandy, strain through cheesecloth and return it to the pot. Bring the broth to a boil and cook it at a rapid boil for about 5 minutes, or until reduced to 1⅓ cups. Add the cream, mustard, dill, pepper and curry. Bring to a boil, whisking, and cook at a slow boil for about 7 minutes, whisking occasionally, until reduced to 1⅓ cups. Remove the pan from the heat and whisk in the cold butter one piece at a time, letting each piece melt before adding another.

Arrange the mussels so that the open sides are pointing up, and drizzle the sauce over the mussels. If desired, serve with crusty French bread.

POINTERS FOR SUCCESS

• Buy the mussels the same day you are planning to cook them. Store them, refrigerated, in an open bag (or punch holes in the bag), placed over ice.
• Don't add salt; the mussel broth is quite salty on its own.

UNDERSTANDING

In the past, it was necessary to soak mussels in salt water or in water with a little cornmeal sprinkled on the top to rid them of their sand. Although this technique was successful, it also resulted in some loss of flavor. Fortunately, mussels these days are often cultivated in less sandy areas, so presoaking them is not usually necessary.

# Party Paella

My friend and colleague Rick Rodgers proclaimed this paella the best he ever tasted. There is a reason: In most paellas served in restaurants, the wonderfully flavored rice seems to stand apart from the chicken and seafood. It took me many years to discover that the simple solution for bringing all the flavors together is to marinate the seafood and chicken before cooking in the olive oil, lemon juice, garlic and herbs.

I loved paella from the moment I first tasted it at the World's Fair in 1964. I had never before encountered the unique Spanish medley of saffron rice, seafood, chicken and spicy sausage. I longed so to taste it again that when my first husband and I moved to New York, and he left me for a few hours to do some of the unpacking, I ran off to Jai Alai, a famous old-time Village restaurant specializing in paella. When he returned to unpacked bags, I didn't dare tell him why.

A year later, Craig Claiborne printed a recipe for paella in *The New York Times*. My twenty-second birthday present was the ingredients for this recipe! I still remember the mysterious, almost unaffordable saffron in its tiny red plastic vial. This recipe was the first of many paellas I have made over the years.

*(continued)*

| INGREDIENTS | MEASURE<br>*volume* | WEIGHT<br>*ounces/pounds* | *grams/kilograms* |
|---|---|---|---|
| extra virgin olive oil | ¼ cup + 2 tablespoons, divided | | |
| lemon juice, freshly squeezed | 1 tablespoon | | |
| 2 large cloves of garlic, smashed | | 0.5 ounce | 14 grams |
| dried thyme, minced | ½ teaspoon | | |
| ground coriander | ½ teaspoon | | |
| salt | 1 teaspoon | | 6 grams |
| 1 lobster, preferably female | | 2 pounds | 908 grams |
| 32 small shrimp, peeled but tails left on | | 1 pound | 454 grams |
| 1 small chicken | | 2.5 to 3 pounds | 1 kilogram 134 grams to 1 kilogram 361 grams |
| chorizo (Spanish sausage), cut into ¼-inch slices | 2 4½-inch-long sausages | 8 ounces | 227 grams |
| lean salt pork, cut into ¼-inch dice* | ¾ cup | 4 ounces | 113 grams |
| 1 small onion, chopped | about ¾ cup | 3.5 ounces | 100 grams |
| 2 medium cloves of garlic, minced | 1 tablespoon | 0.35 ounce | 10 grams |
| whole saffron threads | 1 teaspoon | | |
| capers | 2 tablespoons | 0.75 ounce | 24 grams |
| 2 small plum tomatoes (5.5 ounces), peeled, seeded and chopped | ½ cup | 3.75 ounces | 106 grams |
| 2⅓ cups short-grain rice, preferably Spanish† or Italian Arborio | 2⅓ cups | 1 pound | 454 grams |
| low-salt chicken broth, preferably College Inn, *or* 3 cubes Glace de Volaille (page 209) dissolved in 3½ cups of boiling water with 1 teaspoon of salt | 3½ liquid cups (2 13.75-ounce cans) | 27.5 ounces | 780 grams |
| dry white wine | ½ liquid cup | | |
| black pepper, freshly ground | ¼ teaspoon | | |
| 16 mussels, well scrubbed‡ | | 1 pound | 454 grams |
| 16 small littleneck clams, well rinsed | | 2 pounds | 907 grams |
| small frozen peas, thawed | ½ cup | 2.3 ounces | 65 grams |
| pimientos, drained and cut into strips | 1 4-ounce can | 4 ounces | 113 grams |
| 1 lemon, cut into 8 wedges and seeded | | | |

*Make sure the butcher gives you salt pork that has large strips of meat running through it and is not all fat, which is called fatback.
†Alcazaba paella rice is available through Williams-Sonoma (800-541-2233) and Dean & DeLuca (800-227-7714). Long-grain rice can be substituted if desired.
‡Do not beard the mussels until shortly before cooking or they may die.

In a large bowl, combine the ¼ cup of olive oil, the lemon juice, smashed garlic, thyme, coriander, and salt. Set aside.

Bring a large pot of water to a boil for the lobster. Use large tongs to grasp the lobster on either side of the body and plunge it head first into the water. Cover and boil for about 1 minute or until all movement stops. Use the tongs to lift out the lobster and run it under cold water to stop the cooking. When cool, use a heavy knife and mallet or cleaver to cut it into large serving pieces. Crack the claws to facilitate removing the meat. Add the lobster to the oil marinade.

Rinse the shrimp under cold running water and pat dry with paper towels. Add them to the marinade.

Rinse the chicken under cold running water and pat dry with paper towels. Cut the chicken into pieces at the joints and cut the breast and back sections in half. Slash each piece in several places to enable the marinade to penetrate. Add it to the marinade bowl and stir to coat everything well. Cover tightly and refrigerate for at least 3 or up to 8 hours.

Place the salt pork in a medium saucepan and add cold water to cover. Bring to a boil and cook for 2 minutes. Drain and rinse under cold water. Drain well and pat dry with paper towels.

In the paella pan or roaster, over medium heat, sauté the salt pork with the remaining 2 tablespoons of oil until the pork bits are golden brown, 6 to 8 minutes. With a slotted skimmer, remove the pork bits to a paper towel, leaving the fat in the pan.

Remove the marinating bowl from the refrigerator and remove the shrimp and lobster, leaving behind the chicken and all the garlic pieces. Allow the chicken to sit at room temperature while you sauté the shrimp, lobster and chorizos.

In the fat remaining in the pan, over medium-high heat, sauté the shrimp and lobster, stirring constantly, for 1 to 2 minutes or until just pink. Use a slotted spoon to remove them to a medium bowl.

*(continued)*

Add the chorizo slices to the pan and sauté, stirring occasionally, until browned and cooked, about 10 minutes. Remove them with tongs and set aside.

Add the chicken pieces to the pan, skin side down, and sauté, turning them until browned on all sides, about 5 minutes for the breast pieces, 10 minutes for the others. (Discard the marinade.) If not using a paella pan, sauté the chicken in 2 batches. When browned, transfer to a plate. Pour off and discard all but about 2 tablespoons of fat from the pan. Add the salt pork, onion, minced garlic, saffron, capers and tomatoes to the pan and reduce the heat to low. Stir in the rice and sauté, stirring constantly, for about 3 minutes.

Meanwhile, heat the chicken broth until it is hot.

Add the white wine, then the hot chicken broth to the pan. Sprinkle the rice with the pepper. Place the chicken over the rice. Cover and simmer about 15 to 17 minutes or until the rice is firm but almost tender and almost all the broth has been absorbed.

Meanwhile, *preheat the oven to* 350°F. In a large covered frying pan or 6-quart Dutch oven, bring 1 cup of water to a boil. Add the mussels and clams and steam, covered, about 5 minutes or just until open. Stir them once or twice and remove them to a large bowl one at a time as they open, using tongs so any liquid drains back into the pot. Reserve the liquid.

Add the lobster, shrimp, chorizo and defrosted peas to the chicken and rice mixture. Cover and bake for 7 minutes to heat through. Then sprinkle 1 to 2 tablespoons of the mussel/clam steaming liquid over the rice mixture. Add the pimientos, mussels and clams. Cover and return to the oven for 5 minutes. (Keep the paella hot for up to a half hour by leaving it in the turned-off oven.) Garnish with the lemon wedges to squeeze over the paella if desired.

- Blanching salt pork removes some of the saltiness.
- The female lobster contains the roe and has a wider tail with sweeter meat than the male.
- For the most attractive appearance, leave the lobster in its shell. Removing the shell makes it difficult to find the lobster pieces and distribute evenly among the guests!
- Littleneck clams are more tender and flavorful than cherrystones.
- If using a chicken larger than 3 pounds, cut the thighs, legs and each breast in half with a cleaver so that they will cook through and make a more harmonious presentation.

# EAST COAST SOFT-SHELL CRABS

One of my greatest pleasures is sharing ethnic foods with my young nephew, Alexander, on his annual visits from California. My primary goal has been to show him how much fun and what an adventure new tastes can be. But I have discovered that through food one can impart many other valuable lessons: an appreciation for other cultures, the joy of sharing, the pride of creating, economy of motion, respect for the ingredients, the importance of freshness and quality, to name just a few.

I started with smell, partly because aroma is the most tantalizing part of eating but also because it tells you about freshness and inspires the combination of flavors and creation of the recipe. As I prepared each ingredient, I encouraged Alex to smell it.

I also wanted Alex to be realistic about where the food came from without turning him into a vegetarian because of his fondness for nature and animals. Two summers ago we shared Alex's first lobster. When he started out by kissing the claw, I was a little worried that he would be too sentimental to consider eating it, but he explained that he had kissed it "because it's the saddest part." It reminded me of the scene in *Last of the Mohicans* when the hunter asks forgiveness of the deer he is about to kill.

Last summer was the greatest test to date: soft-shell crab at Alex's request. "I've eaten it before," he claimed. "I doubt it; where you're from, it was probably Dungeness." "That may be, but I want to try it anyway." Who could resist his daring young spirit?

The crab was so fresh it moved in the pan. But when he cut into it and the green liver spurted out I was certain it wouldn't get past his lips. I watched in fascination as he tasted the first mouthful. "Umm . . . this is delicious." But what really melted my heart was that he offered me one of the claws. Never have I been so pleased to have been proven wrong. I could take this kid anywhere.

| INGREDIENTS | MEASURE | WEIGHT | |
| --- | --- | --- | --- |
| | *volume* | *ounces* | *grams* |
| all-purpose flour | 2 tablespoons | 0.5 ounce | 18 grams |
| salt | a large pinch | | |
| black pepper, freshly ground | a few grindings | | |
| unsalted butter | 2 tablespoons | 1 ounce | 28 grams |
| extra virgin olive oil | 1 tablespoon | | |
| 4 soft-shell crabs | | 10 ounces | 285 grams |
| OPTIONAL: freshly squeezed lemon juice | | | |

SERVES: 2

In a shallow bowl, whisk together the flour, salt and pepper.

Heat a large heavy frying pan over medium heat until a drop of water sprinkled in it sizzles. Add the butter with the olive oil. When the foam subsides, dredge each crab on both sides in the flour mixture and place it in the pan. Turn the heat down slightly and sauté for about 3 minutes a side or until golden brown. If desired, add a squeeze of lemon juice.

NOTE: Any leftover crab makes an excellent sandwich.

# DRUNKEN BLUEFISH WITH STEWED TOMATOES

My cousin Marty Bush is a brilliant mixer of gin stingers and martinis. However, the most creative use to which Marty has put gin is in this dish, where he uses it to its finest advantage (only a martini drinker would give me an argument). The gin, with its juniper flavor, gives the tomatoes a special quality that Marty describes as "high octane." But more valuable still, the gin completely cuts the oily quality normally associated with bluefish (the one drawback to one of America's finest native fish). A crusty bread is perfect for dipping in the flavorful pan juices. Any leftover fish and tomatoes is delicious served cold.

| INGREDIENTS | MEASURE | WEIGHT | |
| --- | --- | --- | --- |
| | *volume* | *ounces/pounds* | *grams/kilograms* |
| bluefish fillets | | 3 pounds | 1 kilogram 361 grams |
| 2 medium cloves of garlic, minced | 1 tablespoon | 0.35 ounce | 10 grams |
| salt | 1 teaspoon | | 6.7 grams |
| black pepper, freshly ground | ¼ teaspoon | | |
| paprika | a fine sprinkling | | |
| 3 large ripe tomatoes, sliced ¼ to ½ inch thick | | 1½ pounds | 680 grams |
| aromatic gin, preferably Tanqueray | ½ liquid cup | | |
| unsalted butter, cut into 8 pieces | 2 tablespoons | 1 ounce | 28 grams |
| 2 green onions, sliced (white and green parts) | ½ cup | 1 ounce | 31.5 grams |

SERVES: 6
ADVANCE PREPARATION: 1 hour
PREHEAT THE OVEN TO: 350°F.
BAKING AND BROILING TIME: about 20 to 30 minutes

EQUIPMENT: baking pan large enough to hold the fish in a single layer (an oval gratin dish is ideal and can be brought to the table for serving)

*Preheat the oven to 350°F. at least 15 minutes before baking.*

Place the fillets skin side down in a single layer in the baking pan. Sprinkle with the garlic, salt, pepper and paprika. Lay the tomato slices on top of the fish. Slowly pour the gin on top of the tomatoes, making sure that a little reaches each tomato slice. Dot with the butter, cover tightly with plastic wrap and allow to sit at room temperature for about 1 hour.

Remove the plastic wrap and bake for about 15 minutes, depending on the thickness of the fish, or until the fish is almost tender when flaked with a fork and the flesh in the thickest sections is almost opaque.

While the fish is baking, preheat the broiler.

Place the baking pan under the broiler for about 5 minutes or until the tomatoes are bubbling and beginning to brown. Sprinkle all over with the green onions. Drain off most of the cooking liquid and pour it into a gravy boat to pass on the side. If desired, reduce the sauce to concentrate the flavor.

 POINTERS FOR SUCCESS

• The success of this dish depends on fresh ripe summer tomatoes.

# AUTHENTIC CHINESE ZINGY RED SHRIMP

Chingwan Tcheng, who created this fabulous recipe, is the daughter of Dr. F. T. Cheng (Cheng Tien-Hsi), a renowned international jurist, scholar, diplomat and gourmet who wrote *The Musings of a Chinese Gourmet*. Growing up in Nanking, Europe and the United States, dining in the company of scholars and diplomats, Chingwan had the opportunity to observe which traditional dishes were the most appreciated by diverse palates. Although her formal studies were in the fine arts, she eventually studied with Grace Chu at the China Institute and then went on to open her own school in Tenafly, New Jersey.

I met Chingwan thanks to my Aunt Ruth, who was her devoted student. Every time I visited Aunt Ruth we would spend the entire day chopping and mincing in the intricate and laborious process required to produce a Chinese banquet, offering the guests the ease and pleasure of feasting without ever having to so much as cut a morsel of food.

The Chengs are now living in California, and Aunt Ruth has been living in Florida for years. And of all Chingwan's unique recipes, this simple and delicious shrimp and ketchup combination is the one I still hear about the most.

Make this dish and serve it on a bed of lettuce with rice for a family dinner, or celebrate the Chinese New Year with a banquet of Chinese-Style Honey Mustard Lamb Riblets (page 31), Perfect Crisp Roast Duck (page 140) and Filipino-Inspired Chicken Shrimp (page 33).

| INGREDIENTS | MEASURE | WEIGHT | |
| --- | --- | --- | --- |
| | *volume* | *ounces/pounds* | *grams* |
| 30 medium shrimp, shelled and deveined | | 1 pound | 454 grams |
| MARINADE | | | |
| salt | ½ teaspoon | | 6 grams |
| dry sherry | 1½ teaspoons | | |
| 1 large egg white | 2 tablespoons | 1 ounce | 30 grams |
| cornstarch | 1 tablespoon | 0.25 ounce | 7.5 grams |

*(continued)*

## SAUCE

| | | | |
|---|---|---|---|
| vegetable oil, preferably peanut | 2 tablespoons | | |
| 1 small onion, finely chopped | ¾ cup | 3.5 ounces | 100 grams |
| tomato ketchup | ⅓ cup | 3.25 ounces | 92 grams |
| water | ¼ cup | | |
| sugar | 2 tablespoons | 1 ounce | 25 grams |
| cornstarch | 1 tablespoon + 1 teaspoon | 0.35 ounce | 10 grams |
| salt | ½ teaspoon | | 6 grams |
| vinegar | 1 tablespoon | | |
| frozen baby peas, thawed | 3 tablespoons | 0.75 ounce | 23 grams |

OPTIONAL: lettuce leaves, for garnish

SERVES: 4

ADVANCE PREPARATION: at least 30 minutes or up to 8 hours ahead

EQUIPMENT: wok or large heavy frying pan

*At least 30 minutes or up to 8 hours ahead:*

Pat the shrimp dry with paper towels. In a medium bowl, stir together the marinade ingredients until blended. Add the shrimp and toss to coat well. Cover tightly and refrigerate.

In a wok or large heavy frying pan, over medium-high heat, heat the oil until a slight haze forms over it. Add the shrimp and cook, stirring constantly, until the shrimp turn pink, about 1 minute. With a slotted skimmer, remove them to a bowl.

Turn the heat to medium low, add the onion and cook, stirring occasionally, until limp, about 2 to 3 minutes. In a small bowl, stir together the ketchup, water, sugar, cornstarch, salt and vinegar, and add it to the onions. Cook, stirring constantly, about 3 minutes or until the sauce thickens. Add the shrimp and the peas. Stir well to coat the shrimp, and serve at once. If desired, line the serving plates with a few leaves of lettuce.

# Japanese Chirashi Sushi

One of the things I loved about having a cooking school was the extraordinary people I met from all over the world. Hiroko Ogawa was one of the most talented students ever to come to the Cordon Rose Cooking School. She took every class I offered and we became close friends, spending hours discussing food and cooking. In fact, her little girl Ayako's first words in English were "cherry pie" and "apple pie"! Hiroko in turn taught me enough Japanese to order politely from a sushi bar and even to say afterward that I had eaten well. She also taught me the special skill of making authentic sushi rice and my favorite Japanese dish: *chirashi sushi*. This is one Japanese dish that happens to be most delicious when prepared at home. Perhaps it's because you can leave out anything you may not like and put in all your own favorites. This dish really is a delightful grab bag of surprise treats varying in texture and flavor, its taste salty yet sweet. I love the crisp oceany flavor of the *nori*, the smoky sweetness of the preserved eel, the crunch of the roasted sesame seeds and the plush earthiness of the shiitake mushrooms. The flourless egg noodles are sheer magic and you have to taste the jade-green soy beans to know just how strangely satisfying they are. But I love the vinegared rice so much I sometimes make it just by itself for lunch.

Hiroko returned to Japan several years ago to become the supervisor of a prestigious French-Japanese restaurant. She also teaches baking and writes for Japanese food magazines. When I visited her in Japan, I discovered the

*(continued)*

---

*Sushi.* Sushi is one of the most classic foods in Japan and has been for over a thousand years. It originally developed out of a process for pickling *funa,* a kind of carp. Fish was salted and placed on a bed of vinegar rice where it fermented, producing a lactic acid which acted as a natural preservative. While the vinegar rice was usually discarded, the Japanese soon began to eat it along with the pickled fish. "Chirashi-zushi," or "scattered sushi," is one of the most common variations of this seafood delicacy because it is so simple to make. In Tokyo, cooks prepare "chirashi-zushi" by placing fresh seafood on top of the vinegar rice, while in Osaka they mix the seafood and rice together. Often taken to work for lunch or on weekend outings as a light snack, "chirashi-zushi" is also routinely sold on railway platforms throughout Japan. Here it is called "eki-ben," or "station lunches," and stations become known for the particular type of "eki-ben" they serve. Specialty sushi bars employ a series of chefs to prepare "nigiri-zushi," which demands the manual dexterity and ingenuity of a well-trained craftsman. In fact, a beginning sushi chef must spend about ten years as an apprentice before he can become a sushi master. He diligently observes his teachers and follows their example, learning the secrets of how to cook rice, roll sushi and cut raw fish.

---

charming presentation of using fresh flowers as chopstick holders. On my return I made a Japanese dinner party for twelve friends. (*Chirashi sushi* multiplies easily.) The aperitif was the Strawberry Champagne Punch from *Rose's Celebrations*, an odd mixture of East and West, but everyone loved it. The hors d'oeuvre was another East-West Hiroko-inspired touch: fresh avocado chunks with a dip of wasabi-flavored soy sauce (page 7). The *chirashi sushi* was served with hot sake, and for dessert, Green Tea Ice Cream (page 291) and meringue Green Tea Pine Needles (page 293).

I reproduced this party for my close friends Shirley and Archie Corriher when visiting Atlanta, Georgia. I was delighted to discover that all of the ingredients were available in their local Eastern food store. Everything went beautifully with the possible exception of Archie picking out all the *anago* in his portion. (I ate it for him.)

| INGREDIENTS | MEASURE | WEIGHT | |
|---|---|---|---|
| | *volume* | *ounces* | *grams* |
| VINEGARED SUSHI RICE | | | |
| Japanese or Chinese short-grain rice* | 3 cups | 22.5 ounces | 638 grams |
| water | 3⅓ liquid cups | | |
| unseasoned rice vinegar† | 5 fluid ounces (10 tablespoons) | | |
| sugar | 3 tablespoons | 1.25 ounces | 38 grams |
| salt, preferably uniodized | 4 teaspoons | 1 ounce | 27 grams |
| MARINATED SHIITAKES | | | |
| 12 large (2-inch) dried shiitake mushrooms | 2 heaping cups | 2 ounces | 56 grams |
| sugar | 1 tablespoon | 0.5 ounce | 12.5 grams |
| soy sauce | 1 tablespoon | | |

*Kokuhose brand, available in Korean stores, is a good choice.
†Mitsukan, available is some Japanese food stores, is my favorite brand.

*(continued)*

## EGG CRÊPE NOODLES

| | | | |
|---|---|---|---|
| 3 large eggs | scant 5 fluid ounces | 5.25 ounces | 150 grams (weighed without shells) |
| sugar | 1 tablespoon | 0.5 ounce | 12.5 grams |
| salt | a pinch | | |
| vegetable oil or nonstick spray | about 1 tablespoon | | |
| frozen soybeans in the pod *(edamame)** | 1 cup | 3.5 ounces | 100 grams |

## SEAFOOD

| | | | |
|---|---|---|---|
| water | 3 liquid cups | | |
| salt | 1 ½ teaspoons | 0.35 ounce | 10 grams |
| 2 dozen medium shrimp | | 12 ounces | 340 grams |
| unagi or *anago* (frozen preserved eel)† | 2 4-ounce packages | 8 ounces | 227 grams |
| *nori* (dried seaweed)‡ | 5 sheets | 0.6 ounce | 16.5 grams |

## SESAME SEEDS

| | | | |
|---|---|---|---|
| unhulled Japanese sesame seeds‡ | ¼ cup | 1 ounce | 28 grams |
| black Japanese sesame seeds‡ | 3 tablespoons | 0.75 ounce | 21 grams |

SERVES: 6

ADVANCE PREPARATION: All the ingredients for the sushi can be prepared early in the day. Everything but the *nori* and sesame seeds can be mixed together up to 2 hours ahead, but then must be left at room temperature.

## VINEGARED SUSHI RICE

The rice must be totally clean and then gradually sprinkled with the vinegar mixture in order to attain the sparkling, almost-translucent quality of perfect sushi rice.

Place the rice in a 2-quart or larger covered saucepan. Hold the pan under the faucet, running cold water into the rice while agitating it vigorously with your hand. Drain and repeat immediately. Repeat this process 5 times more (the agitation can be more casual now) or until the drained water runs completely clear. Add the 3⅓ cups of water, cover and allow to soak for at least 30 minutes.

Place the covered pan over medium heat, and bring the water to a boil. When the lid begins to "dance," turn the heat to

*Available at Eastern food stores. *Note:* Elizabeth Andoh, in *An American Taste of Japan,* lists the Japan Food Corporation, 445 Kauffman, South San Francisco, California 94080, as a resource that will tell you where to get Japanese food supplies in your area.
†Defrost the *unagi* either overnight in the refrigerator or for 30 minutes at room temperature.
‡Available at Eastern food stores or by mail order from Katagiri & Company, 224 East 59th Street, New York, New York 10021 (212-755-3566).

very low, and cook for 10 minutes. Remove from the heat and allow the rice to sit and steam for 10 minutes. Stir briefly to equalize the texture. Then empty into a large bowl or roasting pan. (The Japanese traditionally use a large wooden drum, held together by copper staves, a flat wooden paddle to stir and, of course, a fan to cool the rice.)

While the rice is cooking, stir together the vinegar, sugar and salt until the sugar and salt are fully dissolved.

Sprinkle the vinegar mixture gradually over the cooked rice, stirring and fanning the rice constantly. The fanning helps the rice to absorb the vinegar mixture. (A piece of shirt cardboard will do in place of a fan, and a hairdryer set on cool also works wonderfully.) Cover with a damp towel or plastic wrap and set aside at room temperature.

MARINATED SHIITAKES

Place the mushrooms in a small saucepan, and add water just to cover. Allow them to sit for about 30 minutes or until soft.

Add the sugar and soy sauce, bring to a boil over medium heat and simmer until almost all the liquid evaporates. Remove the mushrooms to a cutting board. When cool, remove and discard the stems and slice the caps into 1/8-inch strips. Place in a bowl, cover with plastic wrap and set aside.

EGG CRÊPE NOODLES

A nonstick pan is ideal for these flourless crêpes.

In a small bowl, mix together the eggs, sugar and salt. Pour this mixture through a fine strainer, stirring occasionally with the back of a spoon to speed the process.

Heat the pan over medium heat until it is hot enough to sizzle a drop of water. Reduce the heat to low and brush the pan with a very thin coating of oil (a little more if the pan is not nonstick). Pour in a small amount of the egg mixture and quickly tilt the pan to the left and then down and around to the right so that the batter moves in a
*(continued)*

counterclockwise direction, covering the entire pan. Immediately pour any extra batter back into the bowl. When the top of the crêpe is set, carefully use your fingers to flip it over to cook the other side briefly. It should be dull but not brown. Flip the crêpe onto a clean work surface, and repeat with the rest of the batter. You will need to re-oil the pan between every 2 or 3 crêpes if you are using a nonstick pan, between every crêpe if using an ordinary pan. As each crêpe is finished, flip it on top of the preceding one. When all the batter has been cooked, roll up the stack of crêpes into a long roll and cut into ⅛-inch-thick slices. Toss them gently to unfurl them into long strands. Place in a bowl, cover with plastic wrap and set aside.

Fill a small saucepan with water and bring it to a boil. Place the frozen soybean pods in the water, and when it is boiling again, continue cooking for 5 minutes. Drain at once. When cool, remove the beans from the pods and discard the pods. Place the beans in a small bowl and cover with plastic wrap. Set aside.

SEAFOOD

In a medium covered saucepan, bring the 3 cups of water to a boil. Add the salt and shrimp and, over high heat, return to a boil. Cover immediately and remove the pan from the heat. Allow it to sit for exactly 10 minutes. Then empty the shrimp into a colander. When cool enough to handle, remove the shells and devein the shrimp. Place them in a bowl and cover with plastic wrap. If not serving within 2 hours, refrigerate.

Cut the *unagi* into ½-inch pieces, place it in a bowl and cover it with plastic wrap. If keeping for more than 2 hours before serving, refrigerate.

The best way to crisp *nori* is over a gas flame. It makes it crunchy and turns it a deeper green. Hold each sheet of *nori* with tongs over a medium-low gas flame. Do not allow the *nori* to touch the flame. Wave it over the flame, turning it from one side to the other until it has turned green. If you are using an electric burner, run each sheet of *nori* over it, allowing it to touch the surface of the burner, until it has turned green. With sharp shears, cut the *nori* into ⅛-inch strips. Set it aside uncovered.

## SESAME SEEDS

Heat a dry (unoiled) heavy skillet over medium heat. Dry-roasting the seeds greatly brings out their flavor. Add the brown and black sesame seeds and roast them, swirling the pan constantly, for about 1 minute or until the brown sesame seeds deepen slightly in color. Empty them immediately into a small bowl and set aside uncovered.

## FINAL ASSEMBLY

I like to combine the ingredients with the rice at least 1 hour ahead of serving so that the flavors have a chance to mingle, but I save the *nori* and sesame seeds for the end to have the contrast of the crunch and crisp. I also reserve some of the egg crêpe noodles, as they provide an attractive decor.

Use a flat wooden paddle, a large rubber spatula or your fingers to mix the ingredients. (If using your fingers, combine 2 tablespoons of rice vinegar with 2 cups of water in a small bowl. Use this to dip your fingers as needed to prevent sticking.) Uncover the rice and add the shiitakes and seafood. Strew half the crêpe noodles on top and mix in very gently. Cover with the damp towel or plastic wrap. Do not refrigerate, as cold will ruin the texture of the rice.

Just before serving, mix in the sesame seeds and half the *nori*. Stew the remaining *nori* and egg crêpe noodles decoratively on top.

UNDERSTANDING   I asked Hiroko if it was okay to use old rice that had been stored in the pantry for over a year. She said she had no idea since in Japan they always used the current year's crop. I found out from personal experience, however, that if the rice is well over a year old it will be drier and require more water.

Cooking shrimp in boiling water removed from the heat is a technique I developed that results in the greatest tenderness.

# SALMON STEAK WITH DIJON MUSTARD AND BLACK MUSTARD GRAINS

**B**uttery moist and richly flavorful, salmon is my favorite fish, and King salmon, with its deeper color and fuller flavor, is my preferred variety. This simple dish, with the slightly tangy gilding of mustard and crunch of mustard seeds, is so delicious and elegant, it works with any variety of fresh salmon. I serve it both as a middle-of-the-week family meal and for elegant dinner parties. Steamed Asparagus (page 170) and new potatoes are lovely accompaniments. For very special occasions, Extra-Lemony Hollandaise Sauce (page 204) is the perfect complement.

| INGREDIENTS | MEASURE<br>*volume* | WEIGHT<br>*ounces/pounds* | *grams* |
|---|---|---|---|
| 6 salmon steaks | ¾ inch thick | 2 pounds | 907 grams |
| Dijon mustard | ¼ cup | 2.5 ounces | 72 grams |
| black pepper, freshly ground | to taste | | |
| black mustard seeds* | 2 tablespoons | 0.75 ounce | 21 grams |

SERVES: 6

Preheat the broiler for about 5 minutes.

Line a shallow pan with foil and spray it with nonstick vegetable shortening. Spread one side of each salmon steak with 1 teaspoon of the mustard. Grind a sprinkling of black pepper on top and sprinkle each mustard-coated salmon steak with ½ teaspoon of the mustard seeds.

Broil about 3 inches from the heat for about 3 minutes or until well browned. With two pancake turners, turn each salmon steak. Coat the second side of each with the mustard, pepper and mustard seeds and broil for another 3 minutes or until well browned and just cooked through, but not dry. (An instant-read thermometer should register 125°F.)

*Available in Indian markets (regular mustard seeds can be substituted).

NOTE: Salmon prepared this way is delicious at room temperature and any leftover is also excellent served cold accompanied by cold boiled potatoes, sliced, with Horseradish Mayonnaise (page 203).

# RUSSIAN RIVERS SALMON PIE (Coulibiac)

This is a fabulous one-of-a-kind dish for entertaining. Not only is it spectacular to behold, delicious in flavor and complex in texture, but also all the work is done well in advance, leaving no last-minute preparation. It is also excellent served at room temperature or even cold, the day after baking.

The first time I made this recipe was for my cousins Bill and Joy Howe. It was their first visit to our house and I thought it would be fun to have a Russian theme to honor Bill's and my mutual ancestry. We were all awed by this traditional culinary work of art, and when I served the leftovers cold to some friends for lunch two days later it was again a great hit. As the dish encompasses so many interesting techniques, I started teaching it in my cooking school and this was when I decided to replace the traditional rice with the more delicate couscous. Most of the components of a coulibiac can be made days ahead. My favorite parts are making the brioche and the final assembly. This is a thrilling recipe to prepare, and it's even more fun to share part of the preparation with a friend and make it into a joint dinner venture. Because of its many components, coulibiac is really a meal in itself, requiring only an equally elegant salad, such as Endive and Walnut Salad with Raspberry Walnut Vinaigrette (page 196), and small but decadent Chocolate Pots de Crème (page 288) to round it out.

*(continued)*

## BRIOCHE

| INGREDIENTS | MEASURE | WEIGHT | |
| --- | --- | --- | --- |
| water | ⅓ liquid cup | | |
| sugar | ¼ cup, divided | 1.75 ounces | 50 grams |
| fresh yeast* *or/* | 4 packed teaspoons | 1 ounce | 28 grams |
| dry yeast (*not* rapid-rise) | 1 tablespoon | 0.33 ounce | 9 grams |
| unbleached bread flour | about 3 cups (measured by dip and sweep method) | 1 pound | 454 grams |
| 6 large eggs, at room temperature | | 12 ounces (weighed in the shells) | 340 grams |
| unsalted butter, softened | 20 tablespoons (2½ sticks) | 10 ounces | 284 grams |
| salt | 1½ teaspoons | 0.33 ounce | 10 grams |

## SALMON AND MUSHROOMS

| INGREDIENTS | MEASURE | WEIGHT | |
| --- | --- | --- | --- |
| unsalted butter, softened | 2 tablespoons | 1 ounce | 28 grams |
| 2 salmon fillets (preferably center-cut), skinned and pin bones removed | | 3 pounds | 1 kilogram 360 grams |
| onion, finely chopped | 2 tablespoons | 0.50 ounce | 16 grams |
| shallots, finely chopped | 2 tablespoons | 0.66 ounce | 18 grams |
| salt | 1½ teaspoons | 0.35 ounce | 10 grams |
| black pepper, freshly ground | ½ teaspoon | | |
| fresh mushrooms, thinly sliced | 3¾ cups | 12 ounces | 340 grams |
| fresh dill, chopped | ¼ cup, firmly packed | 0.50 ounce | 14 grams |
| dry white wine or vermouth | 1 liquid cup | | |
| low-salt chicken broth preferably College Inn, or 2 cubes Glace de Volaille (page 209) dissolved in 1 cup of boiling water | 1 liquid cup | 1 ounce | 34 grams |

## VELOUTÉ

| INGREDIENTS | MEASURE | WEIGHT | |
| --- | --- | --- | --- |
| (salmon cooking liquid) | | | |
| unsalted butter | 2 tablespoons | 1 ounce | 28 grams |
| all-purpose flour | 3 tablespoons | 1 ounce | 27 grams |
| cayenne pepper | ⅛ teaspoon | | |
| lemon juice, freshly squeezed | 3 tablespoons | | |
| 5 large egg yolks, lightly beaten | 3 fluid ounces | 3.25 ounces | 93 grams |
| white pepper, freshly ground | a few grindings | | |

*Fresh yeast causes dough to rise faster than dry.

## Dill Crêpes

| | | | |
|---|---|---|---|
| 2 large eggs | 3 full fluid ounces | 3.5 ounces (weighed without shells) | 100 grams |
| milk | ⅔ liquid cup | | |
| unsalted butter, melted | 2 tablespoons | 1 ounce | 28 grams |
| cornstarch | ⅔ cup | 2.66 ounces | 75 grams |
| salt | ⅛ teaspoon | | |
| fresh dill, minced | 2 teaspoons | | |
| fresh parsley, preferably flat-leafed, minced | 2 teaspoons | | |
| clarified butter* | 1 tablespoon | 0.5 ounce | 12 grams |

## Couscous and Egg Filling

| | | | |
|---|---|---|---|
| water | 1 liquid cup | | |
| unsalted butter | 1 tablespoon | 0.5 ounce | 12 grams |
| salt | ½ teaspoon | | |
| black pepper, freshly ground | ⅛ teaspoon | | |
| couscous | ⅔ cup | 4.25 ounces | 121 grams |
| 3 hard-cooked large eggs, shelled and finely chopped† | | 6 ounces | 170 grams |
| fresh parsley, preferably flat-leafed, minced | ¼ cup | 2.25 ounces | 64 grams |
| fresh dill, minced | 1 tablespoon | | 3.5 grams |

## Egg Glaze

| | | | |
|---|---|---|---|
| 2 large egg yolks | 2 tablespoons | 1.25 ounces | 37 grams |
| heavy cream | 2 tablespoons | | |
| unsalted butter, softened | 2 tablespoons | 1 ounce | 28 grams |
| Flaky Tender Pastry (page 118) | | 2 ounces | 56 grams |
| unsalted butter, melted | 24 tablespoons | 12 ounces | 340 grams |

*If you do not have clarified butter on hand, you will need to clarify 3 tablespoons (1.5 ounces/43 grams) of unsalted butter. In a heavy saucepan, melt the butter partially covered to prevent splattering, over medium heat. When it looks clear, cook, uncovered, watching carefully, until the solids drop and just begin to turn pale gold. Immediately pour through a fine strainer or a strainer lined with cheesecloth.

†To hard-cook eggs: Place the eggs in a pan of cold water. Bring to a simmer and cook at a simmer for 20 minutes. Do not allow the water to boil. With a slotted spoon, remove the eggs and place them under cold running water for about 15 seconds. When cool, roll the eggs on the counter, using light pressure to crush the shells evenly for ease in removal.

SERVES: 16

ADVANCE PREPARATION: Make
  brioche at least 1 day or up to
  2 days ahead

PREHEAT THE OVEN TO: 400°F.

BAKING TIME: 1 hour

FINISHED SIZE: 16 inches by 9
  inches

EQUIPMENT: heavy-duty mixer
  such as a KitchenAid, baking
  dish or roasting pan about 14
  inches by 9 inches by 2 inches
  (large enough to hold 2 rows of
  slightly overlapping slices of
  salmon), 6-inch crêpe pan

## BRIOCHE

(prepare 1 day or up to 2 days ahead)

PROOF THE YEAST: In a small bowl, combine the water (ideally a tepid 100°F. if using fresh yeast, a little warmer, 110°F., if using dry; (do not use hot water, or the yeast will die), 1 teaspoon of the sugar and the yeast. If using fresh yeast, crumble it slightly while adding it. Set the mixture aside in a draft-free spot for 10 to 20 minutes. By this time, the mixture should be full of bubbles. If not, the yeast is too old to be useful and you must start again with newer yeast.

MAKE THE SPONGE: Place ⅔ cup of the flour and 2 of the eggs in the large mixer bowl and whisk until mixed. Add the yeast mixture and whisk until smooth. Sprinkle the remaining 2⅔ cups of flour over the mixture, but do not mix it in. Cover tightly with plastic wrap (preferably Saran brand) and let stand for 1½ to 2 hours.

In a medium-size heavy saucepan, melt 4 tablespoons of the butter, partially covered to prevent spattering, over medium heat. Do not stir. When the butter looks clear, cook, uncovered, watching carefully, until the solids drop and turn dark brown. Watch carefully, as when the bubbling noise quiets, all the water has evaporated and the butter can burn easily. Remove immediately from the heat and pour the butter and brown solids into a medium bowl. When cool, stir in the remaining softened butter.

MAKE THE DOUGH: In a small bowl, whisk together the remaining sugar and the salt until well combined. Add this mixture together with the remaining 4 eggs to the sponge, and beat on medium speed with the flat beater for about 5 minutes or until the dough is smooth, shiny and very elastic and begins to clean the bowl. If the dough starts to climb up the beater, change to the dough hook. Be sure to continue beating until the dough starts to mass together and come away from the sides. Then increase the speed to medium-high and add the browned butter mixture by the tablespoon, beating until it is incorporated.

FIRST RISE: Scrape the dough into a lightly buttered bowl. It will be very soft and elastic. Sprinkle it lightly with flour to prevent a crust from forming. Cover the bowl tightly with plastic wrap (preferably Saran brand), and let it rise in a warm place (about 80°F. but not above, or the yeast will develop a sour taste) until doubled in bulk, 1½ to 2 hours.

Refrigerate the dough for 1 hour to firm it so the butter will not separate. Gently deflate the dough by stirring it with a rubber scraper and return it to the refrigerator for another hour so that it will be less sticky to handle.

REDISTRIBUTING THE YEAST AND FINAL RISE (6 HOURS TO 2 DAYS, CHILLED): Turn the dough onto a lightly floured surface and gently press it into a rectangle, flouring the surface and dough as needed to keep the dough from sticking to your hands. Fold the dough into thirds (as you would a business letter), brushing off any excess flour, and again press it out into a rectangle. Fold it again into thirds and dust it lightly with flour on all sides. Wrap it loosely but securely in plastic wrap and then place it in a large zip-seal bag or wrap it in foil and refrigerate for 6 hours or up to 2 days to allow the dough to ripen and firm.

SALMON AND MUSHROOMS

(can be prepared a day ahead)

*Preheat the oven to 400°F.*

Butter the baking dish with the softened butter.

Cut each salmon fillet on the bias into slices about ½ inch thick.

Sprinkle the onion, shallots, ¾ teaspoon of the salt and ¼ teaspoon of the pepper into the baking dish. Arrange the salmon slices in 2 parallel rows on top. Sprinkle with the remaining salt and pepper. Scatter the mushrooms over the salmon and sprinkle with the dill.

Heat the wine and chicken broth until hot and pour it on top of the salmon and mushrooms. Cover the dish with aluminum foil and bake for 10 minutes. The salmon should be barely opaque. (It will continue cooking when baked in the brioche.) Turn off the oven. Pour the accumulated cooking liquid into a medium saucepan. Remove the

*(continued)*

mushrooms to a small bowl and set aside. Allow the salmon to cool, draining any liquid that forms into the saucepan.

## VELOUTÉ

Bring the salmon cooking liquid to a full boil. Turn the heat to low.

In another medium saucepan, over medium-low heat, melt the butter. Over low heat, add the flour and cook for 1 minute, whisking constantly. Add the hot liquid all at once, whisking rapidly. Add the reserved mushrooms and simmer over very low heat, stirring often, for 20 minutes. Whisk in the cayenne pepper and lemon juice and then the egg yolks. Continue cooking for 30 seconds, whisking rapidly. The sauce will be very thick. Remove it from the heat and add the white pepper. Spread the sauce evenly over the salmon and allow it to cool. Press a piece of plastic wrap, lightly sprayed with nonstick vegetable spray, on top, and refrigerate until cold (at least 1 hour).

## DILL CRÊPES

(can be prepared up to 2 days ahead and refrigerated, or can be prepared well ahead and frozen for up to 3 months)

In a blender container, place all the ingredients for the crêpes except for the clarified butter, and blend at high speed for 10 seconds. Alternatively, in a large bowl, combine the cornstarch, salt and pepper. Slowly stir in the milk. Use a hand-held electric or rotary beater, beat in the eggs one at a time, beating about 1 minute after each addition. Beat until the batter is smooth. Beat in the dill, parsley and melted butter.

Heat the crêpe pan over medium-high heat until hot enough to sizzle a drop of water. Brush it lightly with some of the clarified butter and pour a scant 2 tablespoons of batter into the center. Immediately tilt the pan to the left and then down and around to the right so that the batter moves in a counterclockwise direction, covering the entire bottom of the pan. Cook until the top starts to dull and the edges begin to brown, about 15 to 20 seconds. Use a small metal spatula to lift the upper edge and check to see if the crêpe is golden brown. Then, grasping the edge of the crêpe with your fingers, flip it over, and cook for 10 seconds, or just until lightly browned. Invert the pan over the counter and the crêpe will release.

It is fine to place 1 crêpe on top of another if using them the same day. If refrigerating or freezing the crêpes, however, separate them with pieces of wax paper or they may stick to each other.

This recipe makes about 18 crêpes. Don't worry if the first ones don't come out perfectly; you need only 14.

### COUSCOUS AND EGG FILLING

(can be prepared up to 2 days ahead and refrigerated)

In a small covered saucepan, bring the water and butter to a boil. Add the salt and pepper and slowly stir in the couscous, making sure the water boils continuously. Simmer over low heat, stirring constantly, until almost all of the water is absorbed. Cover and allow to sit for 5 minutes. Fluff with a fork and let cool, uncovered.

Combine the couscous with the chopped eggs, parsley and dill, mixing lightly with a fork.

### FINAL ASSEMBLY

Remove the salmon from the refrigerator, and divide it in half lengthwise down the center.

On a lightly floured counter, gently deflate the dough by kneading it lightly with floured hands. Roll it into an 18-inch by 21-inch rectangle.

Arrange 8 overlapping crêpes, in 2 rows, down the center of the rectangle, leaving a wide border (about 3 inches) on all sides. Sprinkle the crêpes with about one third of the couscous mixture, in a long rectangle down the center. Place half of the chilled salmon, mushroom side down, on top of the couscous mixture. Sprinkle the top of the salmon with another one third of the couscous mixture. Place the remaining salmon on top, mushroom side up,
*(continued)*

and sprinkle with the remaining couscous mixture. Cover with 6 overlapping crêpes.

In a small bowl, whisk together the egg yolks and cream for a glaze.

Bring one long side of the brioche up over the filling, and brush it well with the yolk-cream mixture. Bring the opposite side of the brioche dough over to enclose the filling, overlapping the 2 sides of the dough. Trim the edges of the dough if necessary to keep an attractive shape.

Bring up the short sides of the brioche, pinching to enclose the filling. Trim the edges if necessary. (Do not tuck the excess more than about ½ inch underneath or the ends will be significantly higher than the middle after baking.)

Use the softened butter to butter a large baking sheet, at least 16 inches long. Place the coulibiac seam side down on the baking sheet. A large rimless baking sheet works well to flip it over. Allow it to rest and begin to rise for 15 minutes.

Using a decorative cookie cutter, cut 2 round or oval steam vents in the top of the coulibiac; these vents can be decorated by surrounding them with slightly larger rings of scalloped pastry dough.

Roll out the Flaky Tender Pastry about ⅛ inch thick and cut into decorative shapes. Brush the coulibiac all over with the yolk mixture and decorate with the flaky pastry shapes. Keep in mind that during baking, the flaky pastry shrinks while the brioche grows, so if you make long strips, do not tuck them under the brioche or they will break! Brush the decorations with the egg glaze.

Tear off a 4½-foot length of 12-inch-wide heavy-duty aluminum foil. Fold it over into thirds to make a long band about 4 inches wide. Brush it with about ¼ cup of the melted butter, or spray it with nonstick vegetable shortening, and arrange it snugly around the coulibiac, buttered side against the brioche. Fasten the band at the top with a large paper clip. Run a cord around the center of the band to keep it in place. This supports the sides of the coulibiac, which are vulnerable to collapse during the initial stages of baking, before the dough is firm and set. Make sure that the bottom of the foil band goes all the way down to the bottom and touches the pan all around.

Place the coulibiac in a warm draft-free place for 30 minutes.

*Preheat the oven to 400°F.*

Bake the coulibiac 15 minutes; lower the heat to 375°F. and continue baking for 10 minutes. Turn it around in the oven for more even baking, cover *loosely* with a piece of aluminum foil (do not crimp it, or the pastry will steam) and continue baking 20 minutes. Remove the piece of foil and bake 15 minutes more.

Remove the coulibiac from the oven and pour ¼ cup of the remaining melted butter into each steam vent. Slip a large rimless baking sheet under the coulibiac and transfer it to a serving platter. Allow it to sit for 30 minutes before serving. (Use a wide pancake turner or spatula, pressed up against the cut end to support the coulibiac.)

Using a serrated knife, cut the coulibiac into 1-inch slices. Pass the remaining melted butter.

NOTE: Also traditional in the egg and rice filling is *vesiga*, the spinal fluid of sturgeon. I have tried it and the gelatinous texture is not to my taste.

POINTERS FOR SUCCESS

• When using yeast, always begin by proofing it to make sure it is alive. If using fresh yeast, smell it to be sure it doesn't have a sour odor. To proof the yeast, use warm water (hot water would kill it).

UNDERSTANDING

BRIOCHE
Unlike a cake, which is primarily a starch structure, bread depends on protein in the form of gluten to create its framework. The higher the protein content of the flour, the stronger the structure will be and the finer the grain of the bread (directly the opposite of cake). This dough is exceptionally wet. Just enough extra flour is added to handle it for shaping, resulting in a very light, soft brioche.

*(continued)*

I do not use rapid-rise yeast, because the flavor development and texture are superior with slower rising.

CRÊPES

Cornstarch in place of flour absorbs the liquid more readily, making it possible to use the batter without resting, and results in more tender crêpes. The crêpes are used in the coulibiac not only for flavor and texture, but also to keep the brioche from getting soggy!

FLAKY TENDER PASTRY

Although scraps of brioche can be used for decoration, flaky pastry provides a better color contrast.

# FLAKY TENDER PASTRY

This recipe is easy to make and perfect for shaping decorations for the coulibiac (page 109). The food processor method is the easiest because the dough gets handled less and stays more chilled, but the hand method will produce just as good a crust.

| INGREDIENTS cold | MEASURE volume | WEIGHT ounces | grams |
|---|---|---|---|
| unsalted butter | 8 tablespoons | 4 ounces | 113 grams |
| bleached all-purpose flour | 1⅓ cups (measured by dip and sweep method) | 6.5 ounces | 184 grams |
| salt | ½ teaspoon | | 3.3 grams |
| ice water | 2 to 3 tablespoons | | |

FOOD PROCESSOR METHOD

Divide the butter into two parts: 5 tablespoons (2.5 ounces) and 3 tablespoons (1.5 ounces). Cut the butter into ½-inch cubes, keeping the two parts separate. Wrap each portion with plastic wrap (preferably Saran brand) and refrigerate for at least 15 minutes.

Place the flour and salt in a food processor with the metal blade and process for a few seconds to combine. Add the larger amount of butter cubes and process for 20 seconds or until the mixture resembles fine meal. Add the remaining butter cubes and pulse for 20 seconds or until the pieces of butter are the size of small peas.

Add 2 tablespoons of the ice water and pulse 6 times. Pinch the dough together between your fingers. If it does not hold together, add another tablespoon of water and pulse 3 times. Try pinching it again and if necessary, add the remaining water, pulsing 3 times to incorporate it. Process for a few seconds, just until the dough forms a ball.

Remove the dough to a piece of plastic wrap (preferably Saran brand), and flatten it into a disc. Wrap it in the plastic wrap and refrigerate for at least 30 minutes or up to 2 days.

## HAND METHOD

Place the flour and salt in a medium bowl and whisk to comine. Use a pastry cutter or two knives to cut the butter into the flour, the first part into fine meal, the second into small peas just as with the food processor method. When adding the ice water, sprinkle it on, tossing the mixture lightly with a fork. Use your hands to gather the dough together and knead it briefly on the counter until it forms a smooth ball. Wrap the dough in plastic wrap and flatten it into a disc. Refrigerate it for at least 45 minutes or up to 2 days.

## ROLLING THE DOUGH

Using a pastry cloth and sleeve, rubbed with flour, or 2 sheets of plastic wrap or wax paper, sprinkled lightly with flour, roll the dough into a rectangle about ⅛ inch thick.

KEEPS: 2 days refrigerated.

# SPICY SOUTHERN FRIED CHICKEN

Fried chicken is a very special once-in-a-great-while treat, so when I eat it, I want it to be perfect. For me, this means a thin, spicy, crunchy but greaseless crust with a moist, tender interior. These criteria eliminate all the fast food places and since I don't live in the South, to have it the way I want it I have to make it myself.

When I prepare this dinner, for once I throw all thoughts of health, texture or color compatibility to the winds in favor of the top favorite things in which I revel: biscuits or Mashed Potatoes (page 162), with Bittersweet Fudge Brownies (page 308) and Triple Vanilla Lover's Ice Cream (page 284) for dessert. Everything is shades of brown and white. No one ever complains.

| INGREDIENTS | MEASURE volume | WEIGHT ounces/pounds | grams/kilograms |
| --- | --- | --- | --- |
| 1 chicken, preferably free range | | 3 pounds | 1 kilogram 361 grams |
| buttermilk | 1 quart | | |
| white vegetable shortening | 2½ cups | 1 pound 0.75 ounce | 480 grams |
| bacon fat, preferably from corncob smoked bacon, or additional shortening* | ½ cup | 3.75 ounces | 107 grams |
| all-purpose flour | 1 cup, (measured by dip and sweep method) | 5 ounces | 145 grams |
| salt | 1 teaspoon | 0.25 ounce | 6.7 grams |
| black pepper, freshly ground | ¼ teaspoon | | |
| OPTIONAL: cayenne pepper | ¼ teaspoon | | |

*Available through mail order from Harrington's, Main Street, Richmond, Vermont 05477 (802-434-4444).

*(continued)*

*Southern Fried Chicken*. In the eighteenth and nineteenth centuries, most Americans prepared chicken quite simply, often boiling or steaming it. In the South, however, cookbooks have contained recipes for fried chicken for over 150 years. Fried chicken has become synonymous with Southern cuisine, but it is only within the last fifty years that people have been able to prepare it all year round. In the antebellum South, chicken was considered a luxury food to be served only on special occasions like holidays, Sundays or when guests visited. In the 1940s, chicken farmers began to employ temperature-controlled environments to raise young chicks specifically for frying. Before this, young tender poultry was attainable only during the spring and summer because hens sit on their eggs during warm months. There are a whole host of regional variations on southern fried chicken and many families have their own carefully guarded recipes for this treasured dish passed down from generation to generation. It is common to marinate the chicken in milk or salt water or skin it before frying. Cooks often bread the chicken with seasoned flour or batter. Some discerning cooks claim that the only way to capture the chicken's succulent flavors is to fry it in a cast-iron skillet. In days gone by, Southerners often served fried chicken with corn cakes, fried cornmeal mush or "chicken biscuits" (biscuits fried in pan drippings).

SERVES: 4

ADVANCE PREPARATION: at least 2 hours ahead or the night before

EQUIPMENT: heavy 11- to 12-inch skillet, preferably cast iron, with cover

*Night before or at least 2 hours ahead:*

Cut the chicken into pieces, separating it at all the joints, and cutting the breast and back sections in half. Rinse the chicken pieces under cold running water and place them in a bowl large enough to hold them with a little room to spare. Add the buttermilk, cover tightly with plastic wrap and refrigerate until an hour before cooking. (Or set aside at room temperature for 2 hours.)

Place the shortening in the skillet and heat over medium heat to 375°F. Add the bacon fat.

While the shortening is heating, place the flour, salt, pepper and optional cayenne pepper in a brown paper bag and shake to blend.

Remove the dark meat pieces of chicken (thighs, drumsticks and backs) from the buttermilk and shake off the excess. Drop them in the bag and shake to coat with the flour mixture. With tongs, gently place the chicken pieces in the hot fat, skin side down. Cover and cook over medium heat 10 minutes. Turn the chicken pieces and continue cooking uncovered for another 10 minutes or until deep golden brown. If the chicken is browning too quickly, lower the heat. Remove the chicken to drain on brown paper bags and continue with the remaining white meat pieces. The breast should be cooked covered for 5 minutes, turned, and cooked covered another 5 minutes. The wings take only 10 minutes and there is no need to turn them as they get submerged.

UNDERSTANDING    The bacon fat adds a delicious ever so slightly smoky flavor. If fried at the correct temperature, and not over-cooked, the chicken absorbs very little fat.

The buttermilk tenderizes the chicken and adds a subtle sweetness.

# FRIDAY NIGHT ROAST CHICKEN WITH PAPRIKA

This roast chicken is moist and juicy with a very crispy skin, a beautiful bronze color with a rosy blush of sweetly savory paprika. When I was growing up, it was standard Friday night fare. In our house, Shabbus, the Jewish Sabbath, was always the same. It began early in the day with a trip to the butcher for the freshly killed kosher chicken. Shopping with Grandma was always an embarrassing experience because she came with the attitude that if she didn't adequately insult the butcher with her superior knowledge of quality, she would be offered less than the best meat. I guess Morris was used to it; though he played his part, acting offended, he always offered me a piece of that wonderful garlicky hard salami along with his smile.

When we got the chicken home, Grandma would singe the pin feathers and sprinkle it with kosher salt according to tradition. Then she made soup using the neck, giblets, feet and even the unborn eggs. The liver was transformed into chopped liver. In the late afternoon, but well before sundown—when all work activity must cease according to Orthodox law—with the chicken sizzling in

*(continued)*

the oven, my grandmother, schooled in the Orthodox tradition as the daughter of a rabbi, would wash her hair, cover her head with a silk kerchief and quietly light the Shabbus candles in the heavy brass candlesticks that had belonged to her mother.

A typical Shabbus menu in our house would begin with a little sweet red wine for the grown-ups, pink grapefruit for the kids. Then came the blessing for the Challah (page 56), spread with chopped liver (page 28), and the chicken soup. Finally the chicken was served, often accompanied by a light coleslaw (see *Rose's Celebrations*). Dessert was a simple fruit cup or, depending on the season, fresh fruit.

I have always loved Shabbus. But it wasn't until one day at the airport, when the Lubovichers, a religious sect given to spreading the joy of Judaism, handed me a miniature set of candlesticks and candles, with instructions for lighting them and a description of the meaning of this Sabbath tradition, that I realized the significance of its beauty: the woman, as keeper of the home, inviting in the values of family and peace.

| INGREDIENTS room temperature | MEASURE volume | WEIGHT ounces/pounds | grams/kilograms |
|---|---|---|---|
| 1 chicken, preferably free range | | 3.5 to 4 pounds | 1 kilogram 588 grams to 1 kilogram 814 grams |
| 1 large clove of garlic, cut in half and peeled | | 0.25 ounce | 7 grams |
| goose fat or unsalted butter | 1 tablespoon | 0.50 ounce | 14 grams |
| kosher salt (Diamond brand)* | 2 teaspoons | | 12 grams |
| black pepper, freshly ground | a few grindings | | |
| cayenne pepper | a pinch or 2 | | |
| fresh rosemary† | several branches | 0.50 ounce | 14 grams |
| paprika | a sprinkling | | |

*If using Morton brand or table salt, use only 1 teaspoon.
†If you cannot obtain fresh rosemary, sprinkle the inside of the chicken with 1 teaspoon dried rosemary. I highly recommend growing your own fresh rosemary. It grows well even indoors, and the dried is just not the same.

SERVES: 3 to 4
PREHEAT THE OVEN TO: 425°F.
BAKING TIME: 45 minutes
INTERNAL TEMPERATURE (THIGH):
  180°F.

*For the crispest skin, allow the chicken to sit uncovered in the refrigerator overnight. (Place it on a rack, preferably V-shaped, in a pan to catch any juices.) Remove the chicken from the refrigerator 1 hour before roasting and discard any juices.*

*Preheat the oven to 425°F. at least 15 minutes before roasting.*

Rub the chicken all over with the cut garlic, reserving the garlic, and then rub it all over with the goose fat or butter. Stir together the salt, pepper and cayenne pepper and sprinkle inside and out with this mixture. Place the cut garlic in the cavity and add the fresh rosemary. Fold back the wing tips under the back. Leave the chicken untrussed.* Place breast side up on a rack in a roasting pan.

Place the chicken in the oven and baste. Roast for 45 minutes, basting every 15 minutes with the pan drippings. (Keep the oven door open as briefly as possible when basting.) Turn the chicken over so that it is breast side down and roast 15 minutes longer for a 3½-pound bird, 30 minutes for a 4-pound bird. Test for doneness by tipping the chicken tailward. The juices should run clear and golden. About 10 minutes before the estimated time of doneness, sprinkle the chicken all over with the paprika.

Leave the chicken on the rack for 15 to 30 minutes before carving so that it can reabsorb its juices and the skin remains crisp.

NOTE: For pan gravy, add 1 cup of water or dry white wine to the roasting pan and bring it to a boil on top of the range, stirring to release the browned bits from the bottom of the pan. Boil, stirring constantly, until reduced to ⅓ cup. Pour into a gravy boat and serve with the chicken.

POINTERS
FOR SUCCESS

• Store paprika in the refrigerator to keep it from darkening.

UNDERSTANDING

The paprika is sprinkled on the chicken toward the end of cooking so that it does not burn and turn dark brown.

*Untrussed, the chicken cooks and browns more evenly.

# TANDOORI CHICKEN

You don't need a special oven or exotic spices to reproduce the authentic flavor of India's most popular and glorious chicken dish. Tandoori chicken, marinated first in lemon/lime juice, then in yogurt and spices, is flavorful but not fiery, juicy and tender and easy to prepare. This is my favorite of all chicken recipes.

I was once invited to attend a wedding in India and to stay with the groom's family. This was a uniquely wonderful opportunity to witness and participate in the many elaborate wedding preparations and ceremonies that last for weeks. But the finest part, for me, was that not only did my hostess, Mrs. Puri, know a great deal about food, she also had one of the best cooks in Delhi. I was treated to the best meals I have ever eaten in my life. Every night I couldn't wait until dinner; it was always subtle and different and delightfully spicy. Even the scrambled eggs for breakfast had minced fresh green chilies. The entire house was perfumed with spices and I wanted to stay forever, but that fantasy was crushed one morning when I heard Mrs. Puri screaming to Mr. Puri in Hindi what sounded to be "Rose, Rose, Rose." I later discovered that it was actually "rose, rose, rose," which in Hindi means "every day . . . !" (and apparently had to do with his behavior, thank God—not mine).

During the month of my stay, the only time we ever ate in a restaurant was at Moti Mahal (Chicken Palace). It was explained to me that chicken tandoori is best made in a tandoor oven, which most people don't have at home. But when I returned to America, with the taste of tandoori chicken still in my memory, and a tandoori chicken recipe in my suitcase, I discovered to my delight that using my Weber charcoal domed grill is perhaps an even more delicious method to enhance these wonderful Eastern spices, and a conventional oven works well too. Over the years I also discovered the most important secret: The longer you let the chicken marinate in the spices, the more tender and flavorful it gets.

Anyone who has ever come to visit us in the country

*(continued)*

*Tandoori Chicken.* In Indian cooking, the type of stove one uses often influences the flavor and texture of the food. Indian stoves have changed very little since ancient times. A "choola," a wood- or coal-burning stove, is still a standard feature of the Indian kitchen, more often than not built directly into the floor. The woman of the house designs the choola to suit her individual needs. The tandoori stove is the cousin of the choola. However, instead of being built into the floor, it is built underground, usually with bricks. Cooks originally baked flatbreads like "nan" and "parathas" in the tandoori stove, but it became popular for a wide variety of foods. Tandoori cooking seals in the natural juices of meat and poultry so that they don't become dry and tough.

during the summer has been treated to chicken tandoori. And they often request it for their next visit. Not only is it festive and delicious, the fact that you can do all of the preparation days ahead and only need twenty minutes grilling time makes it practical as well. In India, cochineal dye is used to paint the chicken its traditional fiery red hue, but here a little red food color does the trick. I especially love to make chicken tandoori in July when the edible yellow and orange daylilies are in bloom, as they make a stunning contrast against the red chicken.

I always serve this zesty, flavorful recipe with cool Raita (page 190) and fragrant Pistachio Saffron Pilaf (page 181). Beer or Zinfandel wine or the non-alcoholic Lassi (page 319) are good accompaniments for this spicy dish.

| INGREDIENTS | MEASURE | WEIGHT | |
| --- | --- | --- | --- |
| | *volume* | *ounces/pounds* | *grams/kilograms* |
| 2 3- to 3½-pound chickens, preferably free range | | 6 to 7 pounds | 2 kilograms 722 grams to 3 kilograms 175 grams |
| salt | 1 tablespoon + 1½ teaspoons | 1 ounce | 30 grams |
| lemon juice, freshly squeezed | ¼ liquid cup | | |
| lime juice, freshly squeezed | ¼ liquid cup | | |
| plain yogurt | 1 liquid cup | 9 ounces | 255 grams |
| 4 medium cloves of garlic, quartered | | 0.75 ounce | 20 grams |
| fresh ginger, peeled and minced | 2 teaspoons | 0.25 ounce | 7 grams |
| cumin seeds | 1 teaspoon | | |
| ground coriander | 1 teaspoon | | |
| turmeric | ½ teaspoon | | |
| cayenne pepper | 1 tablespoon | 0.25 ounce | 7 grams |
| black pepper, freshly ground | ½ teaspoon | | |
| ground cinnamon | ¼ teaspoon | | |
| ground cloves | a large pinch | | |
| liquid red food color | 1 teaspoon | | |

## GARNISHES

long green chili peppers

1 large sweet onion, preferably Vidalia or Bermuda

vegetable oil

fresh coriander sprigs

lemon and lime wedges

|  |  |  |
|---|---|---|
|  | 8 ounces | 227 grams |
| 1 tablespoon |  |  |

SERVES: 6
ADVANCE PREPARATION: at least 24
  hours or up to 3 days ahead

*Twenty-four hours or up to 3 days ahead:*

Rinse the chickens under cold running water and pat dry with paper towels. Cut the chickens apart at all the joints, and cut the breast and back sections in half. Remove as much skin as possible. Slash each piece in several places to enable the marinade to penetrate.

Place the chicken in a large bowl. Sprinkle with the salt, add the lemon and lime juices and toss to coat well. Set aside for 30 minutes.

Place the yogurt, garlic, and spices in a food processor or blender and blend on high speed until well mixed, about 1 minute. Pour the mixture over the chicken, turning to coat all the pieces on all sides. Cover tightly with plastic wrap (preferably Saran brand) and refrigerate for at least 24 hours.

Prepare a fire for grilling: Heat the coals and grease the rack lightly.

Remove the chicken from the marinade, reserving the marinade. Using a wad of plastic wrap, the back of a spoon or a small brush, dab it with food color. With tongs, place the chicken on the grill, arranging the thicker dark meat portions over the hottest part of the coals. Grill, covered, brushing with the marinade every 5 minutes, and turning to brown evenly, until the juices run clear when pierced with the tip of a knife. The breast and wings will take about 15 minutes and the rest about 20. (The marination makes the chicken cook faster than usual.) Grill the hot chili peppers alongside the chicken, turning often, until they are blackened and limp.

*(continued)*

While the chicken is cooking, heat a large heavy pan, preferably cast-iron, until very hot. Cut the onion in half lengthwise and then slice each half into thin lengthwise slices. Add the oil to the hot pan, and tilt the pan to coat it evenly. Add the onions. Cook over medium-high heat, stirring constantly, for about 3 minutes or until browned but still crisp. Remove at once to paper towels.

To serve, place the chicken on a large serving plate. Garnish with the onions, grilled chili peppers, fresh coriander, lemon and lime wedges and fresh *day*lilies. (The edible variety is the one *without* the spots.) The chicken is delicious both hot and at room temperature.

NOTE: To roast the chicken in an oven, preheat the oven to 400°F. Place the chicken on a lightly greased rack in a roasting pan and bake for 20 to 30 minutes or until the juices run clear when the chicken is pierced with the tip of a knife. Alternatively, if you have a clay cooker, place the chicken in it without soaking it, and bake in an *unpreheated* 475°F. oven for 30 minutes. Uncover and continue cooking about 10 minutes or until done. This method simulates the tandoor oven: It maintains all the juices and extracts all the fat, and while the chicken gets stewed more than dry roasted, the flavors are delicious. (The La Cloche clay cooker also works well for one chicken. Bake in a *preheated* 475°F. oven for 20 minutes; uncover and continue cooking about 10 minutes or until done. Drain off and discard the fat and liquid that accumulate). Serve hot or at room temperature.

POINTERS
FOR SUCCESS

• Using plastic wrap as a paintbrush is the best method because it makes it easiest to apply—and red food color stains.

# ETHIOPIAN DORO WAT

This sumptuously spicy chicken dish has the same flavor components as Indian tandoori chicken except cumin—and, in addition to all the other spices, it contains fenugreek, paprika, allspice and nutmeg. But the character of the dish is changed most dramatically because it is stewed rather than dry cooked.

Traditionally, the *berberé* paste, which incorporates many of the spices also present in the sauce, is prepared in large quantities and then used for many other Ethiopian recipes as well. But because this stew is the only Ethiopian dish I prepare, I have incorporated the *berberé* into the sauce in one step to save time without altering flavor.

When I was in college, one of my favorite teachers, Dorothy Bryant, became engaged to an African prince, John Ogundapay. Before leaving for Africa, she invited me for a traditional dinner she had learned to cook for her fiancé. It consisted of one chicken cut into pieces and stewed with about three-quarters of a can of cayenne pepper. To temper the heat, she prepared farina, which apparently was similar to a root starch called *fufu* served in Africa. She explained to me that John had taught her to make these dishes and liked to eat them every night, though she herself was getting quite bored with them. But this was a first for me and I thought the dinner utterly exotic and absolutely sensational. I was also spellbound by the demonstration Prince Ogundapay gave me on the talking drum on which he skillfully produced the sounds of actual African words that could carry for miles in the jungle.

I, in turn, invited Dorothy and John for dinner to my one-room apartment in the Village a few weeks later. I prepared this *doro wat* because it seemed similar enough in character to their dish to please John and different enough in spices to intrigue Dorothy. I also served a Spicy Lentil Salad (page 172). I didn't, however, have anything to compare with a talking drum so I invited my oldest and most erudite friend, L. S. Colby, who entertained them royally.

*(continued)*

*African Kwanzaa*
Ethiopian Doro Wat
Creamy Polenta
Spicy Lentil Salad
Raita
Brazilian Quindin Sweets

Nowadays, in true melting pot spirit, I have added creamy Polenta (page 173, minus the Parmesan) to the menu. Its subtle flavor and bright yellow color harmonize perfectly with the bold red-brown sauce of the *doro wat*.

| INGREDIENTS | MEASURE *volume* | WEIGHT *ounces/pounds* | *grams/kilograms* |
|---|---|---|---|
| **NITER KEBBEH (SPICED CLARIFIED BUTTER)** | | | |
| unsalted butter, cut into ½-inch pieces | 8 tablespoons | 4 ounces | 113 grams |
| onion, coarsely chopped | 2 tablespoons | 0.5 ounce | 16 grams |
| 2 medium cloves of garlic, minced | 2 teaspoons | 0.25 ounce | 7 grams |
| fresh ginger, peeled and finely chopped | 1 teaspoon | | 3.5 grams |
| turmeric | ¼ teaspoon | | |
| 1 cardamom pod, crushed with the flat of a knife | | | |
| cinnamon stick | ½-inch piece | | |
| ½ whole clove | | | |
| nutmeg, freshly grated | a pinch | | |
| 2 chickens, preferably free range | | 6 to 7 pounds | 2 kilograms 722 grams to 3 kilograms 175 grams |
| salt | 1 tablespoon + 1½ teaspoons, or to taste | 1 ounce | 30 grams |

*Doro Wat.* For years, Western writers from Ernest Hemingway to Isak Dinesen to Robert Ruark have recorded the natural beauties of the East African landscape. Its rolling, grassy plains dotted with thorn trees have been the setting for numerous films. The third most populous country on the continent, Ethiopia's history dates back to antiquity. Its former royal family (overthrown in the early 1970s) descended from Menelik I, the son of King Solomon and the Queen of Sheba. "Ethiopia" means "burnt face" and was first used by the Greeks to describe the inhabitants of what they thought to be the southernmost part of the world. While coffee is Ethiopia's main export, it also has given us a rich and savory collection of ethnic foods. One of the most notable is Doro Wat, a spicy chicken stew. Traditionally, Ethiopian cooks serve Doro Wat on thin sourdough pancakes called "injera." Instead of silverware, each person is provided with his own injera which he tears into small pieces, folds around bits of the tender chicken, dips in the spicy sauce, and eats. The truly dexterous Doro Wat eater is able to do this without touching the stew or the lips with the fingers. The underlying injera, which becomes saturated with the zesty sauce of the Doro Wat sitting on top of it, is considered a special treat and is usually eaten at the end of the meal by those who can stomach the concentration of the hot spices.

BERBERÉ

| | | | |
|---|---|---|---|
| paprika | ¾ cup | 3 ounces | 83 grams |
| cayenne pepper | 2 teaspoons | | |
| 12 pods cardamom, crushed* | ½ teaspoon | | |
| fenugreek seeds, crushed* | ½ teaspoon | | |
| nutmeg, freshly grated | ¼ teaspoon | | |
| ground ginger | ¼ teaspoon | | |
| black pepper, freshly ground | ⅛ teaspoon | | |
| ground cloves | a pinch | | |
| ground cinnamon | a pinch | | |
| ground allspice | a pinch | | |
| (*Niter Kebbeh*) | (6 tablespoons) | (2.5 ounces) | (73 grams) |
| 3 medium onions, finely chopped | 4 cups | 18 ounces | 510 grams |
| 3 large cloves of garlic, minced | 2 tablespoons | 0.75 ounce | 20 grams |
| fresh ginger, peeled and finely chopped | 2 teaspoons | 0.25 ounce | 7 grams |
| red wine | ½ liquid cup | | |
| water | 1½ liquid cups | | |
| 6 hard-cooked large eggs, peeled† | | | |
| black pepper, freshly ground | a few grindings | | |
| salt | to taste | | |
| OPTIONAL: flatbread (pita), yogurt, farina, rice or polenta (page 173), for accompaniment | | | |

SERVES: 6

NITER KEBBEH

In a small heavy saucepan, over medium heat, heat the butter, stirring often, until it is melted and foaming. Reduce the heat to very low. Add the onion, garlic, ginger, turmeric, cardamom, cinnamon, clove and nutmeg and swirl the pan to mix them together. Simmer uncovered, without stirring, about 30 minutes or until the butter is clear and the milk solids have turned brown. Strain

*Remove the hulls from the cardamom pods and crush the seeds, together with the fenugreek seeds, in a mortar and pestle or in a coffee or spice grinder.
†To hard-cook: Place 6 eggs in a large pan of cold water. Bring to a simmer and cook at a simmer for 20 minutes. Do not allow the water to boil. With a slotted spoon, remove the eggs and place them under cold running water for about 15 seconds. When cool, roll the eggs on the counter, using light pressure to crush the shells evenly for ease of removal.

*(continued)*

through a cheesecloth-lined strainer into a large enameled or noncorrodible Dutch oven. Gather the edges of the cheesecloth together and squeeze to release all the butter.

While the butter is clarifying, marinate the chickens: Rinse the chickens under cold running water and pat them dry with paper towels. Cut the chickens at all the joints, and cut the breast and back sections in half. Remove as much skin as possible. Slash each piece in several places to enable the marinade to penetrate.

Place the chicken in a large bowl. Sprinkle with the salt, add the lemon juice and toss to coat well. Set aside for 30 minutes while you mix the spices for the berberé.

BERBERÉ

In a small frying pan, stir together the paprika, cayenne pepper, crushed cardamom and fenugreek seeds, nutmeg, ground ginger, black pepper, ground cloves, ground cinnamon and ground allspice. Over low heat, stirring constantly, toast the spices for 1 minute. Remove the pan from the heat and set it aside.

THE RED PEPPER STEW

Over medium heat, heat the *niter kebbeh* in the Dutch oven. When it is sizzling, add the onions to the pan and sauté, stirring often, until browned around the edges, about 8 minutes. Reduce the heat to low, add the garlic and ginger and cook 1 minute. Stir in the *berberé* spice mixture and cook, stirring constantly, for 3 minutes to blend the flavors. Stir in the wine and water, raise the heat to high and bring to a boil, stirring constantly. Reduce the heat slightly and boil, stirring constantly, for about 5 minutes or until the liquid is thickened. Reduce the heat to very low.

Pat the chicken dry with paper towels and add it to the sauce. Stir to coat the chicken with the sauce, and arrange the breasts on top. Cover tightly and simmer for 20 minutes or until the breasts are tender. Remove the breasts and wing pieces to a deep serving plate. Cover with foil and keep warm. With the tines of a fork, pierce the eggs all over, about ¼ inch deep. Add them to the sauce, turning them gently to coat them. Cover tightly and continue cooking 10 minutes or until the dark meat is cooked through. Remove the remaining chicken, skim any fat from the surface and simmer for a few minutes or until thickened. Stir constantly so that the sauce does not scorch. Sprinkle with the black pepper and salt to taste. Serve immediately. Any leftover *doro wat* is even more delicious the following day.

NOTE: If you wish to have the authentic experience of ragingly hot *doro wat* juxtaposed with the blandest possible grain accompaniment, make farina: Use 1¼ cups of farina (quick-cooking cream of wheat), 1 teaspoon of salt and 6 cups of water. Bring the water to a boil. Add the farina slowly, whisking often to prevent lumps, and simmer over medium-low heat, whisking often, until thickened, 8 to 10 minutes.

# CLASSIC CHICKEN CACCIATORE PICCANTE

*Italian Columbus Day*
Fried Sicilian Artichokes
Classic Chicken Cacciatore
   Piccante
Fried Polenta
Tiramisù

This dish has become so "American" no one even thinks of it as ethnic anymore. I made this recipe for one of my oldest family friends, Neil Bernstein, over twenty years ago and he is still talking about it. I would have to suspect sentiment if it weren't for the fact that I adore this version of the classic Italian dish as well.

What are the secrets that make it extra special? One is the carrots, which add a natural sweetness to the tomato sauce. The other is the splash of red wine vinegar, which gives a piquant flavor. I came up with this idea one day when I ran out of the red wine!

*(continued)*

| INGREDIENTS<br>room temperature | MEASURE<br>volume | WEIGHT<br>ounces/pounds | grams/kilograms |
|---|---|---|---|
| 1 chicken, preferably free range | | 3½ pounds | 1 kilogram<br>588 grams |
| unsalted butter | 1 tablespoon | 0.5 ounce | 14 grams |
| extra virgin olive oil | 1 tablespoon | | |
| chopped onion | 1½ cups | 5.5 ounces | 160 grams |
| chopped carrot | ½ cup | 2.25 ounces | 64 grams |
| chopped celery | ½ cup | 2 ounces | 60 grams |
| salt | ½ teaspoon | | |
| black pepper, freshly ground | ¼ teaspoon | | |
| 1 medium clove of garlic, minced | 1 teaspoon | | 3 grams |
| 1 can imported plum tomatoes, undrained | 1¾ cups<br>(1 14-ounce can) | 14 ounces | 397 grams |
| 1 can tomato sauce | scant liquid cup<br>(1 8-ounce can) | 8 ounces | 227 grams |
| 1 bay leaf | | | |
| red wine | 3 tablespoons | | |
| red wine vinegar | 1 tablespoon | | |
| sugar | 1 teaspoon | | 4 grams |
| fresh basil, minced* | 3 tablespoons | 0.5 ounce | 15 grams |
| fresh parsley, preferably flat-leafed, minced | 2 tablespoons | 0.25 ounce | 8 grams |

SERVES: 4

Rinse the chicken under cold running water and pat it dry with paper towels. Cut the chicken into pieces, separating it at all the joints, and cutting the breast and back sections in half. Allow to sit for 30 minutes.

*Optional:* If you like the neck and gizzard, rinse them under cold running water and, in a small saucepan, simmer, partially covered, in water to cover with a split clove of garlic and 2 black peppercorns. The neck will be tender in about 30 minutes, the gizzard in 40 minutes. Use a skewer to test for doneness. Remove along with the garlic and peppercorns and reduce the liquid to 1 tablespoon. Set aside.

In a heavy 12-inch frying pan or Dutch oven, over medium heat, melt the butter with the oil. When sizzling, add the chicken pieces without crowding and brown them

*Or 1 teaspoon dried.

well, turning them on all sides, and removing the pieces as they are browned. Set the chicken aside. Drain off all but 2 tablespoons of the oil from the pan.

Add the onion, carrot, celery, salt and pepper to the pan and sauté, stirring often, until the vegetables are golden brown. Add the garlic and cook 1 minute. Add the tomatoes, tomato sauce and bay leaf and simmer uncovered, stirring occasionally, 20 minutes, breaking up the tomatoes with the stirring spoon.

Add the browned chicken and any drippings, the optional reserved 1 tablespoon of broth, the wine, wine vinegar and sugar. Simmer, covered, 20 minutes or until the breasts are tender. Remove the breasts and wing pieces and continue cooking, uncovered, to finish cooking the dark meat and thicken the sauce, about 10 minutes. Skim any fat from the surface of the sauce and sprinkle with the basil and parsley. Return the breasts and wings to the sauce, and serve.

# Capon with Savory Bulgur Stuffing

> **Mideastern Thanksgiving**
> Dolmadakia
> Capon with Savory
>   Bulgur Stuffing
> Lebanese Spinach
> Triple Vanilla Lover's Ice
>   Cream

This could actually be the most fabulous thing you ever put into your mouth. My guests all thought so the day of its creation. We kept going back for more of the wheaty crunchy bulgur, flavored with the juices of the capon, punctuated with sweet little bursts of currant.

Capon for Thanksgiving is actually an old family tradition started by my grandmother, who grew up in Russia and did not quite comprehend the symbolic significance the turkey plays in an American Thanksgiving. When her children were young and her family small, she served capon, "explaining" that it was a small turkey.

*(continued)*

| INGREDIENTS | MEASURE *volume* | WEIGHT *ounces/pounds* | *grams/kilograms* |
|---|---|---|---|
| 1 capon | | 9 pounds | 4 kilograms 82 grams |
| 1 large clove of garlic, halved | | 0.25 ounce | 7 grams |
| unsalted butter, softened | 2 tablespoons | 1 ounce | 28 grams |
| salt | 1 teaspoon | 0.25 ounce | 6.7 grams |
| black pepper, freshly ground | several grindings | | |
| CAPON STOCK | (makes 2½ cups) | | |
| vegetable oil | 1 tablespoon | | |
| reserved giblets | | | |
| 1 small onion, coarsely chopped | ½ cup | 2.25 ounces | 64 grams |
| 1 large carrot, coarsely chopped | ½ cup | 2 ounces | 57 grams |
| white wine | ½ liquid cup | | |
| water | 3 liquid cups | | |
| low-salt chicken broth, preferably College Inn, *or* 2 cubes Glace de Volaille (page 209) dissolved in 1¾ cups of boiling water | 1¾ liquid cups (1 13.75-ounce can) | 13.75 ounces | 390 grams |
| 2 parsley sprigs | | | |
| dried thyme | ¼ teaspoon | | |
| 3 whole black peppercorns | | | |
| 1 small bay leaf | | | |
| Bulgur and Currant Stuffing (page 176) | 1 recipe | | |
| white wine | 1 liquid cup | | |

SERVES: 8
PREHEAT THE OVEN TO: 325°F.
ROASTING TIME: about 3½ hours
RESTING TIME: 20 minutes to
  1 hour
INTERNAL TEMPERATURE (THIGH):
  180°F.

Rinse the capon under cold running water and drain well. Remove any fat from the cavity and set it aside. Reserve the giblets (not the liver). Pat the capon dry with paper towels. Rub the capon all over with the cut garlic and then rub it all over with the butter. Sprinkle the capon inside and out with salt and pepper, and refrigerate while you make the stock. *Remove from the refrigerator 1 hour before roasting.*

CAPON STOCK

In a medium saucepan, heat the oil over medium-high heat. Add the reserved giblets, and cook, stirring often, until browned, about 10 minutes. Add the onion and carrot and cook until the onion is softened. Pour in the wine, water and chicken broth and bring to a simmer. Skim off any foam on the surface. Add the parsley, thyme, peppercorns and bay leaf and simmer, uncovered, for at least 2 hours.

Strain the capon stock, discarding the giblets and vegetables. Measure the stock. You should have 2½ cups. If you have more, boil to reduce it to 2½ cups; if less, add water. If you are making the stock ahead, cool it to room temperature, cover and refrigerate. When the fat solidifies on the surface, scrape it off. Alternatively, skim the fat from the surface with a large spoon. You will need ½ cup stock for the bulgar stuffing and the rest for the gravy.

*While the stock is simmering, prepare the stuffing (see page 176).*

*Preheat the oven to 325°F. at least 15 minutes ahead of roasting.*

Spoon about 2 cups of the stuffing into the capon. Do not pack it in as it will expand during baking. Tie the wings to the sides of the bird or truss in the following manner: Place a long piece of twine under the capon, near the tail. Bring it up over the ends of the legs, cross it over and bring each piece down under the leg ends, bringing the legs together. Pull the ends of the twine toward the back of the bird so that the twine runs along the sides, under each leg and across the wings, holding them in place. Tie the twine together securely with a knot at the back of the bird.

Place the capon on a strong rack in a roasting pan. Place the reserved capon fat in the pan. Pour the wine into the pan. Roast the capon, basting every 30 minutes with the liquid in the bottom of the pan, for about 3½ hours or until an instant-read thermometer inserted in the thigh (not touching the bone), reads 180°F.

Allow the capon to rest for at least 20 minutes before carving.

*Meanwhile, make the gravy:* Pour the pan drippings into a liquid measuring cup or bowl and let them stand 5 minutes. Skim off the clear yellow fat that rises to the surface. Return the dark juices to the roasting pan and

*(continued)*

pour in the remaining 2 cups of reserved capon stock. Place the roasting pan over 2 burners and reduce juices over medium-high heat to 1 cup, stirring and scraping often to dislodge the delicious browned bits on the bottom and sides of the pan, about 10 to 15 minutes. Pour the juices into a sauceboat to pass at the table, and carve the capon.

# PERFECT CRISP ROAST DUCK

Duck, with its rich moist flesh and flavorful crispy skin, can be the most delicious of all poultry. However, when not cooked properly, it can be greasy with fat, the flesh overcooked and dry and the skin soft and uninteresting. Because I love duck so much and even in restaurants have more often than not been disappointed, I set out years ago to find a way to roast duck that would eliminate the maximum fat while maintaining the juiciness.

The solution turned out to be extraordinarily simple: Boiling water is poured over the skin to tighten it, then the duck is air-dried (which can be accomplished overnight in the refrigerator). During roasting, the skin of the duck is pricked, the oven temperature is kept very high to release the fat and boiling water is poured on the duck to keep it moist and to prevent the fat from splattering. The resulting duck is virtually fat-free, moist but with crisp skin and it cooks in under an hour.

My duck dinner menu includes peppery Kasha Varnishkes (page 177), creamed onions with a sprinkling of dill and a robust cabernet such as Jordan or a Merlot such as St. Francis. Hot Fudge Sundaes (pages 283–287) round out what is one of my favorite meals.

For a delightful variation, try this version of Peking Duck: shortly before roasting, rub the duck all over with a mixture of 1 teaspoon of malt sugar or honey and 2 teaspoons of soy sauce. Allow it to dry for at least 15 minutes. When basting with the boiling water, add 1 teaspoon of soy sauce each time. Serve with Plum Sauce (page 35) and green onions. Green Tea Ice Cream (page 291) would be the perfect dessert.

*(continued)*

ROSE'S MELTING POT

| INGREDIENTS | MEASURE<br>*volume* | WEIGHT | |
| --- | --- | --- | --- |
| | | *ounces/pounds* | *grams/kilograms* |
| 1 Long Island duckling | | 4½ to 5 pounds | 2 kilograms to 2 kilograms 268 grams |
| salt | 1 teaspoon | | 6.7 grams |
| black pepper, freshly ground | ½ teaspoon | | |
| 1 large clove of garlic, cut in half | | 0.25 ounce | 7 grams |
| 1 large apple, quartered | | 7 ounces | 200 grams |

SERVES: 3 to 4
PREHEAT THE OVEN TO: 450°F.
ROASTING TIME: 45 minutes
INTERNAL TEMPERATURE (THIGH): 180°F.

EQUIPMENT: roasting pan with slotted rack*

*One day ahead:*

Remove all loose fat from the duck. Pour boiling water over the skin. Sprinkle it lightly inside and out with salt and pepper. Place the duck on a rack (preferably a V-shaped rack) in a pan to catch any juices, and refrigerate for 24 hours.

*Remove the duck from the refrigerator 1 hour before roasting.*

*Preheat the oven to 450°F.*

Fold the wing tips back under the back of the duck and wrap foil around the wings to protect them from burning. Place the garlic and apple in the duck's cavity and prick the duck all over, being careful not to go deeper than the fat layer.

Pour ¼ cup boiling water on top of the duck. Roast for 15 minutes. Remove it from oven, prick and add ¼ cup boiling water again and return it to the oven. Repeat this procedure every 15 minutes until the duck has roasted for at least 45 minutes (not including time out of the oven). Test for doneness by tipping the duck tailward. The juices should run almost clear with barely a tinge of pink. An instant-read thermometer inserted in the thigh, not touching the bone, should read 180°F. Leave the duck on the rack for 15 minutes before carving so that it can reabsorb its juices and the skin remains crisp.

*The rack keeps the duck fat from spattering in the oven and makes it unnecessary to pour off the fat during roasting.

If desired, after carving, place the back under the broiler for a few minutes to crisp the skin.

NOTE: For a totally fat-free duck, when removing the fat, make a 2-inch-long incision in either side of the duck's cavity, between the leg and thigh joints, and remove the long strip of fat that is wrapped around the top of the leg. I also like to hang the duck in a cool spot for several hours with a fan blowing on it. This yields the crispest skin and the least fat of all.

# GRILLED SMOKY TURKEY

People had been telling me for years how easy and delicious it is to cook a whole turkey on a charcoal grill, but I never really believed them. I'd picture a twelve-pound turkey and then consider everything I knew about grilling, and I couldn't reconcile the two. For one thing, I have never been willing to add coals during the grilling process, a necessity for the longer cooking required for a large bird. The thought of lifting the grill rack with a heavy turkey on top in order to add more coals was nothing short of terrifying. Also, I couldn't imagine how the turkey, which doesn't cook evenly in an oven, could possibly cook evenly on the grill. But when my new Weber "Performer" charcoal grill arrived, it looked so beautiful and functional, it gave me the confidence to ignore my reservations and give the turkey a try.

Actually, I've never really enjoyed grilling; it's the results I adore. When Elliott and I first married, he did the grilling while I tended to the rest of the meal. A perfect arrangement, I thought, until the meat started getting too well done. Clearly it was sabotage: He disliked grilling enough to ruin the meat in order to get me to take over the task. It worked.

Since that time I've gone the gas grill route, but I'm always disappointed with the less "charcoal-y" flavor. I've tried self-starting coals but hate the smell and sparks that fly up when emptying them from the starting chimney. At last Weber has come up with the perfectly designed grill

*(continued)*

that eliminates all my grilling problems and actually makes the process a pleasure. The "Performer" has a small propane tank that readily ignites the coals neatly contained in two sturdy metal baskets on the lower grate. After about thirty minutes, when the coals are evenly aglow with a light coating of gray ash, the baskets can be left together or separated for indirect grilling. An upper grate has butterfly-style hinges on two opposing sides, making it easy to add coals when necessary. And an enclosed container beneath the grill catches the ashes, preventing them from blowing about and making emptying them a snap.

When I used the indirect method of grilling, together with the domed lid, my twelve-pound turkey cooked perfectly—no, magnificently—in less than two hours. No turning, no basting: All I had to do was add six coals to each basket after one hour of grilling. The skin, though not crisp, was evenly deeply bronzed, the dark meat fabulously succulent and the breast meat the moistest and most flavorful I have ever experienced. What could be more perfect, close to effortless and yet impressive for a summer or Labor Day party. And those of you who live in climates where grilling in November is possible can have an unforgettable Thanksgiving turkey!

| INGREDIENTS | MEASURE | WEIGHT | |
| --- | --- | --- | --- |
| | *volume* | *ounces/pounds* | *grams/kilograms* |
| 1 turkey | | 12 to 14 pounds | 5½ to 6½ kilograms |
| 2 large cloves of garlic, halved | | 0.50 ounce | 14 grams |
| salt | 2 teaspoons | 0.50 ounce | 13.5 grams |
| black pepper, freshly ground | to taste | | |
| OPTIONAL: 2 large bunches of fresh thyme | | 2 ounces | 56 grams |
| OPTIONAL: a large bunch of fresh sage | | 1 ounce | 28 grams |

SERVES: 12 to 14

ROASTING TIME: about 1¾ hours

RESTING TIME: 30 minutes to 2
  hours

INTERNAL TEMPERATURE (THIGH):
  175°F.

EQUIPMENT: charcoal grill with a
  domed cover, a foil drip pan

*Optional*: For an extra-smoky flavor, soak a few handfuls of wood chips in water for at least 30 minutes (no more than one quarter of the coals, or they will extinguish the fire).

*Remove the turkey from the refrigerator 1 hour before grilling.*

Rinse the turkey under cold running water and drain well. Pat dry with paper towels. Rub the cut sides of the garlic cloves all over the outside and inside of the turkey and reserve. Sprinkle the turkey inside and out with the salt and pepper. Insert the fresh herbs, if desired into the neck and body cavities together with the garlic cloves and close the openings with metal skewers. Wrap the wings loosely with foil.

Follow the directions for your grill to prepare a fire for indirect grilling. When the coals are all lit, place the drip pan in the center, between the two piles of coals. Drain the optional wood chips and scatter them on top of the coals. Place the turkey in the center of the grill. Cover it with the domed lid and allow it to cook undisturbed for 1 hour.

Add 6 fresh coals to each side of the fire, cover and continue cooking for 45 minutes or until an instant-read thermometer inserted into the thigh, not touching the bone, reads 175°F. (If you cook a larger turkey, and after the second hour the turkey is not done, add 6 more coals to each side and continue cooking). Do not rely on the pop-up thermometers sometimes found in turkey breasts as they often result in overcooking.

Allow the turkey to rest for at least 30 minutes or up to 1 hour before carving.

NOTE: This is also a fabulous method for cooking leg of lamb. Remove the lamb from the refrigerator about an hour before grilling. Make at least 10 small slits all over the lamb and insert slivers of garlic and fresh rosemary. Sprinkle with salt and pepper. A 7-pound leg of lamb cooked with this method takes 45 minutes to an hour (125°F. in the thickest part of the meat to 140°F. in the thinnest section).

# BISTRO-STYLE PORK CHOPS WITH LIMA BEANS

This special recipe was created many years ago when I was camping out in Vermont. The purpose of the trip was to show a visiting French chef from the Auvergne the splendor of the New England autumn leaves, but he, in turn, showed me something equally exciting about lima beans. When we arrived late in the afternoon at our campsite, we found that the little general store in town had fresh pork chops but the only vegetable left was frozen baby lima beans. "Ça va," said Michel. After partially frying the pork chops in the blackened cast-iron skillet, he adeptly defrosted the frozen limas on top of the chops and then flavored them by sautéing them briefly in the pan juices. It was simple and splendid fare.

Serve this hearty dish with a mesclun (mixed baby greens) salad, dressed with California Heirloom Salad Dressing (page 198).

| INGREDIENTS | MEASURE | WEIGHT | |
|---|---|---|---|
| | *volume* | *ounces/pounds* | *grams* |
| vegetable oil | 1 tablespoon | | |
| 4 shoulder pork chops, ½ to ¾ inch thick | | 1¾ to 2 pounds | 794 to 907 grams |
| salt | ¾ teaspoon, divided | | |
| black pepper, freshly ground | ¼ teaspoon | | |
| 2 medium cloves of garlic | | | 10 grams |
| 2 packages frozen baby lima beans, partially thawed* | 4 cups | 1 pound 4 ounces | 567 grams |
| unsalted butter | 1 tablespoon | 0.50 ounce | 14 grams |
| dried thyme | ½ teaspoon | | |

*For fresh limas, separate the large ones from the small and medium ones, when you shell the beans. Instead of cooking them with the pork chops, boil in lightly salted water, adding the small and medium beans after the large ones have cooked for 10 minutes. Continue cooking about 5 minutes, or until just tender when pierced with a skewer. Drain, and sauté in the pan juices.

SERVES: 4

Heat a heavy 10-inch skillet over medium-high heat until hot. Add the oil and heat until a film appears over the oil. Add the pork chops and cook for about 5 minutes or until golden brown on the bottom. Tilt the pan to one side and use a wadded-up paper towel to absorb and discard the fat. Sprinkle the pork chops with ¼ teaspoon of the salt and half of the pepper, and turn the chops. Split each garlic clove in half and smash it with the flat of a chef's knife. Place a smashed garlic clove on top of each pork chop.

Cover the pan and turn the heat to low. Cook 25 minutes. Sprinkle the lima beans on top of the pork chops, season with the remaining ½ teaspoon of salt and ⅛ teaspoon of pepper and continue cooking for 10 minutes or until the lima beans are just tender when pierced with a skewer.

Remove the chops to serving plates and keep warm. Scrape the garlic cloves into the lima beans and add the butter and thyme. Turn up the heat to medium and sauté for 3 to 5 minutes, until the beans become glossy and lightly browned, stirring to release the browned bits in the bottom of the pan. Serve the beans alongside the chops.

POINTERS
FOR SUCCESS

• Frozen baby lima beans have a better, firmer texture than mature frozen lima beans. Be sure to cook them just until tender or they will become pasty. Fresh lima beans have the best texture of all but, of course, are time-consuming to pod.

# PORK CHOPS WITH GERMAN SWEET-AND-SOUR KRAUT

*German Oktoberfest*
Grilled Portobello
   Mushrooms
Authentic Russian
   Pumpernickel Bread
Pork Chops with German
   Sweet-and-Sour Kraut
Mashed Potatoes (without
   caramelized pears)
Black Forest Marzipan and
   Cherry Brownies

This favorite down-home family meal is a little unusual, but everyone seems to love the tangy with its slightly caramelized sweetened edge, which keeps the pork chops moist and flavorful. The tiny apple cubes maintain their shape, adding a soft juicy texture and harmonious flavor. And if you like the spiky/peppery taste of caraway, you will welcome its addition to this dish. I have been making this recipe for thirty years. The apple component was added fifteen years ago, the caraway five years later. This is how a good simple dish evolves over time. I think it has reached its final permutation. This food cries out for an accompaniment of Mashed Potatoes (page 162), but leave out the caramelized pears.

| INGREDIENTS | MEASURE | WEIGHT | |
| --- | --- | --- | --- |
| | *volume* | *ounces/pounds* | *grams* |
| sauerkraut, preferably packed in plastic bags, drained | 2 16-ounce bags | 2 pounds | 907 grams |
| vegetable oil | 1 tablespoon | | |
| 4 shoulder pork chops, ½ to ¾ inch thick | | 1¾ to 2 pounds | 794 to 907 grams |
| salt | ¼ teaspoon | | |
| black pepper, freshly ground | ¼ teaspoon | | |
| 1 medium McIntosh apple (6 ounce), peeled, cored and diced | 1 cup | 4 ounces (peeled and cored) | 113 grams |
| light brown sugar | ½ cup, packed | 3.75 ounces | 108 grams |
| OPTIONAL: caraway seeds | ¾ teaspoon | | |

In a colander, drain the sauerkraut thoroughly.

Heat a heavy 10-inch skillet over medium-high heat until hot. Add the oil and heat until a film appears over the oil. Add the pork chops and brown on the bottom, about 5 minutes. Tilt the pan to one side and use a wadded-up paper towel to absorb and discard the fat. Turn the chops over. Sprinkle them with the salt and pepper and arrange the sauerkraut on top. Sprinkle the sauerkraut with the apple, brown sugar and optional caraway seeds and toss lightly with a fork to mix.

Cover the pan and turn the heat to low. Cook 30 minutes. Uncover the pan, turn up the heat slightly and cook 5 minutes longer or until any liquid evaporates and the sugar caramelizes slightly. Remove the pork chops to serving plates and keep warm. Continue cooking the sauerkraut, stirring lightly with a fork, for another 5 minutes or until evenly browned. Serve the sauerkraut alongside the pork chops.

# PORK LOIN WITH PRUNES AND APPLES

I created this elegant and hearty Danish-inspired recipe as part of my first food story assignment (apples from soup to nuts) when I worked in the test kitchens at *Ladies' Home Journal.* I consider it to be one of my top recipes for entertaining, and apparently so did the *Journal* as it reappeared in their anniversary issue as one of the top one hundred recipes in their one hundred years of publication. Several years later, when I taught a cooking class in Scarsdale (to which I jokingly referred as the "Scarsdale diet"), several students did not eat pork so I prepared the recipe with veal with excellent results. The liltingly sweet touch of crème de cassis in the sauce is sheer magic.

Make this recipe for the grandest dinner party of the season.

*(continued)*

| INGREDIENTS | MEASURE | WEIGHT | |
| --- | --- | --- | --- |
| *room temperature* | *volume* | *ounces/pounds* | *grams/kilograms* |
| center-cut pork loin roast (bone-in) | | 4.5 to 5 pounds | 2 to 2½ kilograms |
| 1 box whole pitted prunes | 2 cups | 12 ounces | 340 grams |
| port wine | ½ liquid cup | | |
| salt | ¼ teaspoon, or to taste | | |
| black pepper, freshly ground | ⅛ teaspoon, or to taste | | |
| unsalted butter | 1 tablespoon | 0.50 ounce | 14 grams |
| vegetable oil | 1 tablespoon | | |
| dry white vermouth | 1 liquid cup | | |

GARNISH

| | | | |
| --- | --- | --- | --- |
| 2 Red Delicious apples | | 14 ounces | 400 grams |
| unsalted butter | 1 tablespoon, divided | 0.50 ounce | 14 grams |

SAUCE

| | | | |
| --- | --- | --- | --- |
| unsalted butter | 2 tablespoons | 1 ounce | 28 grams |
| all-purpose flour | 2 tablespoons | 0.6 ounce | 18 grams |
| heavy cream | ¼ liquid cup | | |
| crème de cassis or sweet red vermouth | ¼ liquid cup | | |

ADVANCE PREPARATION: Allow to
sit at room temperature for 1
hour before roasting
PREHEAT THE OVEN TO: 325°F.
ROASTING TIME: 1½ to 2 hours
INTERNAL TEMPERATURE: 170°F.
SERVES: 8

Using a sharpening steel or a sharp long narrow knife, pierce through the center of the pork loin from one end to the other, twisting slightly to form a tunnel. Use the handle of a wooden spoon to push as many prunes as possible into the tunnel (about ⅔ cup). If time allows, let the pork sit at room temperature for 1 hour before roasting.

Place the remaining prunes in a heat-proof bowl. Heat the port until hot and pour it over the prunes. Cover the bowl tightly with plastic wrap and set aside. (Turn the prunes after about an hour to moisten the other sides.)

*Preheat the oven to 325°F.*

Sprinkle the pork on all sides with the salt and pepper.

In a Dutch oven or covered roasting pan large enough to hold the pork loin, over medium-high heat, heat the butter with the oil until melted. Brown the pork evenly on all sides. (This will take about 15 minutes.) Remove the pork and discard the fat.

Return the pork to the Dutch oven, fat side up, and pour in the white vermouth. Cover and roast for 1½ to 2 hours or until an instant-read thermometer, inserted toward the middle but not touching the bone or prunes reads 170°F. Remove the meat to a heated serving platter and set aside in a warm place. Set the Dutch oven aside.

MAKE THE GARNISH: Slice the apples into rounds about ¼ inch thick. Use a small scalloped or plain cutter to remove the core from each slice.

In a large frying pan, preferably nonstick, melt about 1 teaspoon of the butter over medium-low heat. Arrange as many apple slices as will fit in a single layer in the pan. Sauté the apples until golden brown on both sides, about 3 minutes per side, using a pancake turner to turn them. Remove the slices to a plate and cover with foil. Continue cooking, adding the remaining butter as needed, until all the slices are sautéed. Set aside in a warm place.

MAKE THE SAUCE: Pour the pan drippings and browned bits into a 2-cup liquid measure.* Skim off and discard as much of the fat that rises to the surface as possible. Add water if necessary to equal 1 cup. Set aside.

In the Dutch oven, over medium-low heat, melt the butter. Add the flour and cook for 1 minute, stirring constantly. Gradually pour in the pan drippings, stirring constantly. Add the heavy cream and crème de cassis or red vermouth and taste for seasonings. Add salt and pepper if desired. Cook over low heat, stirring constantly, until thickened. Set aside, covered.

To serve, drain the prunes, reserving the port. Place the sautéed apple slices, alternating with the prunes, on either side of the roast. (Return any remaining prunes to the port to serve on the side.) Pour a little sauce onto each portion of meat, and serve the remainder in a gravy boat.

*If you have a gravy separator, first pour the drippings into it to remove the fat.

# Grandma Sarah's Lamb with Prune Glaze

This unusual combination of lamb and prunes is so succulent and gloriously flavorful it was my favorite recipe growing up and still remains one of my top ten. It has elicited rave reviews such as: "The best thing I've ever put in my mouth" and "It was so good I didn't want to share!"

Grandma grew up in "The Old Country" (Russia, near Minsk). Although this recipe seems Slavic in inspiration, she claimed that the idea of adding the prunes was hers. She said it just seemed to her that they would go well with the lamb. Knowing how she viewed prunes as Nature's cure-all, I suspect she was really looking for an irresistible way to get us to eat them!

Although this recipe was originally for a stew, I prefer to boil down the liquid and juices until just enough remains to glaze the lamb. This gives it extra moisture and richer color and flavor. Grandma simmered the meat in a large pot on top of the stove for at least an hour and a half, but in the pressure cooker, this recipe cooks to a perfection of melting tenderness in only about thirty minutes.

I like to serve this glorious dish with a bold red cabernet (though Grandma certainly didn't).

*(continued)*

| INGREDIENTS | MEASURE<br>*volume* | WEIGHT<br>*ounces/pounds* | *grams/kilograms* |
|---|---|---|---|
| all-purpose flour | 3 tablespoons | 1 ounce | 27 grams |
| salt | 2 teaspoons | 0.50 ounce | 13 grams |
| black pepper, freshly ground | ¼ teaspoon | | |
| cayenne pepper | a big pinch | | |
| lamb shanks, cut into thirds (2- to 3-inch pieces) | | 5 pounds | 2 kilograms<br>268 grams |
| vegetable oil | 3 tablespoons | | |
| 1 large onion, thinly sliced | 2 cups | 8 ounces | 227 grams |
| 2 ribs celery (including leafy portion), thinly sliced | 1 cup | 3 ounces | 90 grams |
| 1 large clove of garlic, minced | 2 teaspoons | 0.25 ounce | 7 grams |
| fresh thyme leaves* | 2 teaspoons | | |
| 1 bay leaf | | | |
| water | 1 ½ liquid cups | | |
| 21 1½-inch red-skin potatoes, scrubbed (if using larger ones, cut them in half) | | 2 pounds | 907 grams |
| pitted prunes | 2 cups, firmly packed | 12 ounces | 340 grams |

SERVES 6 to 8

EQUIPMENT: 6-quart pressure cooker

In a gallon-size heavy-duty plastic bag, combine the flour, salt, black pepper and cayenne pepper and shake to mix. Add the lamb a few pieces at a time and toss to coat with the flour mixture. If any of the flour mixture remains, set it aside.

Heat a large heavy frying pan, preferably cast-iron, until hot. Add 1 tablespoon of the oil and heat until a film appears over the oil. Over medium-high heat, brown the lamb in batches, adding only as much lamb as will fit in the pan without crowding, until well browned on all sides, about 8 to 10 minutes, adding more oil as necessary to keep the lamb from sticking. Remove the lamb to a bowl and set aside.

Add any remaining oil to the pan, and sauté the onions and celery until the onions are golden-brown and the celery wilted. Sprinkle on any remaining flour mixture, stir in the garlic and cook, stirring, for about 30 seconds. Then

*Or ½ teaspoon dried.

spoon the mixture into the pressure cooker. Top with the lamb. Add the thyme, bay leaf and water.

Cook at full pressure for 20 minutes. Release the pressure (using the quick-release technique), stir and add the potatoes and prunes. Cook at full pressure for 10 minutes. The meat should be almost falling-off-the-bone tender and the potatoes firm but done. If necessary, continue cooking, without pressure, until the potatoes are just done.

With a skimmer, remove the lamb and vegetables to a large serving platter, and cover with foil to keep warm. Tilt the pan and skim off the fat from the top of the sauce. Bring the sauce to a boil and reduce to about 1 cup, or until very thick, stirring often, about 5 to 10 minutes. Film it over the meat.

### TRADITIONAL METHOD

Brown the lamb and sauté the vegetables as directed above, but transfer the mixture to a Dutch oven instead of a pressure cooker. Increase the water to 4 cups, and bring to a boil over medium-high heat. Reduce the heat and simmer, partly covered, for 1 hour. Add the potatoes and cook 30 minutes longer. Add the prunes and cook about 30 minutes longer or until the potatoes are tender. Reducing the gravy to 1 cup will take about 15 minutes.

NOTE: A tablespoon of leftover sauce, added to the cooking water, is a fabulous enhancement to wild rice. It deepens the color and the flavor in an undefinable but intense way.

# JEWISH DELI SMOKED TONGUE

$M$y friend Rick Rodgers calls tongue Jewish ham. I agree that it is as close as you can come to that hauntingly smoky, meaty flavor, but it is even more succulent. When I was growing up, my grandmother would occasionally buy a whole pickled tongue at the kosher butcher's and simmer it with a few peppercorns and a bay leaf for three to four hours, until tender. When cold, she would peel it and slice it fairly thick for sandwiches between slices of Jewish rye bread, which we would pack for outings at the beach. I loved it then and I love it now, but I still can't eat it without remembering the few grains of sand that always found their way into the sandwich (and the admonition from my mother that we could not go back into the ocean until a full hour of digestion had taken place).

Our favorite weekend restaurant in recent years, the Beaver House in Stroudsburg, Pennsylvania, serves one-inch chunks of smoked tongue with pumpernickel rolls and zippy English mustard. I have combined the past and present in this attractive and delectable presentation for festive occasions.

| INGREDIENTS | MEASURE<br>*volume* | WEIGHT<br>*ounces/pounds* | *grams/kilograms* |
| --- | --- | --- | --- |
| 1 smoked beef tongue | | 4 pounds | 1 kilogram<br>814 grams |
| 1 medium onion, stuck with 3 whole cloves | | 6 ounces | 170 grams |
| 2 large cloves of garlic unpeeled, halved | | 0.5 ounce | 14 grams |
| 4 parsley sprigs | | | |
| 1 bay leaf | | | |
| whole black peppercorns | 1 teaspoon | | |
| prepared mustard, preferably Colman's English | 1 small jar (½ cup) | 4.6 ounces | 130 grams |
| 1 loaf pumpernickel or rye bread | | | |

COOKING TIME: about 3 hours
SERVES: 12

EQUIPMENT: heavy, preferably oval, covered pot large enough to hold the tongue

Place the tongue in the pot, and add enough cold water to cover it by a few inches. Bring it to a simmer over high heat. Reduce the heat to low and simmer, covered, for 45 minutes per pound, until fork-tender. Cool completely in the cooking liquid.

Peel the tongue and trim off the root end. Use a thin-bladed sharp knife to cut slices of tongue as thin as possible (no more than ⅛ inch thick), starting from the tip and working toward the back.

On a large serving platter, arrange the slices in overlapping circles, starting with the wider back pieces at the outside perimeter and working towards the center, placing the darker tip pieces in the very center to form a rosette. Serve with mustard and pumpernickel or rye bread.

---

*Tongue.* Always considered a delicacy among Jews, tongue has been an important dish in Jewish cooking for centuries. In the Book of Genesis, we are told that when three angels came to Abraham he prepared a special feast for them. It is traditionally believed that tongue with mustard was served at this holy banquet. Today, tongue is often eaten at Ashkenazic seders as well as at many other holiday meals, including Rosh Hashanah (Jewish New Year).

---

# RARE PRIME RIBS OF BEEF

Let's face it: There is no cooking aroma better or more enticing than roasting beef sizzling in the oven. Roast prime ribs of beef is, for us, a special-occasion family dinner, often served at Christmastime. It is always accompanied by Yorkshire Popovers (page 66), which are a smaller version of the classic English Yorkshire pudding, prepared with the roast's savory drippings. Regretfully, though, it is difficult for today's beef to compete with my memories of the aged beef of years past. A simple technique for home aging, however, described by Jane Freiman* does wonders to tenderize the meat and heighten the beefy flavor; in fact, using this technique, I prefer the less expensive choice grade to prime!

My favorite technique for assuring a perfect roast, one that has a browned and crusty exterior with a perfectly rare interior all the way through, is one invented by the late Ann Seranne (who happened, ironically, to be known as a rare and somewhat crusty individual herself). I had once been told that she lived quite near my former house in Hainesburg, New Jersey, and had always hoped to meet her. One day, in the local pharmacy, I overheard an old woman putting the pharmacist in his place in no uncertain terms. In a moment of illuminated daring, I asked if she happened to be Ann Seranne. "And who are you?" she asked, confirming my suspicion.

(Note: This technique requires a well-insulated oven. An alternate method is also given.)

*Italic* English Christmas*
Rare Prime Ribs of Beef
Yorkshire Popovers
Gratin de Pommes de Terre
Mixed Greens Salad with
   California Heirloom Salad
   Dressing
Lemon and White Poppy
   Seed Surprise Cake
Rosy Cran-Raspberry Butter
   Bars

*Dinner Party*, Harper & Row, 1990.

ROSE'S MELTING POT

| INGREDIENTS | MEASURE | WEIGHT | |
| *room temperature* | *volume* | *ounces/pounds* | *grams/kilograms* |
| --- | --- | --- | --- |
| 1 standing rib roast* | | 5 to 6 pounds | 2 kilograms 268 grams to 2 kilograms 722 grams |
| all-purpose flour | 1 tablespoon | | |
| kosher salt (Diamond brand)† | 1 tablespoon | | |
| black pepper, freshly ground | ¼ teaspoon | | |

ADVANCE PREPARATION: Allow the roast to sit at room temperature 1 to 2 hours before roasting.
PREHEAT THE OVEN TO: 500°F.
BAKING TIME: 25 to 30 minutes roasting time plus at least 2 hours standing time
SERVES: 6

Remove the roast from the refrigerator 1 to 2 hours before roasting.

*Preheat the oven to 500°F. at least 15 minutes before roasting.*

In a small bowl, whisk together the flour, salt and pepper. Rub the roast on the top and sides with the flour mixture.

Place the roast in a roasting pan and roast for 25 minutes for a 4½-pound roast, 30 minutes for a 5-pound roast (about 5 to 6 minutes a pound). Do not open the oven door. Turn off the heat and allow the roast to sit undisturbed for at least 2 hours or up to 4 hours.

If your oven is not well insulated (say the door does not close firmly), roast the beef for 15 minutes at 450°F., and then reduce the heat to 325°F. and continue roasting until an instant-read thermometer, inserted toward the center of the roast, reads 120°F. to 125°F. This method will take about 15 minutes per pound. Allow the roast to stand for at least 20 minutes before carving to reabsorb its juices.

Present the roast surrounded by Yorkshire Popovers (page 66). Pass the meat juices in a gravy boat.

NOTE: If you buy prime meat, part of what you are paying for is its aging by the butcher. If you buy supermarket choice-grade meat, it benefits greatly from the following 3- to 5-day aging process: Place a roasting pan a little

*Ask for a "first cut," cut from the ribs closest to the loin. Be sure to buy either prime grade or choice. Prime is more tender but choice has more flavor. If the butcher offers you the short ribs, freeze them to make the Beef and Barley Soupless in *Rose's Celebrations* (William Morrow, 1992).
†If using Morton brand or table salt, use only 1½ teaspoons.

*(continued)*

larger than the roast on a refrigerator shelf. Line it with a few paper towels to absorb the drippings. Unwrap the roast and place it, fat side up, on a shelf directly above the pan. Allow it to sit for 3 to 5 days. Trim off any dried areas. From a 5-pound roast you will lose about 10 ounces in trimmings and 5 ounces in liquid. A supermarket or butcher prime roast of this weight costs about fifty cents more per pound than the choice that has been home aged. I find that the advantage to prime beef is more tenderness and the advantage to choice beef is more flavor.

*Timetable for other size roasts (2- to 4-hour sitting period remains the same):* 8- to 9-pound roast: 40 to 45 minutes initial roasting time: Serves 10 to 12. 11- to 12-pound roast: 55 to 60 minutes initial roasting time. Serves 14 to 16.

# SIDE DISHES

# MASHED POTATOES WITH CARAMELIZED PEARS

This felicitous combination of pear and potato was inspired by a Swiss friend, chef Peter Bührer. The caramelized pear adds just the right element of tangy sweetness, harmoniously playing against the smooth, mellow, earthy potato. My daughter Beth's boyfriend, Peter Dawes, when asked if he preferred mashed potatoes fluffy or with more substance replied, "I never thought about it; I love mashed potatoes so much I accept them any way they come!" After tasting these, however, he pronounced them the best he had ever eaten.

My preference is to keep the pear flavor subtle, but for a more pronounced pear taste it's fine to double the amount of pears. To accompany a dish that already has caramel and fruit overtones, such as the Bistro-Style Pork Chops with Lima Beans (page 146), simply leave out the caramelized pears. With the pears, these are an appropriate and appreciated accompaniment to Spicy Southern Fried Chicken (page 121), Friday Night Roast Chicken with Paprika (page 123) or Rare Prime Ribs of Beef (page 158).

| INGREDIENTS room temperature | MEASURE volume | WEIGHT ounces/pounds | grams/kilograms |
|---|---|---|---|
| 1 Bartlett pear | | 7 ounces | 200 grams |
| sugar | 2 tablespoons + 1 teaspoon | 1 ounce | 30 grams |
| water | ¼ liquid cup | | |
| white wine or water | 1 tablespoon | | |
| 4 large boiling potatoes | | 2½ pounds | 1 kilogram 134 grams |
| unsalted butter | 4 tablespoons | 2 ounces | 57 grams |
| heavy cream | 1 liquid cup | | |
| salt | 1 teaspoon | | 6 grams |
| nutmeg | a grating | | |
| white pepper, freshly ground | a few grindings | | |

(continued)

Peel, core, and thinly slice the pear.

In a small, heavy saucepan, over medium heat, stir together the sugar and water until the sugar is fully moistened. Heat, stirring constantly, until the mixture boils. Stop stirring completely and allow it to cook until it turns a deep amber. (There will be a scant 2 tablespoons of caramel.) Immediately add the pear slices. Turn them over to coat them with the caramel. Add the wine or water, and boil over high heat, stirring to dissolve the caramel, for about 5 minutes or until most of the liquid has evaporated. Empty the pears into a bowl and set aside.

Peel and quarter the potatoes. Place them in a medium saucepan and add cold water to cover them by a few inches. Boil for 20 minutes or until just tender when pierced with a skewer or sharp knife.

Drain the potatoes thoroughly, and put them through a ricer or sieve or mash them.* Stir in the butter and caramelized pears with a wooden spoon. Heat the cream and add it gradually to the potatoes, whisking briefly. Whisk in the salt, nutmeg and pepper and taste to adjust the seasoning. Do not overwhisk. Keep warm until ready to serve.

 POINTERS
FOR SUCCESS

- After purchasing potatoes, keep them in a cool place, but not in the refrigerator or they will develop an undesirable "sweet" flavor.
- Slicing the pears as thin as possible makes them almost melt into the potatoes.

*The secret to silky-smooth mashed potatoes is to press them through a ricer or sieve. Using a food processor or blender will make them pasty, while mashing them with a potato masher will never make them as smooth.

ROSE'S MELTING POT

# SWISS RÖSTI POTATOES

I first learned about rösti potatoes from Charlotte, a Swiss friend who, at the time, was living in America. This golden fried grated potato cake, crunchy on the outside, meltingly textured on the inside, was the only dish from her native land she talked about with passion, and I became very curious. She claimed that the two secrets to perfect rösti are using the right size grater and precooking the potatoes far enough in advance to maintain the coarse tender-crisp texture.

On my first trip to Switzerland, finding a rösti grater was a high priority. And although it is nice to have the traditional size, an ordinary coarse grater also works well. The most important part, however, is undercooking the potatoes and cooking them far enough ahead of frying so that they firm up and hold their shape. The Swiss say two to three days is ideal. Although lard or butter is traditional, my first choice in this instance is goose fat because I adore its flavor with fried potatoes.

In Switzerland, rösti are usually served with sausages. I also enjoy them with Perfect Crisp Roast Duck (page 140) and roast chicken (page 123).

(continued)

---

*Rösti Potatoes.* Indigenous to South and Central America, the potato has been cultivated for over 4,000 years and was a staple of the Incas. Its name comes from the Caribbean Indian word for the sweet potato, "batata." Introduced to Europe around 1570 by Spanish explorers it immediately became a mainstay of the peasantry. Until about 1780, discerning French cooks refrained from using the potato because it was thought to cause leprosy. It arrived in the United States, via Ireland, in about 1720. Today it is grown around the world. In Switzerland, the grated potato pancake, or rösti, is the quintessential dish of the German-speaking Swiss. It is a bit like hash browns only crustier. Over the years, rösti has come to be associated with the Sarine River, which is jokingly referred to as the "Rösti-graben," the dividing line or "ditch" between the French- and German-speaking sections of the country. To make rösti, the Swiss grate parboiled potatoes and place them in a hot skillet with butter where they are cooked until the bottom layer is crispy brown. The potato cake is then turned and browned on the other side and cut into wedges. Originally, rural farmers ate rösti for breakfast with a cup of hot coffee. Today it is usually served as a light midday snack or dinner entrée. It is the perfect companion to almost any meat or fish dish.

---

| INGREDIENTS | MEASURE | WEIGHT | |
| --- | --- | --- | --- |
| | *volume* | *ounces* | *grams* |
| 4 medium boiling potatoes, halved | | 26 ounces | 737 grams |
| salt | ½ teaspoon | | |
| 1 large onion, (8 ounces/227 grams), chopped medium-fine | 1⅔ cups | 7.5 ounces (chopped) | 210 grams |
| sugar | a pinch | | |
| goose fat* or butter | ¼ cup (4 tablespoons) | 2½/2 ounces | 71/56 grams |
| black pepper, freshly ground | a few grindings | | |

ADVANCE PREPARATION: at least 6 hours or up to 3 days ahead
SERVES: 4 to 6

EQUIPMENT: 10-inch (measured across the bottom) heavy skillet, preferably nonstick, with curved as opposed to sloped sides for the nicest shape

In a large saucepan of boiling salted water (about 1 teaspoon of salt), cook the potatoes for about 15 minutes or until the outside feels tender but the center of the potato still feels quite firm when a sharp knife is inserted. With a slotted skimmer or tongs, gently lift out the potatoes and place them in a bowl of ice water to cool. When cool, drain the potatoes on paper towels and refrigerate them, covered, for at least 6 hours.

About 45 minutes before serving time, peel the potatoes and grate them coarsely. Sprinkle them evenly with the salt and toss gently.

In the frying pan, over medium heat, melt 3 tablespoons of the goose fat or butter. Add the onions and sugar and sauté, stirring occasionally, for about 5 minutes, or until the onions are softened but not beginning to color. Add the potatoes and, with a fork, gently mix the onions into them. Using a pancake turner, press the mixture gently together to make it adhere. Grate the pepper on top and cook for about 7 minutes or until golden brown on the bottom. (When you shake the pan, there will be a slight scraping sound once the bottom of the potatoes is crisp.)

To turn the potatoes, place a large flat plate or cookie sheet over the top of the pan and invert. Add the remaining tablespoon of fat to the pan and swirl it around to coat the pan evenly. Slide the potato cake back into the pan. Press it together again with the spatula to be sure the

*Available in specialty stores such as Dean & DeLuca, 560 Broadway, New York, New York 10012 (212-431-1691; outside New York, 800-227-7714).

potatoes adhere, grind more pepper over the top and cook for another 7 minutes or until the second side is golden brown. Unmold it onto a serving plate. Cut into wedges and serve immediately. If necessary, keep it warm in a low oven with the door partly ajar.

Any leftover rösti can be refrigerated and recrisped on a baking sheet under the broiler until heated through.

POINTERS
FOR SUCCESS

- It is essential to undercook the potatoes when boiling them so that they remain firm and separate when grated and fried.
- If the onions begin to brown before you add the potatoes, they will get too brown during the rest of the cooking.
- Use a fork to stir the onions and potatoes, as a spoon would tend to mash them.

UNDERSTANDING

The larger the skillet, the larger the surface area of the rösti and the more crisp potatoes in proportion to the soft inside.

Salt is added to the potatoes when they are in the bowl rather than in the frying pan for the most even distribution.

# GRATIN DE POMMES DE TERRE
## (GrahTAN duh pahm duh tare) (Scalloped Potatoes)

**French Bastille Day**
Walnut Fougasse
Cold Garlicky Mediterranean
  Mussels
Salmon Steak with Dijon
  Mustard and Black
  Mustard Grains
Steamed Asparagus with
  Extra-Lemony Hollandaise
  Sauce
Gratin de Pommes de Terre
Endive and Walnut Salad
  with Raspberry Walnut
  Vinaigrette
Chocolate Pots de Crème

Since I never could make up my mind which version of this popular French potato dish I loved most—*gratin dauphinois*, with its cream sauce, or *gratin savoyard*, with its chicken broth–based sauce—I finally decided to combine the best features of both, resulting in a less rich but more flavorful gratin! In this version, most of the milk and cream gets absorbed into the potatoes, but a small amount thickens slightly around the potato slices, giving them a creamy/crunchy texture.

This is one of the most superb potato dishes I know. It has elicited such comments as "I didn't know potatoes could taste this way!" It works brilliantly to dress up a simple roast, such as Friday Night Roast Chicken with Paprika (page 123) or Rare Prime Ribs of Beef (page 158), chops or even baked ham.

| INGREDIENTS | MEASURE volume | WEIGHT ounces/pounds | grams |
|---|---|---|---|
| potatoes, preferably Yukon gold or russets, pared | about 6 cups, sliced | 1½ pounds | 750 grams |
| milk | 1 liquid cup | | |
| heavy cream | ¼ liquid cup | | |
| 1 chicken bouillon cube or 2 cubes Glace de Volaille (page 209)* | | | |
| 1 large clove of garlic | | 0.25 ounce | 7 grams |
| unsalted butter | 1 tablespoon | 0.50 ounce | 14 grams |
| black pepper, freshly ground | a few grindings | | |
| Gruyère cheese, grated | 1 to 2 tablespoons | | 3 to 6 grams |

*If using the homemade chicken concentrate, add ¼ teaspoon salt to the milk-cream mixture.

EQUIPMENT: shallow 1½-quart
baking dish (my favorite is a 9-
inch by 7¾-inch oval copper
gratin pan); if using Pyrex,
decrease the oven temperature
to 375°F.

*Preheat the oven to 400°F.*

Use the 2-mm. food processor slicing blade or a sharp knife to slice the potatoes into thin rounds. Set them aside without rinsing them.

In a small saucepan, combine the milk, cream and bouillon cube and simmer for 3 to 5 minutes, stirring occasionally, until the bouillon cube has dissolved. Set aside.

Meanwhile cut the garlic clove in half. Remove the skin and use the cut side of each half to rub the baking pan. Add the garlic to the simmering milk mixture.

Use half the butter to grease the baking dish. Cut the remainder into about 6 small pieces and refrigerate them.

Layer the potato slices into the pan, grinding a little pepper over each layer. Remove and discard the garlic from the milk mixture, and pour it over the potatoes.

Sprinkle the top of the potatoes with the Gruyère and scatter the reserved bits of butter over it. Place in the oven and bake about 60 to 70 minutes or until golden brown and tender when pierced with a sharp knife tip. If the surface becomes very browned before the potatoes are tender, cover it loosely with foil. Serve hot.

UNDERSTANDING    Washing or rinsing the sliced potatoes would wash away the starch, which is necessary to thicken the sauce and hold the potatoes together.

After purchasing potatoes, keep them in a cool place, but not in the refrigerator or they will develop an undesirable "sweet" flavor.

---

*Gratin dauphinois.* In French cooking, a "gratin" is any dish with a crusted or browned surface. This cooking technique developed in the mid-seventeenth century. Gratin dauphinois originated in the area of the Alps known as the Dauphiné and has since generated many different versions, which may include milk, eggs, or cream along with potatoes and cheese.

# STEAMED ASPARAGUS

The first-of-the-season asparagus, perfectly cooked, with or without hollandaise, is the uncontested heralder of spring. Because it is one of my favorite vegetables, I enjoy it year-round. It is wonderful both hot and cold the next day with a simple vinaigrette.

| INGREDIENTS | MEASURE<br>*volume* | WEIGHT<br>*ounces/pounds* | *grams* |
|---|---|---|---|
| fresh asparagus | | 2 pounds | 907 grams |
| salt | ¼ teaspoon | | |

SERVES: 8

EQUIPMENT: fish poacher or large covered frying pan

Rinse the asparagus under cold running water. Trim the base ends so that each spear is approximately the same length and any part of the stalk that is not bright green has been removed.

Place the asparagus on the rack of the fish poacher or in the frying pan and add about 2 cups of boiling water. Cover and simmer over medium-low heat for 10 to 12 minutes, depending on the size, until the asparagus feels tender when pierced with a skewer or a single spear, when lifted with tongs, curves. For even cooking, use tongs to lift the asparagus on the bottom to the top partway through cooking.

Remove the asparagus at once to a serving plate, sprinkle with the salt and cover with plastic wrap to keep it warm and prevent shriveling. (The asparagus is also delicious cold.)

POINTERS
FOR SUCCESS

• Peeling the lower part of the stalks is not usually necessary unless the asparagus is sandy or tough. If you bend each asparagus spear to break off the bottom, the tough part will snap off automatically. I prefer to cut them all to the same length for ease in handling and appearance.

# LEBANESE SPINACH

This method for cooking spinach is the most simple and flavorful one I know. It was taught to me many years ago by a cellist whose father had grown up in Lebanon and was a close friend of Kahlil Gibran (author of *The Prophet*). The small amount of olive oil softens the slight astringency of the spinach and the smashed garlic stays with the spinach only long enough to release its perfumed oils. This would be a fine side dish for Capon with Savory Bulgur Stuffing (page 137).

| INGREDIENTS | MEASURE<br>*volume* | WEIGHT<br>*ounces/pounds* | *grams* |
|---|---|---|---|
| fresh spinach | | 1 pound | 454 grams |
| extra virgin olive oil | 1 tablespoon | | |
| 1 medium clove of garlic, smashed | | | 5 grams |
| salt | to taste | | |
| black pepper, freshly ground | to taste | | |

SERVES: 4

Wash the spinach well to remove any grit. Remove and discard any coarse stems.

Place the olive oil and garlic in a large pot with a tight-fitting cover. Set over medium heat and cook for about 3 minutes or until the garlic starts to sizzle. Place the spinach leaves on top, without shaking off any water that clings to the leaves. Sprinkle with salt and pepper. Cover tightly, reduce the heat to medium low and cook for 15 to 20 minutes or until the spinach is wilted and tender. Stir gently, and discard the garlic clove. Drain and serve.

# SPICY LENTIL SALAD

This cold, spicy salad is a refreshingly tasty complement to the hot spicy stew called Ethiopian Doro Wat (page 131) or to Tandoori Chicken (page 126), but it would also complement less spicy poultry dishes such as Capon with Savory Bulgur Stuffing (page 137) or Friday Night Roast Chicken with Paprika (page 123).

| INGREDIENTS room temperature | MEASURE volume | WEIGHT ounces | grams |
|---|---|---|---|
| dried lentils, preferably French* | 1¼ scant cups | 8 ounces | 227 grams |
| salt | 1½ teaspoons, divided | 0.25 ounce | 6.7 grams |
| extra virgin olive oil | 3 tablespoons | | |
| lemon juice, freshly squeezed | 2 tablespoons, or to taste | | |
| black pepper, freshly ground | ⅛ teaspoon | | |
| sugar | a pinch | | |
| 2 medium cloves of garlic, minced | 2 teaspoons | 0.25 ounce | 7 grams |
| 1 medium onion, chopped | 1 cup | 4.5 ounces | 128 grams |
| ½ 6-inch-long fresh green chili pepper, coarsely chopped | 1 scant tablespoon | 0.3 ounce | 9 grams |
| fresh coriander leaves | 1 cup | 0.5 ounce | 14 grams |

MAKE AHEAD: at least 2 hours or up to 3 days
MAKES: 4½ cups
SERVES: 6

*At least 2 hours or up to 3 days ahead:*

Rinse the lentils, pick out any stones and drain well. Place the lentils in a medium saucepan and add water to cover them by at least 3 inches. Add ¼ teaspoon of the salt and bring the water to a boil. Lower the heat and simmer, partially covered, for 20 to 30 minutes or until the lentils are tender but still have a little bite. Drain the lentils immediately, using a strainer, and run cold water through them until they are cool.

*Available in specialty food stores such as Dean & DeLuca, 560 Broadway, New York, New York 10012 (212-431-1691; outside New York, 800-227-7714).

In a 2-quart bowl, whisk together the olive oil, lemon juice, the remaining 1¼ teaspoons of salt, the pepper and sugar. Add the cooled lentils, the garlic, onion and chili pepper. Coarsely chop the coriander, add it to the mixture and mix together until everything is evenly coated. Cover the bowl tightly and set it aside for at least 2 hours at room temperature or refrigerate for up to 3 days, stirring at least once every day.

Just before serving, adjust seasonings with additional lemon juice, salt and pepper.

SERVE: At room temperature or chilled.

KEEPS: Leftover lentil salad freezes well for up to 3 months.

POINTERS FOR SUCCESS

• Marinating the lentils for at least 2 hours allows the flavors to penetrate, making it unnecessary to flavor them during cooking.

# POLENTA (Creamy and Fried)

For me, polenta, with its golden color, subtle corn flavor and light creamy-crisp texture, is the ideal accompaniment to Classic Chicken Cacciatore Piccante (page 135) and Ethiopian Doro Wat (page 131). Of course, it also makes an excellent first course on its own.

This recipe is easy to make either on the stove top or in a microwave oven, but here is a time where the microwave really shines. With the microwave, the polenta cooks in only eleven minutes with only three stirrings, whereas the stove-top method takes forty minutes and must be stirred continuously to prevent lumping.

*(continued)*

| INGREDIENTS | MEASURE | WEIGHT | |
| room temperature | volume | ounces | grams |
|---|---|---|---|
| coarse yellow cornmeal | 1 cup | 5 ounces | 140 grams |
| water | 4 liquid cups* | | |
| salt | ¾ teaspoon | | |
| extra virgin olive oil | 1 tablespoon | | |
| unsalted butter | 2 tablespoons | 1 ounce | 28 grams |
| black pepper, freshly ground | a few grindings | | |
| Parmesan cheese, freshly grated | 2 tablespoons | 0.25 ounce | 8 grams |

SERVES: 4 to 6

EQUIPMENT: (for fried polenta) 9-inch by 13-inch baking dish, lightly buttered or sprayed with nonstick vegetable spray, scalloped round biscuit cutter (optional)

Place the cornmeal in a small bowl and add ½ cup of the water, stirring to moisten it evenly. Allow it to soak for at least 15 minutes.

In a medium-size heavy saucepan, bring the remaining 3½ cups of water to a full boil. Add the salt and oil and then, stirring constantly, add the cornmeal mixture very gradually so that the water never stops boiling. Over low heat, cook the polenta, stirring often, for 40 minutes or until the mixture is very stiff and starts to come away from the sides of the pan.

For Creamy Polenta, stir in the butter and serve at once, sprinkled with the pepper and cheese.

For Fried Polenta, scrape the creamy polenta into the prepared pan and press it to about a ½-inch thickness (it will come only to about 2 inches from one short side of the pan). Cover with plastic wrap and cool completely.

Use a scalloped round biscuit cutter to cut rounds or a sharp knife to cut diamond shapes from the polenta. Knead the scraps together, roll with a rolling pin to ½ inch thick and cut out. Continue until all the polenta has been cut and shaped.

In a large heavy frying pan, over medium heat, melt 1 tablespoon of the butter. When bubbling, add about one third of the polenta pieces. Sauté about 3 minutes on each

*The water can be reduced to 2½ to 3 cups to decrease cooking time to about 20 minutes, but the flavor is best with the longer cooking time (if not using the microwave method).

side or until golden brown. Remove to a serving platter and place in a warm oven. Cook the remaining polenta in 2 batches, adding ½ tablespoon of the remaining butter for each batch.

Sprinkle the polenta with freshly ground black pepper and the Parmesan cheese, and serve.

MICROWAVE VERSION (4 servings)

Reduce the water to 3½ cups.

In a 2½-quart microwave-safe dish, combine the water, oil and salt. Gradually whisk in the cornmeal. Cover with a lid or Saran brand plastic wrap, folding back a small corner, and cook on high for 5 minutes. Uncover carefully and whisk well. Recover and cook on high for 2 minutes. Uncover carefully and whisk well. Leave uncovered and cook until very thick, about 2 minutes. Whisk well before spreading out to cool.

NOTE: This was tested in a 700-watt microwave. The exact timing will vary according to the type of microwave used.

VARIATION: For a richer version, after removing the polenta from the heat, stir in 4 tablespoons of softened unsalted butter and 1 cup of grated Parmesan cheese. Spread into the prepared baking pan and cool. Cut into shapes as above, but arrange them overlapping in a buttered baking dish. Drizzle the polenta with 4 tablespoons of melted unsalted butter and sprinkle with more Parmesan. Bake in a preheated 375°F. oven for 15 minutes or until golden and bubbly.

UNDERSTANDING    Soaking the cornmeal prevents lumping when it is added to the boiling water.

# MIDEASTERN BULGUR AND CURRANT STUFFING

I have been preparing bulgur and currants as a side dish for years and often wondered how it would be as a stuffing for capon (page 137). On first try it became an instant favorite. The natural juices of the bird do wonders to enhance the wheaty bulgur.*

This recipe, made without the currants, but with the addition of boiled lentils (see page 172) and onions fried until caramelized turns into a classic Lebanese dish *mjudra*, which I also adore. Use plain brown lentils and save the liquid to cook the bulgur. Serve it with Lebanese Spinach (page 171).

| INGREDIENTS | MEASURE | WEIGHT | |
| --- | --- | --- | --- |
| | *volume* | *ounces* | *grams* |
| extra virgin olive oil | 1 tablespoon | | |
| 2 medium cloves of garlic, lightly smashed | | 0.35 ounce | 10 grams |
| medium bulgur | 3 cups | 16 ounces | 454 grams |
| dried currants | ½ cup | 1 ounce | 28 grams |
| salt | 1 ½ teaspoons | 0.33 ounce | 10 grams |
| sugar | ½ teaspoon | | |
| black pepper, freshly ground | ½ teaspoon | | |
| boiling water | 3 liquid cups | | |
| Capon Broth (page 138) | (½ liquid cup) | | |

MAKES: 7 cups
SERVES: 8

In a medium-size heavy saucepan, with a tight-fitting lid, heat the oil over medium heat. Add the garlic and bulgur and fry, stirring often, for 2 to 3 minutes. Reduce the heat to low. Add the currants, and sprinkle with the salt, sugar and pepper. Add the boiling water and simmer, tightly covered, for 15 minutes. Fluff the mixture with a fork, remove from the heat and allow it to stand, covered, for at least 5 minutes.

*If you would like to serve this as a side dish with lamb or poultry, increase the water to 4½ cups (or use half water and half unsalted chicken broth) and simmer until tender or bake as directed.

Use 2 cups of the bulgur to stuff the capon. Spoon the remaining stuffing into a 2-quart casserole. Sprinkle it with ½ cup of the reserved capon broth, tossing lightly with a fork. Cover tightly and bake along with the capon for the last 30 minutes of cooking.

# KASHA VARNISHKES
## (Buckwheat Groats with Bowtie Noodles)

It is unfortunate indeed that such a splendid grain as buckwheat is burdened by the unappealing name of *groats*. In my family, it was known by its Eastern European name, *kasha*. But whatever it was called, I wouldn't have eaten it as it was prepared by my grandmother, who did the cooking in our family when I was growing up: Her preparation was pale in color, soft and soupy like a cereal and undistinguished in taste. Not for me.

An American friend, however, reintroduced me to Kasha when I grew up, and her recipe was spicy with black pepper and oregano. This blending of Italian spice with Russian/Jewish flavor was amazingly successful. And each grain was appealingly firm and separate. The secret is allowing the buckwheat grains to sit with the raw egg for at least 30 minutes, stirring occasionally to keep them separate. Over the years I have discovered other secrets, such as browning the grains under the broiler after cooking to add crunch and deepen the color; adding sautéed mushroom slices, and sometimes a little dried porcini mushrooms, for extra flavor intensity; using stock instead of water and adding the bowtie noodles for the classic *kasha varnishkes*. Goose fat is another fabulous flavor enhancement. This has become my favorite grain dish and my traditional accompaniment to Perfect Crisp Roast Duck (page 140). The earthy, spicy, wheaty flavor goes so well with the rich crispy duck, I can't bear to vary it.

*(continued)*

*Kasha Varnishkes.* In medieval Russia, a "kasha" referred to a "feast." Today "kasha" describes any porridge-like dish prepared with grain that is cooked in water, milk or broth. It is among the oldest Russian foods and still forms a standard part of the diet of most Slavs, especially the rural peasantry. Buckwheat—whole, medium, or finely ground— is the most popular grain used in making kashas, but millet and oats are not uncommon substitutes. Semolina and rice are two grains more frequently found in kashas prepared in upper-class Russian homes, semolina because it is from a more expensive wheat and rice because it is imported. In every Russian kitchen, one finds a special clay pot for cooking kasha, which can be eaten at any meal of the day. Usually it is brought to the table along with soup. At breakfast or lunch, Russians eat kasha with milk ("milk soup"), much like modern cereal.

| INGREDIENTS room temperature | MEASURE volume | WEIGHT ounces/pounds | grams |
|---|---|---|---|
| OPTIONAL: dried porcini mushrooms, well rinsed | | 0.50 ounce | 14 grams |
| kasha, coarse ground | 1 cup | 5.6 ounces | 160 grams |
| 1 large egg | | 2 ounces (weighed in the shell) | 57 grams |
| goose fat* or unsalted butter | ¼ cup/4 tablespoons | 2.5/2 ounces | 71/56 grams |
| 1 large onion, chopped | 2 cups | 9 ounces | 255 grams |
| sugar | 1 teaspoon | | 4 grams |
| fresh mushrooms, sliced | 5 cups | 1 pound | 454 grams |
| garlic, minced | 1 teaspoon | | 3 grams |
| salt | 1 teaspoon, or to taste | | 6.7 grams |
| black pepper, freshly ground[†] | 1½ to 2 teaspoons | | 3 to 4 grams |
| dried oregano | 1 tablespoon | | |
| low-salt chicken broth, preferably College Inn[‡] | 1¾ cups (1 13.75-ounce can) | 13.75 ounces | 390 grams |
| bowtie noodles (farfalle) | 2 cups | 4.5 ounces | 128 grams |
| goose fat* or unsalted butter | 1 tablespoon | 0.50 ounce | 14 grams |

*Available in specialty stores such as Dean & DeLuca, 560 Broadway, New York, New York 10012 (212-431-1691; outside New York, 800-227-7714).
[†]If you love the heightened bite of black pepper, use the larger amount.
[‡]Or 3 cubes of Glace de Volaille (page 209) dissolved in 3 cups boiling water. If the chicken broth is not low-salt, omit the salt.

*(continued)*

Soak the optional porcini mushrooms in about ½ cup of warm water for 10 minutes or until softened. (The soaking water may later be added to make up part of the 1¾ cups of chicken broth.) When soft, drain, cut them into small pieces and set aside.

With a fork, stir together the kasha and egg. Set it aside to dry for 30 minutes, stirring occasionally with the fork.

In an 11-inch or larger skillet (at least 11 inches, preferably broiler-proof), with a tight-fitting lid, melt the ¼ cup of goose fat or butter. Add the onions, sprinkle with the sugar and fry, stirring often, until deep golden brown, about 7 minutes. Add the sliced mushrooms and garlic, cover and cook for about 5 minutes or until the mushrooms give up their liquid. Then continue cooking uncovered, stirring occasionally, until the liquid evaporates and the mushrooms are lightly browned, about 7 minutes.

Add the kasha mixture, salt, pepper and oregano and cook, stirring constantly, for 3 minutes. Stir in the broth and porcini mushrooms, cover tightly and simmer 20 minutes or until the liquid is absorbed. Remove from the heat.

Meanwhile, cook the bowties according to the package directions. Drain, and stir in the 1 tablespoon of goose fat or butter. (The recipe may be prepared up to this point 6 hours in advance of serving.)

If the skillet is not broiler-proof, turn the kasha mixture into a broiler pan or baking pan. Add salt to taste. Broil several inches from the heat, stirring occasionally for even browning and to prevent scorching, 7 to 10 minutes. Mix in the bowties and broil for about 3 minutes just to crisp the top edges of the bowties slightly. Serve hot.

# PISTACHIO SAFFRON PILAF

This special rice pilaf, inspired by Julie Sahni,* is my traditional accompaniment to tandoori chicken. It is golden and fragrant with saffron and the faintly lemony quality of my favorite spice, cardamom. It's a treat to encounter the sweet bursts of golden raisins and the soft crunch of pale green pistachios.

| INGREDIENTS | MEASURE | WEIGHT | |
|---|---|---|---|
| | volume | ounces | grams |
| basmati rice | 1½ cups | 10 ounces | 280 grams |
| cold water | 2½ liquid cups | | |
| ghee† | 3 tablespoons | 1 ounce | 28 grams |
| shelled unsalted pistachio nuts, blanched‡ and coarsely chopped | 3 tablespoons | 1 ounce | 28 grams |
| finely chopped onion | ⅓ cup | 1.5 ounces | 42 grams |
| stick cinnamon | 2½-inch stick | | |
| 9 cardamom pods § | ⅜ teaspoon (ground) | | |
| saffron threads | ¾ teaspoon | | |
| salt | 1¾ teaspoons | 0.5 ounce | 12 grams |
| milk | ¾ liquid cup | | |
| golden raisins | ⅓ cup | 1.66 ounces | 48 grams |

SERVES: 6

Place the rice in a colander and rinse it under cold water until the water runs clear. Place the rice in a small bowl, and add the 2¼ cups of cold water. Cover and allow it to soak for at least 30 minutes.

When ready to cook, drain the rice, reserving the water.

*Classic Indian Cooking, William Morrow, 1980.
†If you do not have ghee (or clarified browned butter) on hand, you will need to clarify 5 tablespoons (2.5 ounces/71 grams) of unsalted butter. In a heavy saucepan, melt the butter over medium heat, partially covered to prevent splattering. When the butter looks clear, cook uncovered, watching carefully until the solids drop and begin to brown. Pour immediately through a fine strainer or a strainer lined with cheesecloth. (I like to make larger amounts as it stores well for months, refrigerated, and indefinitely frozen.)
‡To blanch, simply boil them for a minute and the peels will slip off.
§Crush in a mortar and pestle or in a coffee or spice grinder. Ground cardamom can be substituted but is less aromatic.

(continued)

*Pistachio Saffron Pilaf.* Saffron, a deeply aromatic and richly colored spice (the English word comes from Arabic for "yellow"), is made from the stigmas of the saffron crocus, which are plucked by hand and dried. Approximately 75,000 to 100,000 of these delicate flower parts are needed to produce a single pound of the dried spice, making it the most expensive seasoning in the world. Despite this fact, saffron has been a vital ingredient in Indian cuisine for thousands of years and is also used in perfumes, medicines, dyes, and sacred religious rituals. The Arabs introduced saffron to Europe in the Middle Ages, and in Germany during the fifteenth century a person could be burned at the stake or buried alive for defiling this treasured spice. Rice, on the other hand, has rarely created such impassioned fervor. Rather, it has been a common culinary staple for three quarters of the world's people for centuries. With over 10,000 varieties, rice is carefully chosen and graded according to its size, shape, color, fragrance, age, taste, and texture. *Basmati* is widely considered to be the most desirable long-grained rice for authentic Indian cooking. It is mainly grown in Pakistan, Dehra Dun in northern India, and the Bihar State, also in northern India. In all three areas, local farmers ritualistically harvest, husk and winnow *basmati* by hand as they have done for generations. Such minimal processing preserves both the agricultural traditions of these regions and the valuable nutrients of the rice itself.

In a medium-size heavy saucepan, heat the ghee over medium heat until melted. Sauté the pistachio nuts for about 2 minutes or until lightly browned, stirring often. Remove them with a slotted spoon, and set aside.

Add the onions to the pan and sauté until they turn pale and limp, about 3 minutes, stirring often. Add the cinnamon and sauté for 1 minute. Add the drained rice and sauté until the rice is thoroughly coated with the ghee, about 3 minutes. Add the cardamom, saffron, salt, raisins, the reserved soaking water and the milk and bring to a boil, stirring to keep the rice from settling. Reduce the heat and simmer, partially covered, for 10 minutes or until most of the liquid is absorbed and the surface of the rice is filled with steamy holes. Do not stir.

Cover the pan tightly and turn off heat, but do not move it from the hot burner. Allow the rice to sit undisturbed for 15 minutes. Fluff with a fork and spoon into a serving bowl. Garnish with the pistachio nuts.

 POINTERS FOR SUCCESS • The milk can be replaced with water. The milk, however, contributes a slight sweetness.

SIDE DISHES

# THE VERY BEST LUCHSHON KUGEL

(Luchshun KUHgul) (Noodle Pudding)

If French be the language of high-flown romantic love, then surely Yiddish is the language of adorable affection. One thing, however, the two languages do have in common is that terms of endearment are often food-related. *Kugel*, which translates as "pudding," is one of the most popular pet names bestowed upon children. This is not only because the word sounds cuddly and comforting, it is because the dish also happens to taste that way. Contrast this with the French "mon petit chou" (my little cabbage). Need I say more?

Luchshon kugel is traditionally a slightly sweet pudding made with flat egg noodles, cottage cheese, cream cheese and an egg-milk custard. This glorious kugel recipe is based on one from my friend Lora Brody's childhood. Lora has raised this beloved traditional Jewish dish to new heights. A tangy crunchy topping with apricot blankets the custardy, slightly creamy noodles. Lora says this noodle pudding makes an excellent brunch dish and is equally wonderful eaten cold the next day. Because it is substantial and contains no meat, kugel is an ideal dairy meal but would also be delicious with sliced Jewish Deli Smoked Tongue (page 156) or roast chicken (page 123).

---

*Luchshon Kugel.* Traditionally, kugel is associated with the Jewish holidays, particularly Chanukah, the Feast of Lights, an eight-day celebration commemorating the Battle of the Maccabees in 165 B.C.E. In Eastern European Jewish households, they eat kugel as a dessert on the Sabbath. It is usually served after a hot cholent, which is a kind of stew. Often kugel is baked directly with the cholent. Placed in a covered clay pot, the kugel is then put in the center of the larger iron cholent pot, and potatoes or beans are added to support the kugel pot. Such a technique prevents the kugel from drying out. It is served as a dessert or a main dish, and Jewish cooks enhance the flavor of kugel by adding a whole host of ingredients—raisins, sugar, fruit, spices, pieces of bread soaked in egg.

---

| INGREDIENTS | MEASURE | WEIGHT | |
| --- | --- | --- | --- |
| | *volume* | *ounces/pounds* | *grams* |
| unsalted butter, melted | 6 tablespoons | 3 ounces | 85 grams |
| ¼-inch-wide egg noodles | | 1 pound | 454 grams |
| 6 large eggs | 1 liquid cup plus 3 tablespoons | 10.5 ounces (weighed without shells) | 300 grams |
| sugar | ¼ cup | 1.75 ounces | 50 grams |
| sour cream | 1 liquid cup | 8.5 ounces | 242 grams |
| cottage cheese | 1 ¾ cups | 1 pound | 454 grams |
| whole-milk ricotta | 1 cup | 8 ounces | 227 grams |
| cream cheese, softened | | 4 ounces | 113 grams |
| milk | 2 liquid cups | | |
| OPTIONAL: raisins | 1 cup | 5 ounces | 144 grams |
| salt | 1 teaspoon | | 6.7 grams |

TOPPING

| | | | |
| --- | --- | --- | --- |
| sliced almonds, coarsely chopped | ⅔ cup | 1 ounce | 28 grams |
| unsalted butter, melted | 2 tablespoons | 1 ounce | 28 grams |
| light brown sugar | ¼ cup, firmly packed | 2 ounces | 54 grams |
| apricot preserves | 1 cup | 12 ounces | 340 grams |

PREHEAT THE OVEN TO: 350°F.
BAKING TIME: 80 to 90 minutes
SERVES: 12 to 16

EQUIPMENT: large rectangular baking dish, about 13 inches by 11 inches (at least 6 quarts)

*Preheat the oven to 350°F. at least 15 minutes before baking time. Have the oven shelf in the middle position of the oven.*

Use a small piece of plastic wrap to dip into the melted butter and lightly coat the inside of the baking dish.

Bring a large pot of water to a boil. Add 4 teaspoons of salt, stir in the noodles and boil until just barely tender but still firm (al dente), about 4 minutes. Drain and place in the prepared dish.

In a large bowl, whisk together all the remaining ingredients except the topping. Pour evenly over the noodles. (The mixture will be very soupy at this point.) Bake for 30 minutes.

MEANWHILE, PREPARE THE TOPPING: In a small saucepan, combine all the topping ingredients. Just before the 30-minute baking period is up, cook the topping over medium

*(continued)*

heat, stirring constantly, until bubbling and well combined.

Drop the topping by spoonfuls over the noodles and spread it evenly. Return the kugel to the oven for 50 minutes to 1 hour or until the top is browned and bubbly. Serve warm.

POINTERS
FOR SUCCESS

• To make half the recipe, use a 9-inch square baking dish and divide the pudding ingredients in half. For the topping, use ⅓ cup of almonds, 1 tablespoon of butter, 1½ tablespoons of light brown sugar and ¼ cup plus 2 tablespoons of apricot preserves. Bake about 50 minutes more or until bubbly and done.

# CLASSIC AMERICAN LEMON-LIME MOLD

I didn't grow up eating Jell-O; in fact, when I first encountered it in the cafeteria at college I took an immediate dislike to the smooth wobbly texture and insipid candy-like flavor. A classmate sitting next to me taught me, however, that it was great as a tactile sensation for squeezing through one's fingers. (She said she learned this when helping her mother clean up after dinner.) I've never enjoyed the flavor of canned pineapple either.

All this changed one year when Roey Samson, a sister-in-law who happens to share the same birthday as mine, invited us for Thanksgiving dinner and prepared this attractive mold. Perhaps it was the sour cream that made it all come together but I was astonished by how well the refreshingly tart and creamy side dish complemented the turkey. Roey obligingly sent me the recipe with a note requesting one in return that was equally easy to prepare.

| INGREDIENTS | MEASURE | WEIGHT | |
| --- | --- | --- | --- |
| | *volume* | *ounces* | *grams* |
| crushed pineapple | 1 20-ounce can | 20 ounces | 567 grams |
| lemon Jell-O | 1 package | 3 ounces | 85 grams |
| lime Jell-O | 1 package | 3 ounces | 85 grams |
| sour cream | 2 liquid cups | 16 ounces | 454 grams |

MAKE AHEAD: at least 6 hours or up to 2 days
SERVES: 12

EQUIPMENT: 6-cup decorative mold, lightly oiled

Place a strainer over a medium bowl and drain the pineapple well, reserving the juices. (There will be a full cup of the pineapple.) Set the pineapple aside and pour the juices into a 4-cup liquid measure. (There will be about 1¼ cups of juice.) Add enough water to the juices to equal 2½ cups. Whisk in the lemon and lime Jell-O until dissolved. Chill or stir over ice water until the Jell-O just begins to thicken. Whisk in the sour cream and crushed pineapple and pour the mixture into the mold. Refrigerate for at least 6 hours or up to 2 days. (The mold will keep longer but the flavor dulls slightly.)

To unmold, chill the presentation plate. Moisten the plate with water so that it will be easy to reposition and center the soufflé. Dip the mold in warm water for 20 seconds. If using the Tupperware mold, remove the large lid and invert it onto the plate. Remove the small upper lid. This releases the suction and the mold will drop from the container onto the plate. If using a container without this upper lid, dip it in the water until the mold slides when tilted. Release the suction by slipping a long spatula or knife blade between the side of the mold and the container, all the way to the top. Garnish with slices of Spiced Apple Rings (page 192).

POINTERS FOR SUCCESS

• Do not use fresh pineapple, as it will keep the gelatin from setting.

# RHUBARB COMPOTE

I have always thought of rhubarb as a dessert, but its fresh acerbic flavor also makes an excellent foil for rich meats such as duck or goose. Elliott prefers his rhubarb barely sweetened; I prefer it sweet/tart with four ounces of sugar per pound. For small amounts of rhubarb, a microwave works beautifully, but for a pound or more, use the stove-top method.

| INGREDIENTS | MEASURE | WEIGHT | |
| --- | --- | --- | --- |
| | *volume* | *ounces* | *grams* |
| fresh rhubarb, cut in ½-inch pieces | 2 cups | 8 ounces | 224 grams |
| sugar | 2 to 4½ tablespoons | 1.14 to 2 ounces | 32 to 57 grams |

MAKES: about 1 cup
SERVES: 3

To cook the rhubarb in a microwave oven, place it in a microwave container, preferably with a cover, and sprinkle the sugar on top. Allow it to stand for at least 10 minutes or until the rhubarb starts to lose some of its liquid and dissolves the sugar.

If the container does not have a lid, use a sheet of plastic wrap to cover it, turning back a small amount at one corner to allow the steam to escape. Microwave on high power for 3½ minutes or until the rhubarb feels tender when pierced with a skewer. Allow the rhubarb to cool completely. Refrigerate it for 2 hours or up to 2 days. It will thicken completely on chilling.

To cook the rhubarb on the stove top, in a heavy medium saucepan, combine the rhubarb and sugar. Let it stand at room temperature for at least 15 minutes or until the rhubarb exudes some juice.

Bring the mixture to a boil over moderately high heat, stirring constantly. Reduce the heat to low, cover and simmer, stirring occasionally, until the rhubarb is tender and the liquid thickened, 7 to 10 minutes. Remove from the heat and allow it to cool without stirring.

NOTE: At some times of the year the rhubarb has more liquid than at other times. If you find that there is too much liquid after cooling, simply drain some off.

# RAITA

This soothing, cool yogurt and cucumber recipe is a traditional accompaniment to fiery or spicy foods such as Tandoori Chicken (page 126) and Ethiopian Doro Wat (page 131).

| INGREDIENTS | MEASURE | WEIGHT | |
| --- | --- | --- | --- |
| | _volume_ | _ounces/pounds_ | _grams_ |
| 1 long thin European seedless cucumber or 1½ ordinary cucumbers | 4 cups when cut into pieces | 1¼ pounds | 567 grams |
| kosher salt (Diamond brand)* | 2 teaspoons | 0.25 ounce | 7 grams |
| OPTIONAL: cumin seed | ½ teaspoon | | |
| plain yogurt | 2 liquid cups | 18 ounces | 510 grams |
| sour cream† | ½ liquid cup | 4.25 ounces | 121 grams |
| OPTIONAL: fresh coriander leaves or burnet‡, torn into pieces, for garnish | 2 tablespoons | | |

ADVANCE PREPARATION: at least 1 hour or up to 1 day ahead
MAKES: 4 cups
SERVES: 6 to 8

_At least 1 hour or up to the day before serving:_

Cut the cucumber into ¼-inch-thick slices and cut each slice into eighths. If using ordinary cucumbers, you may want to cut the cucumbers in half the long way and scoop out the seeds. Place the cucumber in a colander set over a bowl or in the sink and sprinkle it with the salt, tossing lightly. Allow it to sit for 30 minutes to drain its liquid. Rinse under cold running water and pat dry with paper towels.

*If using Morton brand or table salt, use only 1 teaspoon.
†Sour cream rounds out the texture and flavor. Alternatively, you can line a strainer with cheesecloth or use one of the handy devices now on the market to drain some of the excess liquid from the yogurt. The longer you let the yogurt sit, the more liquid will drain out and the thicker it will get.
‡A lacy herb that has a cucumber-like flavor.

In a medium bowl, combine all the ingredients except the coriander and fold together until blended. Refrigerate, tightly covered, until serving time.

To serve, place in a crystal or decorative bowl and garnish with the coriander.

UNDERSTANDING   The casein (milk protein) in the yogurt and sour cream bonds with the capsicum (hot oil) in the chilies in spicy food and washes away the heat.

---

*Raita*. The *Vedas*, the vast religious and philosophical texts of India, outline the laws, morality and knowledge necessary to live and maintain a life of spiritual harmony. One of the most important lessons to learn is how to coexist with the land and its other inhabitants. Because of its agrarian economy, India readily acknowledges the importance of animals, particularly cows, in sustaining communal harmony. Protecting and respecting the land and cows is a religious duty and the basis for a vegetarian diet for hundreds of millions of Indians. They consider milk and milk products—like yogurt—to be perfect, ideal foods that nourish the mind and calm the soul. The *Vedas* liken milk to nectar, and Indian cooks take full advantage of the gastronomic possibilities of dairy products. Raita is one of the most popular yogurt dishes in India. "Rai" are black mustard seeds, and for many Indians Raita is incomplete without them. Often Raita is garnished with herbs like coriander, and in northern India coarsely ground cumin seed is preferred to rai.

---

# SPICED APPLE RINGS

I developed this recipe on a free-lance project for the Ball Canning Company many years ago and it has remained a personal favorite. The juicy, spicy, crimson apple rings are delicious with any full-flavored fowl such as capon, duck or turkey, and make a beautiful garnish for the Classic American Lemon-Lime Mold (page 186). A jar of these apple rings would also make a most welcome stocking stuffer for Christmas.

| INGREDIENTS | MEASURE | WEIGHT | |
| --- | --- | --- | --- |
| | volume | ounces | grams |
| cold water | 4 quarts | | |
| salt | 2 tablespoons | 1.5 ounces | 40 grams |
| cider vinegar | 2 tablespoons | | |
| 12 Golden Delicious apples (7 ounces each) | | 5.25 pounds | 2 kilograms 381 grams |
| water | 3 quarts | | |
| sugar | 1½ cups | 10 ounces | 300 grams |
| liquid red food coloring | 1 tablespoon | | |
| ground cloves | 1½ teaspoons | | |
| ground cinnamon | 2¼ teaspoons | | |
| ground allspice | 2¼ teaspoons | | |

MAKE AHEAD: Apples must stand for 12 hours before processing; after processing, apples must stand for at least 4 days
MAKES: 7 pints

EQUIPMENT: 7 wide-mouth pint canning jars, a water bath canner

In a very large bowl, combine the 4 quarts of cold water, the salt and vinegar and stir until the salt is dissolved.

Wash the apples well and slice them ⅓ inch thick. Use a small scalloped or plain cutter to remove the core from each slice. Soak the apple slices in the salted water for at least 10 minutes, but no longer than 20 minutes, to set the color. Drain the apples.

In a large enamel or nonreactive kettle, bring the 3 quarts of water, the sugar, food coloring and spices to a boil, stirring to dissolve the sugar. Add the apple slices and return the liquid to a boil. Lower the heat and simmer, stirring often, until the apples are barely tender and just beginning to turn translucent around the edges, 5 to 7 minutes.

Remove the kettle from the heat and let cool for 30 minutes. Then place a plate on top of the apples to keep them submerged in the liquid and allow them to sit for 12 hours.

Sterilize the canning jars and lids in boiling water. Pack the apples and liquid into the canning jars, leaving a ½-inch headspace. Wipe any spills on the side of the jars with a clean damp towel. Screw on the caps and place them in a water bath canner. The jars must sit on a rack to allow the water to flow all around them and the water must be high enough to cover them by 1 inch. (They must remain upright to expel any air inside the jars, producing a vacuum, which will seal the jars.) Cover the water bath and bring the water to a boil. Process, covered, for 25 minutes. Remove to racks and cool before checking the seal. (The lids should be slightly concave.) Store in a cool dark place.

KEEPS: several years. Allow to sit for at least 4 days for the color and flavors to develop.

POINTERS FOR SUCCESS

• For ease of preparation, but a somewhat less attractive appearance, the apples can be cored before slicing.

UNDERSTANDING

Golden Delicious apples offer a firmer texture and slightly tarter flavor than red delicious.

# AUNT MARGARET'S NEW ENGLAND BEACH PLUM PRESERVES

I had been hearing about this for years: the annual family expedition to the beach around Labor Day to harvest the native beach plums that most people are perfectly content to leave on the bushes for the birds. Last year, though, Cousin Marion gave me a jar of the resulting thick, deep garnet, glistening preserves and after the first fruity-tangy taste, just perfect as a counterpoint to rich flavorful fowl such as goose, duck (Perfect Crisp Roast Duck, page 140) turkey, squab or Capon with Savory Bulgur Stuffing (page 137). I resolved to join in the annual tradition. So we met this year, three generations, which included Aunt Margaret, her daughter Marion and granddaughter Alexandra. We met in a parking lot and all piled into one car. Aunt Margaret guided us down the morass of winding roads leading to her special site by the bay and there were the beach plum bushes hung with clusters of the small purple orbs, resembling Concord grapes in size and shape. After two hours, we had each picked at least five pounds of beach plums, developed appetites for lunch and caught up on many stories.

The next day I started the pitting process. It was slow— averaging one pound of beach plums an hour—so I called Marion to catch up on some more stories while squeezing the pits from the fruit. I was awed to realize that I, who during the rest of the year can't seem to spare five minutes for relaxation, was spending five hours pitting beach plums and loving it. Precious preserves aside, the real fruit of our harvest was the intimacy and connection this time-honored activity provided.

| INGREDIENTS | MEASURE<br>*volume* | WEIGHT<br>*ounces/pounds* | *grams/kilograms* |
|---|---|---|---|
| beach plums | 4 quarts | 5.66 pounds | 2 kilograms<br>551 grams |
| sugar | 5 cups | 2 pounds 3 ounces | 1 kilogram |

MAKES: 7 half-pints

*Note: Do in 2 batches; pitted or unpitted beach plums can be frozen and then cooked when time allows.*

Pit the beach plums by cutting each in half with a small sharp knife and removing the pit, saving any juices that result from the pitting. You will have about 10½ cups (4 quarts) of pitted beach plums.

In an 8-quart or larger saucepot or deep frying pan,* stir together the beach plums and sugar and allow them to sit for at least 15 minutes or until the sugar is completely moistened by the juices exuded by the fruit.

Over medium-high heat, bring the mixture to a boil, stirring constantly. Simmer over low heat, stirring occasionally, for about 1½ hours or until very thick and reduced to about 6 cups.

Sterilize canning jars and lids in boiling water and fill, leaving a ⅜-inch headspace. Screw on the caps and invert the jars onto a folded towel until cool. (The air trapped in the headspace will travel upward through the hot preserves and be sterilized.) Store in a cool, dark area.

POINTERS FOR SUCCESS

• Include some red (unripe) beach plums. These supply extra pectin (thickening power).
• The sugar in this recipe is a little more than half the weight of the pitted fruit. Taste a little after the preserves have thickened and stir in more sugar if desired, heating until it has dissolved.

*My favorite is the 12-inch by 2-inch Millennium nonstick pan by Farberware. Its large surface area speeds evaporation, it heats evenly and the thickened preserves do not stick to it.

# ENDIVE AND WALNUT SALAD WITH RASPBERRY WALNUT VINAIGRETTE

I adore the crunch of the endive and toasted walnuts tossed in the unforgettable blend of woody walnut oil and bright raspberry vinegar. Serve this on its own, after the main course so that the vinaigrette does not interfere with the dinner wine.

This American salad with Continental overtones would go well after any American or Continental-style dinner. It would also be delicious accompanied by cheese, such as Bleu de Bresse or Brie.

| INGREDIENTS | MEASURE | WEIGHT | |
|---|---|---|---|
| | *volume* | *ounces* | *grams* |
| walnut halves, preferably toasted, coarsely broken | ¾ cup | 2.66 ounces | 75 grams |
| 6 large endive | | 26 ounces | 737 grams |
| Raspberry Vinegar (page 201) | ¼ liquid cup | | |
| 1 shallot, finely minced | 2 tablespoons | 0.66 ounce | 18 grams |
| Dijon mustard | 1 teaspoon | | |
| salt | ½ teaspoon | | |
| black pepper, freshly ground | ¼ teaspoon | | |
| walnut oil | ⅓ liquid cup | | |

SERVES: 8

Place the walnuts on a baking sheet and place in the oven. Turn the heat to 350°F. and toast the nuts for about 15 minutes, or until they are just beginning to darken. Remove the nuts to a clean countertop to cool.

Cut the base from each endive and separate the leaves, trimming off more of the base as you go. Cut the longer leaves crosswise in half, and place the endive in a large salad bowl.

In a small bowl, whisk together the raspberry vinegar, shallots, mustard, salt and pepper. Gradually whisk in the walnut oil. Pour this vinaigrette over the endive. Add the walnuts and toss to blend. Serve at once, or refrigerate for up to 4 hours.

POINTERS
FOR SUCCESS

• Be sure to use fresh walnut oil that is not at all rancid. Store the oil in the refrigerator and it will keep for many months.

UNDERSTANDING

Toasting the walnuts brings out their flavor. Do not over-brown, however, or they will become bitter.

A high proportion of vinegar to oil is necessary when using raspberry vinegar as the oil neutralizes some of the raspberry flavor.

# CALIFORNIA HEIRLOOM
# SALAD DRESSING

My lovely sister-in-law Mia Hiyashi has just come into the family and I'm pleased to be able to offer this recipe from her that has been in her family for three generations. It was originally from a California restaurant. This salad dressing has a wonderfully tangy, sweet/sour flavor and is thick enough to cling nicely to salad greens. It has become an instant favorite (just like her). I serve it on green salads with Friday Night Roast Chicken with Paprika (page 123) and Rare Prime Ribs of Beef (page 158).

| INGREDIENTS | MEASURE | WEIGHT | |
|---|---|---|---|
| | *volume* | *ounces* | *grams* |
| salt | 1 teaspoon | | |
| dry mustard | 1 teaspoon | | |
| celery seed | 1 teaspoon | | |
| paprika | 1 teaspoon | | |
| sugar | 6 tablespoons | 2.5 ounces | 80 grams |
| vinegar | ¼ liquid cup | | |
| salad oil | 1 liquid cup | | |
| onion, grated | 1 tablespoon | | |

MAKES: 1½ cups

In a double boiler, over simmering water, combine all of the ingredients and heat, stirring occasionally, until warm to the touch. Remove from the heat and beat with a rotary or electric beater until thickened. Pour into a cruet or jar and refrigerate until needed. Shake well before serving.

KEEPS: Several weeks refrigerated.

POINTERS FOR SUCCESS

• The water in the bottom container of the double boiler must not touch the upper container.

# VINAIGRETTES, SAUCES AND STOCKS

# RASPBERRY VINEGAR

I have never tasted a commercial raspberry vinegar as pure or flavorful as this simple-to-make homemade version. I sometimes use a few teaspoonsful of this vinegar to deglaze the pan after sautéing chicken or calf's liver, but most often I use it to make the Raspberry Walnut Vinaigrette for Endive and Walnut Salad (page 196).

| INGREDIENTS | MEASURE | WEIGHT | |
| --- | --- | --- | --- |
| | volume | ounces/pounds | grams |
| fresh raspberries | 1½ quarts | 1½ pounds | 680 grams |
| sugar | ½ cup | 3.5 ounces | 100 grams |
| red wine vinegar | 5½ liquid cups | | |

MAKE AHEAD: at least 4 weeks
MAKES: about 1 quart

EQUIPMENT: 1-quart canning jar

Place the berries and sugar in the canning jar, and add enough vinegar to fill the jar. Set the jar, uncovered, on a small rack in a saucepan and pour enough water into the pan to come halfway up the sides of the jar. Bring the water to a boil and simmer for 10 minutes. Remove the jar from the water and let cool on a rack or folded towel.

Close the jar with an airtight lid and shake well. Refrigerate for about 4 weeks.

Strain the vinegar, pressing lightly on the berries to extract the juice. Discard the pulp and seeds. Close tightly and store refrigerated.

KEEPS: At least 2 years.

# PINK MAYONNAISE AMÉRICAINE

People who taste this easy-to-prepare mayonnaise swear they will never make mayonnaise any other way again. The simple secret is the addition of one tablespoon of tomato paste. It makes commercially prepared mayonnaise more delicious as well. And it makes a fabulous BLT (page 223) or lobster or crab salad sandwich (page 229).

| INGREDIENTS<br>room temperature | MEASURE<br>volume | WEIGHT<br>ounces | grams |
|---|---|---|---|
| 1 large egg yolk | 1 tablespoon + ½ teaspoon | 0.5 ounce | 16 grams |
| tomato paste | 1 tablespoon | 0.5 ounce | 16 grams |
| lemon juice, freshly squeezed | 2 teaspoons | | |
| salt | ⅛ teaspoon | | |
| black pepper, freshly ground | ⅛ teaspoon | | |
| sugar | ⅛ teaspoon | | |
| safflower oil | ⅔ cups | | |
| OPTIONAL: fresh dill, washed and dried, stems removed | ½ cup, loosely packed | 0.5 ounce | 14 grams |

MAKES: about ¾ cup

In a food processor, place the egg yolk, tomato paste, lemon juice, salt, pepper and sugar. Process for a few seconds to mix and then, with the motor on, very slowly pour in the oil. By the time all the oil has been added, the mayonnaise will have thickened. Add the optional dill and pulse until finely chopped, scraping the sides of the bowl once or twice.

UNDERSTANDING

All the ingredients for the mayonnaise must be at room temperature or it will not emulsify into a smooth mixture. One egg yolk can absorb as much as two-thirds cup of oil. Less oil will make it less thick but more stable so that it will keep longer. If desired, 2 tablespoons of olive oil can replace an equal amount of the safflower oil. Do not use all olive oil as it will tend to separate sooner.

KEEPS: 1 week refrigerated.

# HORSERADISH MAYONNAISE

This simple sauce is the perfect accompaniment to cold fish, seafood and beef. It is most delicious when made from scratch but also very tasty if made with prepared mayonnaise (use two-thirds cup, and stir in the parsley and horseradish). I serve it with any leftover Salmon Steak with Dijon Mustard and Black Mustard Grains (page 108) and cold sliced Rare Prime Ribs of Beef (page 158).

| INGREDIENTS room temperature | MEASURE volume | WEIGHT ounces | grams |
|---|---|---|---|
| 1 large egg yolk | 1 tablespoon + ½ teaspoon | 0.5 ounce | 16 grams |
| prepared horseradish, drained | 1 tablespoon + 2 teaspoons | 1 ounce | 27 grams |
| lemon juice, freshly squeezed | 2 teaspoons | | |
| salt | ⅛ teaspoon | | |
| white pepper, freshly ground | ⅛ teaspoon | | |
| sugar | ⅛ teaspoon | | |
| safflower oil | ⅔ liquid cup | | |
| fresh parsley, preferably flat-leafed, washed and dried, stems removed | ½ cup, loosely packed | 0.7 ounce | 20 grams |

MAKES: about ¾ cup

In a food processor, place the egg yolk, horseradish, lemon juice, salt, pepper and sugar. Process for a few seconds to mix and then, with the motor on, very slowly pour in the oil. By the time all the oil has been added, the mayonnaise will have thickened. Add the parsley and pulse until finely chopped, scraping the sides of the bowl once or twice.

UNDERSTANDING

All ingredients for the mayonnaise must be at room temperature or it will not emulsify into a smooth mixture. One egg yolk can absorb as much as two-thirds cup of oil. Less oil will make it less thick but more stable so that it will keep longer. If desired, 2 tablespoons of olive oil can replace an equal amount of the safflower oil. Do not use all olive oil as it will tend to separate sooner.

KEEPS: 1 week refrigerated.

# EXTRA-LEMONY HOLLANDAISE SAUCE

What could possibly be more glorious than hollandaise: golden, buttery/lemony, velvet sauce with just the right consistency to cling lovingly to a spear of perfectly Steamed Asparagus (page 170) or gently nap salmon or sole. This is springtime, summertime, and sunshine—simple perfection—sheer poetry. My version of this classic French sauce uses extra lemon juice which enlivens the flavor and seems to lighten the richness.

| INGREDIENTS room temperature | MEASURE volume | WEIGHT ounces | grams |
|---|---|---|---|
| 6 large egg yolks | scant 10 fluid ounces | 10.5 ounces | 300 grams |
| hot water | 2 tablespoons, or more as necessary | | |
| unsalted butter, softened | 16 tablespoons | 8 ounces | 227 grams |
| salt | ½ teaspoon | | |
| cayenne pepper | 2 dashes | | |
| lemon juice, freshly squeezed | 3 tablespoons | | |
| dry mustard | ½ teaspoon | | |

MAKES: about 1⅓ cups

With your fingers or a small spoon, remove the chalaza (the small, thickened ropy part) from each yolk.

In a double boiler, over simmering water, whisk together the yolks and hot water. Add the butter 2 tablespoons at a time, whisking after each addition until the butter is melted and incorporated. Continue whisking until the sauce is thick enough to see the whisk marks, about 8 minutes. If the sauce begins to curdle at any time, remove it from the heat and whisk in a tablespoon or more of hot water before returning it to the heat. Remove the upper container from the simmering water and whisk in the salt, cayenne pepper, lemon juice and dry mustard.

Serve at once or hold, covered, for up to 30 minutes over hot water or in a Thermos. (If not using a Thermos, a piece of plastic wrap can be placed directly on the surface of the sauce to prevent a skin from forming.) To thin, whisk in hot water.

POINTERS
FOR SUCCESS

- The water in the bottom container of the double boiler must not touch the upper container.

UNDERSTANDING

Using the food processor or blender to make hollandaise results in a thinner consistency and less full flavor.

# GLACE DE VIANDE

## (glass duh veeAHND) (Homemade Beef Essence)

In French this recipe is called a *glace* because the reduced broth becomes so concentrated it turns into a glaze. I, however, call it *essence* because this one recipe will enhance and intensify so many others without adding either salt or fat. I like to make a large quantity as the work is about the same but if you don't have a large enough stockpot, it's fine to make half the recipe.

| INGREDIENTS<br>*room temperature* | MEASURE<br>*volume* | WEIGHT | |
| --- | --- | --- | --- |
| | | *ounces/pounds* | *grams/kilograms* |
| chicken bones, veal bones and beef bones (one third each), cut into 2-inch pieces | | 10 pounds | 4 kilograms<br>536 grams |
| 6 carrots, scrubbed and cut into 1-inch chunks | | 1 pound | 454 grams |
| 3 large onions, unpeeled, cut into eighths | | 1½ pounds | 680 grams |
| water | 12 quarts, divided | | |
| 3 large ripe tomatoes, quartered, seeded and coarsely chopped | | 1½ pounds | 680 grams |
| 1 large leek, roots removed, cut in half and thoroughly washed | | 8 ounces | 227 grams |
| 3 celery ribs with leaves, cut into 1-inch pieces | | 7 ounces | 100 grams |
| 1 small bunch parsley, preferably flat-leafed, tied with string | | 2 ounces | 56 grams |
| 2 bay leaves | | | |
| dried thyme | 1 teaspoon | | |
| black peppercorns | ½ teaspoon | | |

*(continued)*

VINAIGRETTES, SAUCES AND STOCKS
205

MAKES: about 2 cups (18 ounces/
510 grams) *glace* or 32 cubes,
about 0.5 ounce/16 grams each
(1 cube + 1 cup water = 1 cup
stock)

EQUIPMENT: large roasting pan;
large stockpot (16 quarts); large
fine strainer; cheesecloth; 2-quart
or larger saucepan or high-sided
skillet, preferably lined with a
nonstick surface; bread pan about
8½ inches by 4½ inches, lightly
sprayed with nonstick vegetable
shortening or lightly oiled

*Place the bones in the roasting pan and brown in a 425°F. oven for 1½ hours, turning the bones once after 45 minutes. Then add the carrots and onions and continue browning for 30 minutes.*

With a slotted skimmer or spoon, remove the bones and vegetables to the stockpot. Discard the fat in the roasting pan and set the pan on one or two burners. Add 2 cups of the water and cook over medium heat, scraping to dislodge the browned bits from the bottom of the pan. Pour this liquid along with the browned bits into the stockpot and add the remaining 11½ quarts of water.

Bring the water to a boil over high heat. Reduce the heat to low and simmer for 1 hour, skimming any scum that rises to the surface. Add the remaining vegetables, the herbs and spices and simmer for at least 10 hours, adding water as necessary so that the bones and vegetables are always covered by at least 2 inches of water. (It's fine to let it simmer overnight, partially covered, but be sure the heat is at the lowest setting possible so that it never boils.)

Use a slotted skimmer or spoon to remove the bones, vegetables and other solids to a strainer suspended over a large bowl. Press them to remove as much juice as possible and then discard the bones and vegetables. Pour all the sauce through the strainer. You will need several large bowls (or a second large stockpot).

Wash the stockpot and return the strained stock to it. Over high heat, reduce the stock to 3 quarts, about 2½ hours.

Pour the stock into a bowl and allow it to cool to room temperature, uncovered. Cover it tightly with plastic wrap (preferably Saran brand) and refrigerate for several hours or overnight. The fat will congeal on the top; remove and discard it.

Suspend the fine strainer over a 4-quart or larger pot and line it with dampened cheesecloth. Heat the stock and pour it through the strainer into the pot. Over high heat, reduce the stock to 6 cups, stirring occasionally with a greased wooden spoon, 1½ to 2 hours.

Transfer the stock to the 2-quart saucepan or high-sided skillet. Scrape any stock clinging to the stirring spoon into the stock. Reduce the sauce over very low heat, to prevent burning, to about 2 cups, about 1 hour. The bubbling surface will be lighter in color but should not be skimmed. The stock will become a very dark and syrupy essence. Toward the very end of the cooking, large sticky bubbles will form on the surface and break. Remove from the heat.

Pour the concentrated stock (*glace*) into the oiled bread pan, scraping out as much of the stock as possible. Set the saucepan aside. Cool the *glace* to room temperature, cover the pan with plastic wrap and refrigerate it for several hours until firmly set.

Meanwhile, add 2 cups of water to the saucepan and heat, stirring constantly to dissolve any remaining beef essence. Reduce the liquid to 1 cup. Cool and refrigerate it. Use this stock within 3 days.

Run a small metal spatula or thin knife between the sides of the bread pan and the *glace* and unmold it onto a cutting board. With a sharp knife, cut it into 32 cubes. (Cut it the short way into eighths, then cut it the long way into fourths.)

PRESSURE COOKER METHOD

When Carl Sontheimer started to market the Cuisinarts pressure cooker, he advised me to buy the largest model available because it was useful for making stock. A 6½-quart pressure cooker makes it possible to do the initial 10-hour cooking of the bones and vegetables in just 2 hours. In a pressure cooker with a 6½-quart liquid capacity you can do half the recipe (half the bones, vegetables, herbs and pepper), using 3 quarts of water; use a large skimmer to remove the bones and debris and then add the remaining half recipe to the same cooking liquid. It takes about 30 minutes to bring it up to pressure when the water is cold plus 1 hour of cooking time, and about 30 minutes for the pressure to go down. Follow the manufacturer's directions for your pressure cooker. Remove the bones and

*(continued)*

solids and strain the stock. You will have about 4 quarts. Refrigerate it and proceed as above.

KEEPS: If refrigerated in an open container, the stock cubes will dry out and harden, losing almost half their weight, and these will keep indefinitely but take longer to reconstitute. (This does not work in a high-humidity refrigerator such as a Traulsen.) If stored airtight in the refrigerator they will keep several months; stored in an airtight container in the freezer, they will keep indefinitely.

UNDERSTANDING    The bones need to be well covered with water to remove the maximum amount of gelatin and juices.

The stock must not be allowed to boil or the fat will become bound into the protein and it will not be possible to make the stock entirely fat-free.

A pan with a nonstick lining is ideal for the final reduction as the stock becomes very syrupy and sticky.

The exact amount of *glace* depends on the amount of gelatin in the bones.

*Demi-glace* (meaning half the concentration) is available in specialty stores. I actually find commercially available *demi-glace* to be one third the concentration of this beef essence. If you use purchased *demi-glace*, use about 3 tablespoons in place of 1 cube.

If you make a smaller quantity of *glace* and have only 1 to 1½ cups, use a 5¾-inch by 3¼-inch 1-pound foil loaf pan, available in supermarkets. Cut the *glace* into eighteen 1-inch by 1-inch by ¾-inch-high cubes (cut the short way into sixths; then cut the long way into thirds).

# Glace de Volaille

(glass duh vohLAHEE) (Homemade Poultry Essence)

Glace de volaille offers the complex intensity of *glace de viande* but is somewhat more subtle. Whenever I cook a chicken (or any fowl), I save the raw gizzard, neck, heart and feet and as much of the cooked carcass as I can salvage and freeze it in heavy-duty plastic freezer bags. At any given time my freezer is always partially filled with such bags, waiting for enough to justify making stock. Usually I get motivated to make stock when I need freezer space.

| INGREDIENTS | MEASURE | WEIGHT | |
| room temperature | volume | ounces/pounds | grams |
| --- | --- | --- | --- |
| chicken and/or duck parts (feet, necks, gizzards, backs, etc.), cut into 2-inch pieces | | 10 pounds | 536 grams |
| water | 12 quarts | | |
| 6 carrots, scrubbed, cut into 1-inch chunks | | 1 pound | 454 grams |
| 2 medium onions, unpeeled, cut into sixths | | 12 ounces | 340 grams |
| 3 large ripe tomatoes, quartered, seeded and coarsely chopped | | 1½ pounds | 680 grams |
| 1 large leek, roots removed, cut in half and thoroughly washed | | 8 ounces | 227 grams |
| 3 celery ribs with leaves, cut into 1-inch pieces | | 7 ounces | 100 grams |
| 1 small bunch parsley, preferably flat-leafed, tied with string | | 2 ounces | 56 grams |
| 2 bay leaves | | | |
| 3 cloves | | | |
| dried thyme | 1 teaspoon | | |
| peppercorns | ½ teaspoon | | |

*(continued)*

MAKES: 2 to 2½ cups (20 ounces/
570 grams if 2 cups) *glace* or 32
cubes, about 0.5 ounce/16 to 18
grams each (1 cube + 1 cup
water = 1 cup stock)

EQUIPMENT: large stockpot (16
quarts); large fine strainer;
cheesecloth; 2-quart or larger
saucepan or high-sided skillet,
preferably lined with a nonstick
surface; bread pan about 8½
inches by 4½ inches, lightly
sprayed with nonstick vegetable
shortening or lightly oiled

Rinse the chicken pieces under cold running water. Place them in the stockpot and add the water. Bring to a boil over high heat. Reduce the heat to low and simmer for 30 minutes, skimming any scum that rises to the surface. Add the vegetables, herbs and spices and simmer for at least 4 hours, adding water as necessary so that the bones and vegetables are always covered by at least 2 inches of water. Be sure the heat is at the lowest setting possible so that it never boils.

Use a slotted skimmer or spoon to remove the bones, vegetables and other solids to a strainer suspended over a large bowl. Press them to remove as much juice as possible and then discard the bones and vegetables. Pour all the sauce through the strainer. You will need several large bowls (or a second large stockpot).

Wash the stockpot and return the strained stock to it. Over high heat, reduce the stock to 3 quarts, about 2½ hours.

Pour the stock into a bowl and allow it to cool to room temperature, uncovered. Cover tightly with plastic wrap (preferably Saran brand) and refrigerate for several hours or overnight. The fat will congeal on the top; remove and discard it.

Suspend the fine strainer over a 4-quart or larger pot and line it with dampened cheesecloth. Heat the stock and pour it through the strainer into the pot. Over high heat, reduce the stock to 6 cups, stirring occasionally with a greased wooden spoon, 1½ to 2 hours.

Transfer the stock to the 2-quart saucepan or high-sided skillet. Scrape any stock clinging to the stirring spoon into the stock. Continue to reduce the stock over very low heat, to prevent burning, to about 2 cups, about 1 hour. The bubbling surface will be lighter in color but this should not be skimmed. The stock will become very dark in color and syrupy. Toward the very end of the cooking, large sticky bubbles will form on the surface and break. Remove from the heat.

Pour the concentrated stock (*glace*) into the oiled bread pan, scraping out as much of it as possible. Set the saucepan aside. Cool the *glace* to room temperature, cover the pan with plastic wrap and refrigerate for several hours until firmly set.

Meanwhile, add 2 cups of water to the saucepan and heat, stirring constantly to dissolve any remaining chicken essence. Reduce the liquid to 1 cup. Cool and refrigerate. Use this stock within 3 days.

Run a small metal spatula or thin knife between the sides of the bread pan and the *glace* and unmold it onto a cutting board. With a sharp knife, cut it into 32 cubes. (Cut it the short way into eighths, then cut it the long way into quarters.)

PRESSURE COOKER METHOD

A large pressure cooker makes it possible to do the initial 4-hour cooking of the bones and vegetables in just 2 hours. In a pressure cooker with a 6½-quart liquid capacity you can do half the recipe (half the bones, vegetables, herbs and pepper), using 3 quarts of water; use a large skimmer to remove the bones and debris and then add the remaining half recipe to the same cooking liquid. It takes about 30 minutes to bring it up to pressure when the water is cold plus 1 hour of cooking time, and about 30 minutes for the pressure to go down. Follow the manufacturer's directions for your pressure cooker. Remove the bones and solids and strain the stock. You will have about 4 quarts. Refrigerate it and proceed as above.

KEEPS: If refrigerated in an open container, the stock cubes will dry out and harden, losing almost half their weight, and these will keep indefinitely but take longer to reconstitute. (This does not work in a high-humidity refrigerator such as a Traulsen.) If stored airtight in the refrigerator they will keep several months; stored in an airtight container in the freezer, they will keep indefinitely.

(*continued*)

The bones need to be well covered with water to remove the maximum amount of gelatin and juices.

The stock must not be allowed to boil or the fat will become bound into the protein and it will not be possible to make the stock entirely fat-free.

A pan with a nonstick lining is ideal for the final reduction as the stock becomes very syrupy and sticky.

The exact amount of concentrated stock depends on the amount of gelatin in the bones. If you include a large amount of chicken feet, which contain more collagen, you will get more essence of the same concentration.

Poultry *demi-glace* (meaning half concentration) is available in specialty stores.* I actually find the commercially available *demi-glace* to be one third the concentration of this chicken essence. If you use purchased *demi-glace*, use about 3 tablespoons in place of 1 cube.

If you make a smaller quantity of essence and have only 1 to 1½ cups, use a 5¾-inch by 3¼-inch 1-pound foil loaf pan, available in supermarkets. Cut the *glace* into eighteen 1-inch by 1-inch by ¾-inch-high cubes (cut the short way into sixths; then cut it the long way into thirds).

*Duck *demi-glace* is available from D'Artagnan (800-DARTAGN).

# BRUNCH

# PERFECT AMERICAN FRENCH TOAST

I hadn't made French toast for years, though I love it for weekend country breakfasts. The reason is an odd one: It's the bread. French toast is one of those simple and wonderful things that if made well is crisp golden brown on the outside with a soft, airy yet moist interior, unsweetened and ready for a liberal lacing of real maple syrup. The problem is, there is only one bread I know of that is perfect for French toast: Wonder Bread, and I don't like it for anything but French toast. It is made with no eggs, milk or dairy products, resulting in a cottony soft, yeasty, airy bread—in short, an ideal yeasty sponge with which to soak up the egg and milk custard. And since my husband no longer eats eggs, and even the smallest loaf ("Small Wonder") has twelve slices, what to do with the rest of it after making the French toast?

So for years I had been having my occasional French toast breakfasts at diners, where I was often faced with disappointment. I always forget, though, when a waitress walks by with those beautiful thick golden slices. I forgot that in the middle is likely to lie a cardboard-hard white portion where, due to the chef's haste, the custard mixture has not reached. There is one diner I know of that almost gets it right. The French toast is great but alas, no **real** maple syrup, only imitation.

So I recently resigned myself to working out a recipe for thick French toast for one serving and freezing the rest of the loaf for future indulgences. It increases easily, however (here I give proportions for 4), and when we have country weekend company, adults and children alike consider this easy-to-make breakfast a special treat.

*(continued)*

---

*French Toast.* Yes, indeed, this breakfast delight comes to us from France. The French call this dish *pain perdu*, which literally means "lost bread." It is prepared using stale bread; French culinary purists advise that the *pain perdu* be at least two days old. In the south of France, cooks traditionally include "pain perdu" as part of feast day meals, particularly Easter when it is served as a dessert.

---

| INGREDIENTS | MEASURE | WEIGHT | |
| --- | --- | --- | --- |
| | *volume* | *ounces* | *grams* |
| 4 large eggs | full ¾ liquid cup | 7 ounces (weighed without shells) | 200 grams |
| heavy cream* | ½ liquid cup | | |
| milk | ½ liquid cup | | |
| pure vanilla extract | ½ teaspoon | | |
| nutmeg, freshly grated | a few gratings | | |
| white Wonder Bread or other soft white bread made without eggs | 8 slices (each 4 inches square by ½ inch thick) | 8 ounces | 227 grams |
| unsalted butter, frozen | 1 tablespoon | 0.50 ounce | 14 grams |
| OPTIONAL: powdered sugar and cinnamon *and* real maple syrup | | | |

SERVES: 4

EQUIPMENT: griddle or large heavy
  frying pan

Place 4 heat-proof dinner plates in the oven and turn the heat to low.

In a medium bowl, combine the eggs, cream, milk, vanilla and nutmeg and whisk lightly just to blend.

If you have a large jelly-roll pan, pour the mixture into it and place the slices of bread close together, in one layer, on top. Allow the bread to sit for a minute or so to soak up the mixture and then turn each slice over to absorb all of the remaining mixture. Move the bread slices around to be sure they pick up all of the egg mixture. Alternatively, dip or brush 1 slice at a time, using a scant ¼ liquid cup per slice.

With a large pancake turner, lift 1 piece of soaked bread and place it on top of another. Repeat with 3 more slices, ending up with 4 stacks of 2 pieces each.

Heat the griddle or frying pan over medium-high heat until hot enough to sizzle a drop of water. Impale the frozen butter on a fork or hold it carefully on either side and run it quickly along the surface of the hot griddle or pan to film it lightly with butter.

Fry 2 stacks of slices at a time (or all 4 if space permits) for about 2 minutes a side or until golden brown.

*Milk can be substituted for the heavy cream.

Cut each stack diagonally in half and arrange on the heated plates. Sprinkle lightly with powdered sugar and cinnamon or pass the maple syrup if desired.

POINTERS
FOR SUCCESS

• When turning the bread over in the egg mixture, it helps to use two pancake turners.
• If desired, the bread can be soaked in the egg mixture, covered tightly and refrigerated overnight, ready for frying in the morning.

VARIATION: Yogurt and Raspberry Sauce French Toast (Prepare the yogurt at least one day ahead.)

Place 2 cups of unflavored plain yogurt in a yogurt strainer or in a strainer lined with several layers of cheesecloth or a coffee filter. Suspend it over a bowl and allow it to sit overnight, refrigerated.

# Raspberry Sauce

| INGREDIENTS | MEASURE | WEIGHT | |
| room temperature | volume | ounces | grams |
| --- | --- | --- | --- |
| frozen raspberries in light syrup | 2 10-ounce packages | 20 ounces | 578 grams |
| sugar | ¼ cup, or more to taste | 1.75 ounces | 50 grams |
| lemon juice, freshly squeezed | 2 teaspoons | | |

MAKES: about 1 cup

Defrost the raspberries overnight in the refrigerator or for several hours at room temperature.

In a medium saucepan, combine the raspberries with the sugar and bring the mixture to a simmer over medium-low heat. Cook, stirring often to avoid scorching, until reduced to about 1⅓ cups, 12 to 15 minutes.

Pass the mixture through a food mill fitted with the fine disc or a strainer to remove the seeds. Stir in the lemon juice. Add more sugar, if desired, to taste. Return the raspberry sauce to the saucepan and heat, stirring constantly.

To serve, pour the raspberry sauce into a serving pitcher and pass to pour over the yogurt and French toast. Scoop about ¼ cup of the thickened yogurt on top of each serving of French toast. Discard or drink the liquid in the bowl.

KEEPS (SAUCE): 10 days refrigerated, 1 year frozen.

POINTERS FOR SUCCESS

• Raspberry seeds are very small and can pass through most food mills. The Cuisinarts power strainer and sieve attachment removes all the tiny seeds in a matter of minutes and is easy to clean. The Squeezo tomato strainer with berry screen attachment, by Vitantonio, is also effective but not as easy to clean.

# LIGHT LEMON PANCAKES WITH RASPBERRY BUTTER

My Swiss friend Erika Leiben made these pancakes for me on a visit to her home in Philadelphia, and they have become my new favorite special breakfast treat. The pancakes are as delicate and lemony as can be. Spread with a thin film of the rosy-hued raspberry butter, they seem to dissolve into thin air.

I like to make the full amount of raspberry butter and freeze any leftover for future lemon pancakes or French toast.

| INGREDIENTS | MEASURE | WEIGHT | |
|---|---|---|---|
| | *volume* | *ounces* | *grams* |
| **RASPBERRY BUTTER** | | | |
| fresh raspberries | 2 cups | 8 ounces | 227 grams |
| water | ¼ liquid cup | | |
| granulated sugar | 2 tablespoons | 1 ounce | 25 grams |
| unsalted butter, softened | 8 tablespoons | 4 ounces | 112 grams |
| powdered sugar | ¼ cup | 1 ounce | 28 grams |
| Chambord (black raspberry liqueur) | 2 teaspoons | | |
| **PANCAKES** | | | |
| whole-milk ricotta | 1 cup | 8 ounces | 227 grams |
| cottage cheese | ½ cup | 4.5 ounces | 130 grams |
| unsalted butter, melted | 8 tablespoons | 4 ounces | 112 grams |
| bleached all-purpose flour | ½ cup (measured by dip and sweep method) | 2.5 ounces | 72.5 grams |
| 6 large eggs, separated | | | |
|    yolks | 3.5 fluid ounces | 4 ounces | 112 grams |
|    whites | ¾ liquid cup | 6.25 ounces | 180 grams |
| sugar | ¼ cup | 1.75 ounces | 50 grams |
| lemon zest, finely grated (yellow portion of peel only) | 2 tablespoons | 0.5 ounce | 12 grams |
| salt | 2 generous pinches | | |
| cream of tartar | ¾ teaspoon | | |

*(continued)*

MAKES: about 53 3-inch pancakes;
1⅓ cups raspberry butter
(enough for 2 batches of
pancakes)
SERVES: 6

## RASPBERRY BUTTER

In a medium saucepan, stir together the raspberries, water and granulated sugar. Over medium heat, bring to a boil, and cook, stirring often, until thickly bubbling and reduced to a scant cup, about 5 minutes. Strain to remove the seeds and cool to room temperature. You will have about ¾ cup. In a food processor, process the raspberry purée with the butter, powdered sugar and Chambord until smooth. Store tightly covered.

KEEPS: 2 weeks refrigerated, 3 months frozen.
*Preheat a griddle or frying pan.*

## PANCAKES

In a food processor fitted with the metal blade, process the ricotta, cottage cheese, butter, flour, egg yolks, sugar, lemon zest and salt until well blended.

In a large bowl, preferably with the whisk beater attachment, beat the egg whites until foamy. Add the cream of tartar and continue beating, gradually raising the speed to high, until stiff peaks form when the beater is raised slowly.

Using a large wire whisk or rubber spatula, fold the whites into the cheese mixture.

The griddle or frying pan should be hot enough to sizzle a drop of water. Lightly butter it and pour on the batter in 3-inch rounds (about 2 tablespoons of batter). Test for doneness by lifting an edge of each pancake with a metal spatula. When golden brown, turn it over and cook for about 1 minute on the other side.

Remove the pancakes to warm plates and keep warm in a low oven while cooking the remaining batter.

POINTERS
FOR SUCCESS

• Avoid preheating the pan for an extended period of time as this delicate batter tends to brown quickly.
• To coat the griddle with a thin film of butter, run a frozen piece of butter lightly across it.

# LEMON POPPY SEED BUTTERMILK PANCAKES

Since the Lemon Poppy Seed Pound Cake is my favorite of all cakes (see *The Cake Bible*) and pancakes are perhaps the favorite of American breakfasts, it was inevitable that I would come up with these special pancakes.

| INGREDIENTS<br>*room temperature* | MEASURE<br>*volume* | WEIGHT<br>*ounces* | *grams* |
|---|---|---|---|
| all-purpose flour | 1⅔ cups (measured by dip and sweep method) | 8 ounces | 227 grams |
| poppy seeds | 3 tablespoons | 1 ounce | 28 grams |
| baking powder | 4 teaspoons | | 19.5 grams |
| lemon zest, finely grated (yellow portion of peel only) | 2 teaspoons | | 4 grams |
| salt | ½ teaspoon | | 3.5 grams |
| 4 large eggs, separated | | | |
|     yolks | 2 full fluid ounces | 2.5 ounces | 68 grams |
|     whites | ½ liquid cup | 4.25 ounces | 120 grams |
| buttermilk | 2 liquid cups | | |
| cream of tartar | ½ teaspoon | | |
| unsalted butter, melted and cooled | 4 tablespoons | 2 ounces | 57 grams |
| pure maple syrup or powdered sugar | | | |

MAKES: about 16 4-inch pancakes
SERVES: 4 to 5

*Preheat a griddle or frying pan.*

In a large bowl, whisk the flour, poppy seeds, baking powder, lemon zest and salt until blended.

In a small bowl, beat the egg yolks and buttermilk to blend slightly.

In a mixing bowl, beat the egg whites until foamy. Add the cream of tartar and beat until stiff peaks form when the beater is raised slowly.

Add the yolk mixture to the flour mixture and mix lightly with a fork until the flour is moistened. Stir in the butter.

*(continued)*

The batter should be lumpy, as overmixing will produce tough pancakes. Add the whites and fold them in with a slotted skimmer or rubber spatula.

The griddle or frying pan should be hot enough to sizzle a drop of water. Lightly butter it and pour on the batter in 4-inch rounds (⅓ cupfuls of batter). Test for doneness by lifting an edge of each pancake with a metal spatula. When golden brown, turn it over and cook 30 seconds to 1 minute on the other side.

Remove the pancakes to warm plates and keep warm in a low oven while cooking the remaining batter.

Serve drizzled with real maple syrup or sprinkled with powdered sugar.

POINTERS
FOR SUCCESS
• Do not overmix the batter.
• To coat the griddle with a thin film of butter, run a frozen piece of butter lightly across it.

UNDERSTANDING
All-purpose flour is preferable to cake flour as it produces a more firm pancake, which is more compatible with the texture of the poppy seeds.

# THE ULTIMATE BLT (on Black Pepper Brioche)

To my mind (not to mention my taste buds), the BLT is the greatest American sandwich under any circumstances, but when prepared with the most flavorful bacon and red ripe tomatoes at the height of the season it is truly at its very best. One summer I started fantasizing about just how much more wonderful still a BLT would be on home-baked bread with homemade mayonnaise. Black pepper brioche, seemed like the perfect complement to the slightly smoky bacon. And if I was going to make my own mayonnaise, it might just as well be tomato mayonnaise to complement the fresh tomato slices. The rest was history.

| INGREDIENTS room temperature | MEASURE volume | WEIGHT ounces/pounds | grams |
|---|---|---|---|
| **BLACK PEPPER BRIOCHE** | | | |
| water | 2 ½ tablespoons | | |
| sugar | 3 tablespoons, divided | 1.25 ounces | 40 grams |
| fresh yeast* *or/* | 2 packed teaspoons | 0.50 ounce | 11 grams |
| dry yeast (*not* rapid-rise) | 1 ½ teaspoons | | 4.5 grams |
| bread flour | about 1 ½ cups (measured by dip and sweep method) | 8 ounces | 227 grams |
| 1 large egg at room temperature + 2 cold large eggs† | | 6 ounces (weighed in the shells) | 170 grams |
| salt | ½ teaspoon | | 3.5 grams |
| black pepper, coarsely ground or butcher grind | 1 ½ teaspoons | | 4 grams |
| unsalted butter (must be softened) | 8 tablespoons | 4 ounces | 114 grams |

*Fresh yeast causes dough to rise faster than dry yeast.
†Only for food processor method; have all 3 eggs at room temperature if not using the food processor.

*(continued)*

### Egg Glaze

| | | | |
|---|---|---|---|
| 1 egg, lightly beaten | 1 tablespoon | | |
| 12 strips bacon, preferably Harrington's corncob smoked* | | 9 ounces | 255 grams |
| 3 medium-size ripe tomatoes | | 1½ pounds | 510 grams |
| Pink Mayonnaise made without the optional dill (page 202) | 1 recipe | | |
| 1 head curly green leaf lettuce, washed and dried on paper towels | | 3.75 ounces | 106 grams |

ADVANCE PREPARATION: at least 1
  day or up to 2 days ahead
PREHEAT THE OVEN TO: 425°F.
BAKING TIME: 30 to 35 minutes
SERVES: 6

EQUIPMENT: food processor with
dough blade or heavy-duty mixer
with dough hook attachment and
paddle beater; 6-cup loaf pan
(8½ inches by 4½ inches by
2½ inches), well buttered

PROOF THE YEAST: In a small bowl, combine the water (a tepid 100°F. if using fresh yeast, a little warmer, 110°F., if using dry), ½ teaspoon of the sugar and the yeast (do not use hot water or the yeast will die). If using fresh yeast, crumble it slightly while adding it. Set the mixture aside in a draft-free spot for 10 to 20 minutes. By this time, the mixture should be full of bubbles. If not, the yeast is too old to be useful and you must start again with newer yeast.

*Available through mail order from Harrington's, Main Street, Richmond, Vermont 05477 (802-434-4444).

### FOOD PROCESSOR METHOD

MAKE THE SPONGE: Place ⅓ cup of the flour and the 1 room-temperature egg in the food processor, fitted with the dough blade, and process for a few seconds until mixed. Add the yeast mixture and stir with a rubber scraper until smooth. Sprinkle the remaining flour over the mixture but do not mix it in. Cover with the food processor cover with the pusher inserted and let stand for 1½ to 2 hours. The wet mixture will rise up through the flour in places.

MAKE THE DOUGH: In a small bowl, whisk together the remaining 2 tablespoons plus 2½ teaspoons of sugar, the salt and pepper until well combined. Add this together with the remaining 2 cold eggs to the sponge and process 1½ minutes or until the dough is smooth and shiny and cleans the bowl. Let rest 5 minutes with the feed tube open. Add the butter in 2 batches of 4 tablespoons each and process for 20 seconds after each addition or until

(continued)

incorporated. (The butter must be soft so as not to overtax the motor of the processor. If the processor should stall, let it rest 5 minutes.)

## HEAVY-DUTY MIXER METHOD

*(All 3 eggs should be at room temperature.)*

MAKE THE SPONGE: Place ⅓ cup of the flour and 1 of the eggs in the large mixer bowl and whisk until mixed. Add the yeast mixture and whisk until smooth. Sprinkle the remaining flour over the mixture but do not mix it in. Cover tightly with plastic wrap (preferably Saran brand) and let stand for 1½ to 2 hours.

MAKE THE DOUGH: In a small bowl, whisk together the remaining 2 tablespoons plus 2½ teaspoons of sugar, the salt and pepper until well combined. Add this mixture together with the remaining 2 eggs to the sponge and beat on medium speed with the paddle beater. If the dough starts to climb up the beater, change to the dough hook. Beat for about 5 minutes or until the dough is smooth, shiny and very elastic and begins to clean the bowl. Be sure to continue beating until the dough starts to mass together and come away from the sides.

Increase the speed to medium high and add the butter by the tablespoon, beating until it is incorporated.

## BOTH METHODS

FIRST RISE: Scrape the dough into a lightly buttered bowl. It will be very soft and elastic. Sprinkle it lightly with flour to prevent a crust from forming. Cover the bowl tightly with plastic wrap (preferably Saran brand) and let it rise in a warm place (80°F. but not above, or the yeast will develop a sour taste) until doubled in bulk, 1½ to 2 hours.

Refrigerate the dough for 1 hour to firm it so the butter will not separate. Then gently deflate the dough by stirring it with a rubber scraper and return it to the refrigerator for another hour so that it will be less sticky to handle.

REDISTRIBUTING THE YEAST AND FINAL RISE (6 HOURS TO 2 DAYS, CHILLED): Turn the dough onto a lightly floured surface and gently press it into a rectangle, flouring the surface and dough as needed to keep the dough from sticking to your hands. Fold the dough in thirds (as you would a business letter), brushing off any excess flour, and again press it out into a rectangle. Fold it again in thirds and dust it lightly on all sides with flour. Wrap it loosely but securely in plastic wrap (preferably Saran brand) and then place it in a large zip-seal bag or wrap it in foil, and refrigerate for 6 hours or up to 2 days to allow the dough to ripen and firm.

BAKE THE BRIOCHE: Knead the dough a few times to deflate it, and shape it into a rectangle. Form it into a loaf to fit the pan by pushing together the long sides and tucking under the short sides. Press the dough into the prepared bread pan, seam side down. Cover the dough lightly with buttered plastic wrap (preferably Saran brand) and allow it to rise in a warm place until it has reached the top of the pan, about 1½ to 2 hours. (Fresh yeast will work faster than dry.)

*Thirty minutes before baking, lower the oven rack to the bottom shelf and place oven tiles or a baking sheet on it. Preheat the oven to 425°F.*

Brush the brioche with the egg glaze, being careful not to drip any on the side of the pan, or it will impede rising. Use a sharp greased knife or single-edged razor blade to make a shallow ¼-inch-deep slash down the center of the loaf almost to the ends.

Place the pan on the tiles or baking sheet and bake for 5 minutes. Lower the heat to 375°F. and continue baking 25 to 35 minutes or until a skewer inserted in the center comes out clean. An instant-read thermometer will register 190°F. If the top crust becomes very brown before the minimum baking time, tent loosely with foil.

Unmold the brioche onto a wire rack and reinvert to cool top side up, covered with a clean towel to keep the crust soft.

*(continued)*

ASSEMBLE THE BLTs: Bake the bacon in a large baking pan for about 10 minutes at 350°F. or until medium crisp. Drain on paper towels and cut each strip in half crosswise.

Cut the brioche into twelve ½-inch slices and place them on baking sheets. Toast the brioche lightly in a preheated 400°F. oven for about 3 to 4 minutes on each side. (Do not place the oven racks above the center position.) The bread should be crisp but not beginning to brown. Cool.

Use a serrated knife to slice the tomatoes into twelve ¼-inch-thick slices, discarding the end pieces.

Spread each slice of toast with about 1 tablespoon of the mayonnaise.* Arrange a piece of lettuce on top of 4 slices, then add 2 slices of tomato, 4 pieces of bacon and another piece of lettuce to each. Top with the remaining slices of toast.

Use a serrated knife to cut the BLTs in half horizontally. Serve at once (although these are also delicious as a lunch-box item).

POINTERS
FOR SUCCESS

- Use bread flour.
- Do *not* use rapid-rise yeast.
- Be sure the yeast is active.
- Do not allow the dough to rise in an area warmer than 80°F. to 85°F.
- Do not allow the dough to rise more than recommended amounts or it will weaken the structure.
- Do not deflate the dough before chilling or the butter will leak out. If this should happen inadvertently, chill the dough for 1 hour and knead the butter back into the dough.
- Unbaked dough can be frozen for up to 3 months.

UNDERSTANDING

Unlike a cake, which is primarily a starch structure, bread depends on protein in the form of gluten to create its framework. The higher the protein content of the flour,

*Be sure to spread it on what will become the insides of the sandwiches so that the pieces will line up evenly.

ROSE'S MELTING POT

the stronger the structure will be and the finer the grain of the bread (directly the opposite of cake). This dough is exceptionally wet. Just enough extra flour is added to handle it for shaping, resulting in a very light, soft brioche.

I do not use rapid-rise yeast because the flavor development and texture are superior with slower rising.

The shorter dough blade attachment of the food processor produces less friction and heat than the metal blade. There is still enough heat generated to actually cook a little of the egg, resulting in little brittle pieces in the bread. I add two of the eggs cold to counter this effect.

VARIATION: Lobster or Crab Salad Sandwiches
Try these variations for an elegant yet lusty sandwich. They were created one day when I was down in the dumps and, shopping at Balducci's, decided to comfort myself with lobster. I had leftover brioche, pink mayonnaise and lettuce. It worked!

For 6 sandwiches you will need 1 pound of cooked lobster tails cut into ½-inch-thick slices (3 cups) or lump crabmeat, picked through to remove any cartilage (3 cups), and 1 recipe of Pink Mayonnaise Américaine (page 202) prepared with dill for the lobster or prepared with 2 tablespoons each (¼ ounce) chopped chives and flat-leafed parsley for the crab.

Place the lobster or crabmeat and ½ cup of the mayonnaise in a medium bowl. With a rubber spatula, fold together the seafood and mayonnaise just until mixed.

Spread the toasted brioche as thinly as possible with some of the remaining mayonnaise. Cover each of 6 of the slices with a lettuce leaf. Arrange the seafood mixture evenly on top and cover with another piece of toasted brioche. Cut the sandwiches in half horizontally and serve at once, or refrigerate until serving time.

NOTE: To cook lobster tails, purchase four 7-ounce frozen Rock lobster tails and allow them to defrost overnight in the refrigerator.

*(continued)*

In a large saucepan, combine 1 cup of water, 1 cup of dry white wine, ¼ teaspoon of salt, ¼ teaspoon of black peppercorns and 2 parsley sprigs. Bring to a simmer and add the lobster tails. Cover and simmer for 10 to 12 minutes or until the shells turn reddish-brown and the lobster meat is opaque when prodded with the tip of a knife.

Drain and cool the lobster completely. Using kitchen shears, snip open the softer underside of the shell. Using both hands, crack open the shell and remove the tail meat. Cut it into ½-inch-thick slices. You will get 1 pound of shelled lobster meat.

# DESSERTS

# MEXICAN KILLER KAHLÚA CHIFFON CAKE

This cake is for the coffee lover. Because of the special spongy quality of chiffon cake, it can be imbued with the coffee and Kahlúa and become delightfully moist without losing any of its wondrously light texture.

I made this cake for a New Year's party last year and studded the glaze with gold dragées. It looked wonderfully elegant but Elliott felt that the hard dragées did not complement the light, soft texture of the coffee chiffon. "Well, what do you suggest?" I demanded, knowing he was right but not expecting a useful answer. To my amazement, he came up with this perfectly harmonious and simple coffee/sugar glaze, which he used to make for his kids' birthday cakes. This cake would be ideal for a Southwestern theme party to include Elliott's Instant-Gratification Summer Margaritas (page 321) and Shrimp, Squid and Chipotle Pasta (page 81).

| INGREDIENTS room temperature | MEASURE volume | WEIGHT ounces | grams |
|---|---|---|---|
| sifted cake flour | 2¼ cups (sifted into the cup and leveled off) | 8 ounces | 225 grams |
| sugar | 1½ cups, divided | 10.5 ounces | 300 grams |
| baking soda | ½ teaspoon | | 2.5 grams |
| salt | ½ teaspoon | | 3.5 grams |
| Medaglio d'Oro instant espresso powder* | 2 tablespoons | | 8 grams |
| water | ⅔ liquid cup | | |
| safflower oil | ½ liquid cup | | |
| 7 large eggs, separated, + 3 additional whites | | | |
| yolks | ½ liquid cup | 4.5 ounces | 130 grams |
| whites | 1¼ cups | 10.5 ounces | 300 grams |
| pure vanilla extract | 1 teaspoon | | |
| cream of tartar | 1¼ teaspoons | | 4 grams |
| Kahlúa | 1 liquid cup | | |

*Available in many supermarkets; most will place a special order if it is not regularly stocked.

(continued)

## MOCHA GLAZE

| | | | |
|---|---|---|---|
| bittersweet chocolate, preferably Lindt | 2 3-ounce bars | 6 ounces | 170 grams |
| Medaglio d'Oro instant espresso powder | 2 teaspoons | | |
| heavy cream | ¾ liquid cup | | |
| Kahlúa | 2 tablespoons | | |

## COFFEE GLAZE

| | | | |
|---|---|---|---|
| Medaglio d'Oro instant espresso powder | ½ teaspoon | | |
| boiling water | 2 teaspoons | | |
| powdered sugar | ½ cup (lightly spooned into the cup) + 1½ tablespoons | 2.5 ounces | 70 grams |

PREHEAT THE OVEN TO: 325°F.
BAKING TIME: 55 minutes
SERVES: 14

EQUIPMENT: ungreased 10-inch 2-piece tube pan, pastry bag fitted with a number 5 plain decorating tube (optional)

In a large mixing bowl, combine the flour, all but 2 tablespoons of the sugar, the baking soda and salt and beat 1 minute to mix. Make a well in the center.

Stir together the 2 tablespoons of Medaglio d'Oro and the ⅔ cup of water until the coffee granules are dissolved.

Add the oil, egg yolks, coffee and water and vanilla to the dry ingredients, and beat 1 minute or until smooth.

In another large mixing bowl, preferably with clean dry whisk beaters, beat the egg whites until frothy. Add the cream of tartar and beat until soft peaks form when the beater is raised. Beat in the remaining 2 tablespoons of sugar and beat until stiff peaks form when the beater is raised slowly. Gently fold the egg whites into the batter with a large balloon wire whisk, slotted skimmer or large rubber spatula until just blended.

Pour the batter into the tube pan (the batter will come to 1 inch from the top) and bake for 55 minutes or until a cake tester inserted in the center comes out clean and the cake springs back when lightly pressed in the center. Invert the pan, placing the tube opening over the neck of a soda or wine bottle to suspend it well above the counter, and cool the cake completely in the pan (this takes about 1½ hours). Brush the surface with ¼ cup of the Kahlúa.

Loosen the sides with a long metal spatula and remove the center core of the pan. Dislodge the cake from the bottom and center core with a metal spatula or thin sharp knife. (A wire cake tester works well around the core.) To keep the sides attractive, press the spatula well against the sides of the pan. Invert the cake onto a greased wire rack and brush the remaining ¾ cup of Kahlúa on the top and sides.

MOCHA GLAZE

Break the chocolate into pieces and process it in a food processor together with the Medaglio d'Oro until very fine. Remove the mixture to a small heat-proof glass bowl.

Heat the cream to the boiling point. Pour three quarters of it over the chocolate. Cover for 5 minutes to allow the chocolate to melt. Gently stir together the chocolate and cream until smooth, trying not to create air bubbles. Pass the mixture through a fine strainer, stir in the Kahlúa and allow to cool until tepid. At a tepid temperature, a small amount of glaze should mound a bit when dropped from a spoon before smoothly disappearing. If the glaze is too thick and the mound remains on the surface or if the glaze seems curdled, add some of the warm remaining cream by the teaspoonful. When the consistency is correct, use it at once, or store and reheat it.

To glaze the cake, set the cake, on its rack, over a pan or a piece of foil to catch the dripping chocolate. Pour the glaze evenly over the top of the cake, allowing it to drip down over the sides. With a small metal spatula, lift the glaze from the bottom surface and apply it to cover the sides of the cake.

Allow the cake to sit at room temperature for at least 2 hours or until the glaze has set. Refrigerating the glazed cake will dull it slightly. Do not apply the coffee glaze until you can touch the mocha glaze with your fingertip without leaving a mark.

Slide a flat cookie sheet or the removable bottom of a tart pan between the cake and the rack and use it to transfer the cake to a flat serving plate.

(continued)

## COFFEE GLAZE

In a small bowl, stir together the Medaglio d'Oro and boiling water. Add the powdered sugar and stir until perfectly smooth. If necessary, add water by the droplet to make the glaze pourable.

Use a pastry bag fitted with a ⅛-inch round decorating tube (number 5) or a spoon to drizzle the coffee glaze over the mocha glaze, allowing it to cascade down the sides of the cake. If desired, garnish with a few chocolate coffee beans.

Store in an airtight container for at least 12 hours before serving.

FINISHED HEIGHT: 4½ inches high in the middle.

STORE: 3 days at room temperature, 10 days refrigerated, 2 months frozen.

SERVE: At room temperature. Cut with a serrated knife.

POINTERS
FOR SUCCESS

• A large balloon whisk or slotted skimmer is ideal for folding in the flour with the least amount of air loss. If using the whisk, periodically shake out the batter that collects inside.

# APPLE UPSIDE-DOWN CAKE

This cake was inspired by the height of the apple season. It is reminiscent of tarte tatin with cake instead of pastry (one could call it gâteau tatin!). The French technique of caramelized apples and walnuts topping a velvety American butter cake is a fabulous combination. I brought it, hot from the oven, to my cousin Marion's house in Westchester for dinner, along with a special treat: Glensfoot cream, which is high in butterfat and not ultrapasteurized. She whipped it in a copper bowl, perfuming it with Jack Daniel's bourbon, and spooned a little onto the top of each portion of cake. It was perfect to temper the sweetness of the cake.

| INGREDIENTS room temperature | MEASURE volume | WEIGHT ounces | grams |
|---|---|---|---|
| **FRUIT TOPPING** | | | |
| 1 pound of apples (about 2 large) peeled, cored and sliced ¼ inch thick* | 2⅔ cups | 13 ounces (cut-up) | 375 grams |
| lemon juice, freshly squeezed | 1 teaspoon | | |
| light brown sugar | ⅓ cup, firmly packed, divided | 2.5 ounces | 71 grams |
| walnuts, coarsely chopped | ⅔ cup | 2.25 ounces | 66 grams |
| unsalted butter, softened | 4 tablespoons | 2 ounces | 57 grams |
| 2 large egg yolks | 2 tablespoons | 1.25 ounces | 37 grams |
| sour cream | ⅓ liquid cup, divided | 2.75 ounces | 78 grams |
| pure vanilla extract | ¾ teaspoon | | 3 grams |
| sifted cake flour† | 1 cup (sifted into the cup and leveled off) | 3.5 ounces | 100 grams |
| sugar | ½ cup | 3.5 ounces | 100 grams |
| baking powder | ½ teaspoon | | |
| salt | ⅛ teaspoon | | |
| unsalted butter (must be softened) | 6 tablespoons | 3 ounces | 85 grams |

OPTIONAL: ⅔ cup of heavy cream, lightly whipped
with 1 tablespoon of good-quality bourbon

*To core apples, cut them in half and use a melon baller to scoop out the core. Slice each half in half and then each piece into 3 pieces.
†Use cake flour without leavening (*not* self-rising); the flour must be bleached.

*(continued)*

PREHEAT THE OVEN TO: 350°F.
BAKING TIME: 35 to 40 minutes
SERVES: 6

EQUIPMENT: 8-inch round cake
   pan (or 9-inch tarte tatin pan)

*Preheat the oven to 350°F. Place a baking sheet on an oven rack in the lower third of oven.*

TO MAKE THE FRUIT TOPPING: In a medium bowl, toss together the apples, lemon juice and 2 tablespoons of the brown sugar. Allow to sit for at least 30 minutes.

Toast the walnuts in the 350°F. oven for 10 minutes or until golden brown. When cool, chop them coarsely and set them aside.

Use 1 tablespoon of the butter to butter the cake pan.

In a small heavy saucepan, preferably nonstick, melt the remaining 3 tablespoons of butter, and add the remaining brown sugar and any liquid that has drained from the apples. Bring it to a boil, stirring constantly, and simmer for about 3 minutes or until thickly bubbling and deep amber. Pour this mixture into the prepared cake pan. Arrange the apple slices, overlapping, in the bottom of the pan. Arrange slices around the sides of the pan as well. Set aside.

TO MAKE THE CAKE BATTER: In a medium bowl, lightly combine the yolks, about ¼ of the sour cream and the vanilla.

In a large mixing bowl*, combine the dry ingredients and mix on low speed for 30 seconds to blend. Add the butter and the remaining sour cream. Mix on low speed until the dry ingredients are moistened. Increase to medium (high speed if using a hand mixer) and beat for 1½ minutes to aerate and develop cake's structure. Scrape down the sides of the bowl.

Gradually add the egg mixture to the batter in 3 batches, beating for 20 seconds after each addition to incorporate the ingredients and strengthen the structure. Scrape down the sides. Scrape the batter into the fruit-lined pan, smoothing it evenly with a rubber spatula. Bake for 35 to 40 minutes or until golden brown, a wire cake tester inserted in the center comes out clean and the cake springs back when pressed lightly in the center. (Test carefully as

*The batter is a bit too scant to mix well in a K5 (KitchenAid). If you do not have a hand-held electric mixer, be sure to use the spade beater and tilt the KitchenAid mixing bowl and scrape the sides often.

the cake may appear done to the eye and still be under-done inside.)

Run a small metal spatula around the sides and invert at once onto a serving plate. Leave the pan in place for 1 or 2 minutes before lifting it. If any apple slices have stuck to the skillet, simply use a small spatula to place them back on the cake. Scatter the toasted nuts on top of the cake.

KEEPS: Wrapped airtight, 1 day at room temperature, 3 days refrigerated, 2 months frozen.

SERVE: Warm or at room temperature. If warm, serve the optional whipped cream on the side instead of on top of the apples.

UNDERSTANDING Although standard for a pineapple upside-down cake, it is better not to use a cast-iron pan for this as it would turn the apples a somewhat gray-green hue.
Use baking apples such as Granny Smith.

# LEMON AND WHITE POPPY SEED SURPRISE CAKE

O ne day, when I was doing a cookie demonstration at Macy's Cellar in New York, a young man, Jonathan Siegman, came up to me and told me that he loved my lemon poppy seed pound cake so much he had created a new variation using white poppy seeds. A few weeks later he sent me a package of the poppy seeds and I couldn't resist trying them immediately. The flavor of the white poppy seeds is milder than that of the black but the most intriguing aspect of the cake is that the poppy seeds blend so completely with the color of the cake crumb, you don't know they're present until you take the first crackly bite.

| INGREDIENTS room temperature | MEASURE volume | WEIGHT ounces | grams |
|---|---|---|---|
| milk | 3 tablespoons | | |
| 3 large eggs | scant 5 fluid ounces | 5.25 ounces (weighed without shells) | 150 grams |
| pure vanilla extract | 1 ½ teaspoons | | |
| sifted cake flour* | 1 ½ cups (sifted into the cup and leveled off) | 5.25 ounces | 150 grams |
| sugar, preferably superfine† | ¾ cup | 5.25 ounces | 150 grams |
| baking powder | ¾ teaspoon | | 3.7 grams |
| salt | ¼ teaspoon | | |
| grated lemon zest (yellow portion of peel only) | 1 tablespoon, loosely packed | | 6 grams |
| white poppy seeds‡ | 3 tablespoons | 1 ounce | 28 grams |
| unsalted butter (must be softened) | 13 tablespoons | 6.5 ounces | 184 grams |
| LEMON SYRUP | | | |
| sugar | ¼ cup + 2 tablespoons | 2.75 ounces | 75 grams |
| lemon juice, freshly squeezed (2 large lemons) | ¼ liquid cup | | |

*Use bleached cake flour, not self-rising.
†You can make it easily by placing regular sugar in a food processor and processing for a few minutes.
‡Available in Indian and Eastern food stores. (Black poppy seeds can be substituted.)

(continued)

EQUIPMENT: 8-inch by 4-inch by
2½-inch loaf pan (4 cups), the
most attractive size, or any 6-cup
loaf or fluted tube pan, greased
and floured; if using a loaf pan,
grease it, line the bottom with
parchment or wax paper and
then grease again and flour

In a medium bowl, lightly combine the milk, eggs and vanilla.

In a large mixing bowl, preferably with the whisk beater, combine the flour, sugar, baking powder, salt, lemon zest and poppy seeds. Mix on low speed for 30 seconds to blend. Add the butter and half the egg mixture. Mix on low speed until the dry ingredients are moistened. Increase to medium speed (high speed if using a hand-held mixer) and beat for 1 minute to aerate and develop the cake's structure. Scrape down the sides of the bowl. Gradually add the remaining egg mixture in 2 batches, beating for 20 seconds after each addition to incorporate the ingredients and strengthen the structure. Scrape down the sides.

Scrape the batter into the prepared pan and smooth the surface with a spatula. The batter will come to almost ½ inch from the top of the 4-cup loaf pan. (If your pan is slightly smaller, use any excess batter for cupcakes.)

Bake 55 to 65 minutes, 35 to 45 minutes in a fluted tube pan, or until a wooden toothpick inserted in the center comes out completely clean. Cover loosely with buttered foil after 30 minutes to prevent overbrowning. *The cake should not start to shrink from the sides of the pan until after it has been removed from the oven.*

NOTE: To get an attractive split down the middle of the crust, wait until the natural split is about to develop (about 20 minutes) and then, with a lightly greased sharp knife or single-edged razor blade, make a shallow mark about 6 inches long down the middle of the cake. This must be done quickly so that the oven door does not remain open very long, or the cake will fall. When the cake splits, it will open along the mark.

Shortly before the cake is done, prepare the lemon syrup: In a small pan over medium heat, stir the sugar and lemon juice until dissolved.

As soon as the cake comes out of the oven, place the pan on a rack, poke the cake all over with a wire tester and brush it with half the syrup. Cool in the pan for 10 minutes. Loosen the sides with a spatula and invert onto a greased wire rack. Poke the bottom of the cake with the wire tester, brush it with some syrup and reinvert onto a greased wire rack. Brush the sides with the remaining syrup and allow it to cool before wrapping airtight in (Saran brand) plastic wrap. Store for 24 hours before serving to give the syrup a chance to be evenly absorbed. Slice with a thin sharp knife into thin slices.

KEEPS: Wrapped airtight, 5 days at room temperature, 1 week refrigerated, 3 months frozen. The texture is most evenly moist when prepared 24 hours ahead of serving.

NOTE: This cake is very attractive made in individual portions. A 6-cake Bundtlette pan made by Nordicware is the perfect size. This recipe will make 6 individual cakelettes, which require about 20 minutes to bake.

POINTERS FOR SUCCESS

- Use *cake* flour that does *not* contain leavening (the flour must be bleached).
- Use superfine sugar for the finest texture.
- Use the correct size pan for the best texture and appearance.
- Be sure to use a wooden toothpick to test for doneness. The cake will spring back when pressed lightly in the center even before it is done. If the cake is underbaked, it will have tough, gummy spots instead of a fine, tender crumb.

# THE SOUTHERN BELLE

When I described my idea for this peach cake to my young cousin Alexandra Bush, she was in the middle of reading *Gone With the Wind.* Knowing that wonderful peaches are grown in the South, she came up with the perfect name for the cake. I am also indebted to my friend Laura Maestro for giving me the idea to broil the peaches for the final dramatic presentation. She was working on the illustrations for *Rose's Celebrations* as I was working on this new cake, and enthusiastically involved herself with this project as well.

The fresh sliced peaches that comprise the delicious and attractive topping are first sprinkled with sugar, which causes them to exude just the right amount of natural juices to moisten the génoise cake layer.

This cake is formal and elegant uncut but has the inviting warmth of a coffee cake when sliced and overlapped on a large serving plate. Lovely for an afternoon tea as well as a fancy dinner.

*(continued)*

| INGREDIENTS room temperature | MEASURE volume | WEIGHT ounces | grams |
|---|---|---|---|

**GÉNOISE**

| | | | |
|---|---|---|---|
| clarified *beurre noisette** | 4 tablespoons | 1.75 ounces | 50 grams |
| pure vanilla extract | 1 teaspoon | | |
| sifted cake flour | ½ cup (sifted into the cup and leveled off) | 1.75 ounces | 50 grams |
| cornstarch | ½ cup (lightly spooned into the cup) − 1 tablespoon | 1.75 ounces | 50 grams |
| 4 large eggs | 6 full fluid ounces | 7 ounces (weighed without shells) | 200 grams |
| sugar | ½ cup | 3.5 ounces | 100 grams |

**PEACH TOPPING**

| | | | |
|---|---|---|---|
| 4 medium ripe but firm peaches, peeled and sliced about ½ inch thick | about 4 cups slices | 20.25 ounces (slices) | 533 grams |
| sugar | ¼ cup | 1.75 ounces | 50 grams |
| lemon juice, freshly squeezed | 1 teaspoon | | |
| pure almond extract | ¼ teaspoon | | |
| unsalted butter, melted | 2 tablespoons | 1 ounce | 28 grams |
| peach brandy (optional) | 2 tablespoons | | |
| light brown sugar | 2 tablespoons, firmly packed | 1 ounce | 30 grams |
| ground cinnamon | ½ teaspoon | | |

**WHIPPED CREAM (OPTIONAL)**

| | | | |
|---|---|---|---|
| heavy cream | 1 liquid cup | | |
| superfine sugar | 1 tablespoon | 0.5 ounce | 13 grams |
| peach brandy | 1 tablespoon | | |
| pure vanilla extract | ¼ teaspoon | | |

*If you do not have clarified browned butter on hand, you will need to clarify 6 tablespoons (3 ounces/85 grams) of unsalted butter. In a heavy saucepan, melt the butter over medium heat, partially covered to prevent splattering. When the butter looks clear, cook uncovered, watching carefully, until the solids drop and begin to brown. Pour immediately through a fine strainer or a strainer lined with cheesecloth.

EQUIPMENT: 9-inch by 2-inch round cake pan, greased, bottom lined with parchment and then greased again and floured; large rectangular baking dish (such as a 13½-inch by 8¾-inch Pyrex); 8-inch cardboard round; foil collar

## GÉNOISE

*Preheat the oven to 350°F.*

Warm the *beurre noisette* until almost hot (110°F. to 120°F.). Place it in a medium bowl, add the vanilla and keep it warm.

Sift together the flour and cornstarch.

In a large mixing bowl set over a pan of simmering water, heat the eggs and sugar until just lukewarm, whisking constantly to prevent curdling. (The eggs may also be heated by placing them, *still in their shells*, in a large mixing bowl in an oven with a pilot light for 3 hours or up to overnight.) Remove the mixing bowl from the heat. Using the whisk beater, beat the mixture on high speed for 5 minutes or until tripled in volume. (A hand beater may be used but it will be necessary to beat for at least 10 minutes.)

Remove 1 scant cup of the egg mixture and thoroughly whisk it into the *beurre noisette*–vanilla mixture.

Sift half the flour mixture over the remaining egg mixture and fold it in gently but rapidly with a large balloon whisk, slotted skimmer or rubber spatula until almost all the flour has disappeared. Repeat with the remaining flour mixture until the flour has disappeared completely. Fold in the butter mixture until just incorporated. Pour immediately into the prepared pan (it will be about two-thirds full).

Bake 25 to 35 minutes or until the cake is golden brown and starts to shrink slightly from the sides of the pan. (No need for a cake tester: Once the sides shrink, the cake is done.) Avoid opening the oven door before the minimum time or the cake may fall. Test toward the end of baking by opening the door slightly; if at a quick glance it does not appear done, close the door at once and check again in 5 minutes.

Loosen the sides of the cake with a small metal spatula and unmold at once onto a lightly greased rack. Reinvert onto another rack to cool. When cool, wrap airtight in plastic wrap (preferably Saran brand).

*(continued)*

PEACH TOPPING

In a medium bowl, combine the peach slices, sugar, lemon juice and almond extract. Toss gently with a rubber spatula and allow to sit for at least 30 minutes. Drain the peaches in a strainer or colander, reserving the juices. Cover with plastic wrap and set aside.

*Preheat the oven to 400°F.*

Brush the baking dish with 1 tablespoon of the melted butter. Place the peach slices in the bottom of the pan, slightly overlapping if necessary, and cover tightly with aluminum foil. Bake for 15 to 20 minutes or until just tender but still firm. Cool completely.

If there are any juices, add them to the reserved drained juice. There should be ½ cup. If you are adding the peach brandy, reduce the juices to 6 tablespoons in a microwave or small saucepan. Allow to cool before stirring in the brandy.

Use a long serrated knife to trim off the bottom and top crust of the génoise. Brush the bottom of the génoise with about half the peach juices. Invert the cake onto the cardboard round. Using a small sharp knife, cut a ¼-inch-deep circle out of the center of the cake, leaving a ½-inch-wide rim around the outer edge of the cake. This provides the well into which the peach slices will be arranged. Brush the remaining syrup on top of the cake.

Starting from the outside edge of the well, arrange the peach slices in concentric circles, generously overlapping them, pit side facing towards the center, to resemble a giant flower. Brush the peach slices with the 1 tablespoon of remaining melted butter, reheating it if solidified.

In a small bowl, stir together the brown sugar and cinnamon. If the brown sugar is lumpy, place it with the cinnamon in a food processor and process until fine. Sprinkle it evenly over the peaches.

TO MAKE THE FOIL COLLAR, cut out a 12-inch circle of foil, preferably heavy-duty. From the center, cut out a circle about 7½ inches in diameter, or large enough to expose all of the peaches but still protect the edges of the cake. Place it on the cake, curving the edges down to protect the sides of the cake.

Place the cake under the broiler and broil for about 5 minutes or until the edges of the peaches begin to brown attractively. Remove the foil collar for the last minute or so of broiling so the edges of the cake brown lightly and become crisp. Use a heavy-duty spatula or pancake turner to lift the cake, still on its cardboard round, to an attractive serving plate.

KEEPS: 1 day at room temperature, 3 days refrigerated.

OPTIONAL WHIPPED CREAM

In a large mixing bowl combine the heavy cream, sugar, peach brandy and vanilla and refrigerate for at least 15 minutes. (Chill the beater alongside the bowl.)

Beat only until soft peaks form or the cream mounds softly when dropped from a spoon.

To serve, cut the cake with a serrated knife. Spoon a large dollop of whipped cream on the side of each portion if desired. Alternatively, arrange slices on a serving plate and garnish with a mound of the whipped cream and extra cooked peach slices.

POINTERS
FOR SUCCESS

• The génoise can be made ahead and frozen (well wrapped) for up to 3 months.

UNDERSTANDING

Compared to a basic layer cake (butter cake) of the same size, the génoise has half the sugar, flour/cornstarch and butter and no chemical leavening or added liquid. This explains why the génoise is "lighter than air!" With the addition of the syrup, however, the sugar level is almost as high as in the butter cake.

Although using cake flour produces the best texture, other flours will work. Using part cornstarch tightens the grain and holds the moisture supplied by the eggs and sugar.

# LA MARJOLAINE

Fernand Point, the renowned chef-owner of La Pyramide in France, invented this wonderful rich layering of crisp dacquoise (nutted meringue) and creamy chocolate and orange fillings. The Marjolaine has since become a classic, considered by many to be one of the most elegant and fabulously indulgent desserts of all times. Instead of the usual praline chocolate ganache used in a Marjolaine, I have chosen the Bernachons' cinnamon ganache* because the faint touch of cinnamon makes it more bitter, balancing the sweetness of the dacquoise.

Granted this dessert is a bit of work to prepare but the payoff is that it serves twenty-two and can be made several days ahead, or even several months ahead and frozen, so it is ideal for a large party. In fact, it would make another ideal candidate for a dessert party but serve it last; it packs a powerful chocolate punch!

| INGREDIENTS | MEASURE<br>volume | WEIGHT<br>ounces | grams |
|---|---|---|---|
| **DENSE CINNAMON GANACHE** | (2¾ cups) | | |
| bittersweet chocolate, preferably Lindt Excellence or Valrhona extra bittersweet | 4 3-ounce bars | 12 ounces | 340 grams |
| ground cinnamon | ½ teaspoon | | |
| heavy cream | 1½ liquid cups | | |
| **LIGHT WHIPPED GANACHE** | (1 cup) | | |
| bittersweet chocolate, preferably Lindt Excellence or Valrhona extra bittersweet | ⅔ of a 3-ounce bar | 2 ounces | 57 grams |
| heavy cream | ½ liquid cup | | |
| pure vanilla extract | ⅛ teaspoon | | |
| **CLASSIC ORANGE BUTTERCREAM** | (1 full cup) | | |
| 2 large egg yolks | 2 tablespoons + 1 teaspoon | 1.3 ounces | 37 grams |
| sugar | ¼ cup | 1.75 ounces | 50 grams |
| water | 2 tablespoons | | |

*See *A Passion for Chocolate* (William Morrow, 1989).

| | | | |
|---|---|---|---|
| unsalted butter (must be softened to cool room temperature) | ½ cup | 4 ounces | 113.5 grams |
| Cointreau | 1 tablespoon | | |
| orange zest, finely grated (orange part only of peel) | 2 tablespoons | 0.5 ounce | 12 grams |

### DACQUOISE

| | | | |
|---|---|---|---|
| water | 2 liquid cups | | |
| whole hazelnuts | 1 cup | 5 ounces | 142 grams |
| baking soda | 3 tablespoons | 1.6 ounces | 45 grams |
| blanched sliced almonds | 1⅓ cups | 4 ounces | 113 grams |
| cornstarch | 3 tablespoons | 0.75 ounce | 24 grams |
| superfine sugar | 1 cup + 2 tablespoons, divided | 8 ounces | 226 grams |
| powdered sugar | 1½ cups (lightly spooned into the cup) | 6 ounces | 170 grams |
| 8 large egg whites | 1 liquid cup | 8.5 ounces | 240 grams |
| cream of tartar | 1 teaspoon | | |

### DECOR

| | | | |
|---|---|---|---|
| unsweetened cocoa | 3 tablespoons | 0.66 ounce | 18 grams |

MAKE AHEAD: at least 1 day or up to 1 week

PREHEAT THE OVEN TO: 325°F.

BAKING TIME: 1 hour

SERVES: 22

EQUIPMENT: 17-inch by 12-inch jelly-roll pan, bottom lined with a nonstick liner* or foil; cooling rack at least the size of the pan

### DENSE CINNAMON GANACHE

Break the chocolate into pieces and process in a food processor, together with the cinnamon, until very fine. Scald the cream† and, with the motor running, pour it through the feed tube in a steady stream. Process for a few seconds until smooth. (Or chop the chocolate finely, place it in a bowl and pour in the scalded cream. Cover; let it sit for 5 minutes and then whisk until smooth.) Transfer to a bowl and allow it to sit for several hours at room temperature, until thickened to frosting consistency. Cover tightly (preferably with Saran brand plastic wrap) until ready to use.

*Available from European Home Products, P.O. Box 2524, Waterbury, Connecticut 06723 (203-866-9683; outside Connecticut, 800-225-0760).
†Heat just to the point when small bubbles appear around the edge.

*(continued)*

KEEPS: 3 days at room temperature, 2 weeks refrigerated, 6 months frozen. To soften ganache after chilling, allow it to warm to room temperature and, if necessary, warm just to soften over hot water or a few seconds in the microwave. Stir gently so that it doesn't get aerated.

## LIGHT WHIPPED GANACHE

Break the chocolate into pieces and process in a food processor until very fine. Scald the cream and, with the motor running, pour it through the feed tube in a steady stream. Process a few seconds until smooth. (Or chop the chocolate finely, place it in a bowl and stir in the scalded cream until smooth.)

Transfer to the large bowl of an electric mixer and refrigerate until cold, stirring once or twice (about 45 minutes). You may speed chilling by setting the bowl in an ice-water bath and stirring frequently. Do not allow the mixture to get too cold or it will be too stiff to incorporate air.

Add the vanilla and beat the mixture just until very soft peaks form when the beater is raised. It will continue to thicken after a few minutes at room temperature. The safest way not to overbeat is to use an electric mixer until the ganache starts to thicken and then continue with a whisk.

If the mixture gets overbeaten and grainy, it can be restored by remelting, chilling and rebeating. Cover tightly (preferably with Saran brand plastic wrap).

KEEPS: 1 day at room temperature.

## CLASSIC ORANGE BUTTERCREAM

Have ready a greased 1-cup heat-proof glass measure near the range.

In a medium bowl, beat the yolks with an electric mixer until light in color.

Meanwhile, combine the sugar and water in a small saucepan (preferably with a nonstick lining) and stir until the sugar is completely moistened. Heat, stirring constantly, just until the sugar dissolves and the syrup is boiling. Stop stirring and boil to the soft-ball stage (238°F.). This will take about 1 minute. Tilt the pan so that the syrup collects in one spot to get an accurate reading. *Immediately transfer the syrup to the glass measure to stop the cooking.*

Using an electric hand-held mixer, on medium speed, beat the syrup into the yolks in a steady stream. Don't allow the syrup to fall on the beaters or they will spin it onto the sides of the bowl. Use a rubber scraper to remove the syrup clinging to the glass measure. Continue beating until completely cool, about 5 minutes.

Gradually beat in the butter until incorporated. Beat in the Cointreau and orange zest. Cover tightly (preferably with Saran brand plastic wrap).

KEEPS: 6 hours at room temperature, 1 week refrigerated, 8 months frozen. Bring to room temperature before using. Rebeat lightly to restore the texture.

DACQUOISE

*Preheat the oven to 350°F.*

In a small saucepan, bring the 2 cups of water to a boil. Add the hazelnuts and baking soda and boil 3 minutes. The water will turn black from the peels. Test a nut by running it under cold water. The skin should slip off easily. If not, boil the nuts for a few more minutes. Drain and rinse the nuts under cold running water.

Place the hazelnuts and almonds on 2 baking sheets. Toast the almonds for 8 to 10 minutes, the hazelnuts 15 to 20 minutes, or until just beginning to color. Allow the nuts to cool completely.

In a food processor, with the grating disc, grate the hazelnuts. Then pulse them together with the almonds, cornstarch, half the superfine sugar and the powdered sugar until finely ground. (Or use a nut grater and then combine the ingredients in a bowl and whisk until well combined.)

*(continued)*

In a 5-quart or larger mixing bowl, beat the whites until frothy. Add the cream of tartar and beat at medium speed while gradually adding 2 tablespoons of the remaining superfine sugar. When soft peaks form when the beater is raised, gradually add the remaining superfine sugar and beat at high speed until stiff peaks form when the beater is raised slowly.

Fold in the reserved nut mixture with a slotted skimmer or large rubber spatula. Immediately pour the mixture into the prepared pan, smoothing it with a spatula, preferably a large offset one, being sure to reach all corners of the pan.

Bake for 1 hour or until crisp and golden. Unmold onto the rack, lift off the pan and remove the nonstick liner or foil. The bottom of the dacquoise may still be slightly soft but will crisp on cooling.

When cool, use a long serrated knife to cut the dacquoise crosswise into 4 equal strips (each will be 4 inches wide by 11 inches long).

ASSEMBLING THE MARJOLAINE

Place 1 dacquoise strip, top side up, on a long rectangular serving platter. Spread 1 cup of the cinnamon ganache evenly on top. Place a second dacquoise strip on top and spread with the whipped ganache. Top with a third dacquoise strip and spread with the orange buttercream. Top with the fourth dacquoise strip, bottom side up. Cover tightly with plastic wrap (preferably Saran brand) and refrigerate for at least 30 minutes to firm the layers.

Slip 4 pieces of wax paper under the dacquoise to keep the serving plate clean. Frost the long sides and top evenly with the remaining cinnamon ganache, leaving the short sides unfrosted. Use an icing comb or fork to make long decorative lines on the sides.

Use a serrated knife to cut a thin slice from either short end to even it. Place a piece of plastic wrap against each cut end to protect it.

To decorate the top of the cake, place the cocoa in a strainer held over the cake and tap the sides of the strainer with a spoon.

Carefully slip out the wax paper. Cover loosely with plastic wrap and refrigerate for at least 12 hours before serving.

To serve, cut ½-inch slices, using a serrated knife dipped in hot water between each slice. Allow the slices to sit at room temperature for at least 20 minutes before serving.

KEEPS: 1 week refrigerated, 3 months frozen, wrapped in plastic wrap and then in aluminum foil.

POINTERS
FOR SUCCESS

### DENSE CINNAMON GANACHE

- Your favorite semisweet or bittersweet eating chocolate will result in the best flavored ganache. If the chocolate is not smooth-textured in bar form it will not be smooth in the ganache either.
- Do not stir the ganache while it is cooling or it will lighten in texture and color.

### LIGHT WHIPPED GANACHE

- The temperature of the mixture is critical when beating. If not cold enough, it will not stiffen; if too cold it will not aerate well. Overbeating causes curdling.

### CLASSIC ORANGE BUTTERCREAM

- To prevent crystallization, do not allow any sugar to fall on the sides of the pan. All the sugar (every crystal) must be moistened before heating. Do not stir after the syrup comes to a boil.
- To keep the temperature from rising too high, remove the syrup from the pan as soon as it has reached 238°F.
- Don't allow the syrup to fall directly on the beaters as it will spin the syrup around the sides of the bowl. Using a hand-held beater makes this easier to avoid.
- Do not rebeat chilled buttercream until it has reached room temperature or it may curdle.

*(continued)*

DESSERTS

255

DACQUOISE

- If you have trouble finding superfine sugar, make your own by processing regular granulated sugar in a food processor. The dacquoise will not be as light and delicate if you use fine granulated sugar instead of superfine.
- Avoid preparing on humid days as the dacquoise will be sticky.
- Do not use parchment or a greased and floured baking sheet as the dacquoise may stick to it.
- To prevent cracking, do not open the oven door during the first three quarters of baking time.
- Use a clean grease-free bowl to beat the egg whites or they will not whip.

# HUNGARIAN DOBOS TORTE

***Dessert Party Extravaganza***
Hungarian Dobos Torte
Apple Upside-Down Cake
La Marjolaine

This marvelously fancy and delicious cake is not often found any more either in cookbooks or bakeries, because it is somewhat of a production to prepare. But I promise, if you follow these instructions, you will succeed in producing a cake that will fulfill your wildest expectations.

I have been hearing about this classic Hungarian cake for as many years as I've known my friend Nancy Blitzer. Every important birthday or other celebration, when Nancy contemplates the menu, she invariably muses, "Well, for dessert I think I'll make a Dobos torte!" Of course she gets many requests for this cake from friends and family. The reasons are obvious: This cake is a tour de force with great variety of texture and flavors. The cake layers are about three sixteenths of an inch thick, the layers of frosting one eighth inch thick—ideal for the frosting lover. But it is the glistening amber glide of caramel on the top of each piece that provides the ultimate magic. Make this cake the star of a dessert party.

## CAKE

| | | | |
|---|---|---|---|
| 9 large eggs, separated | | | |
|    yolks | ⅔ liquid cup | 5.75 ounces | 167 grams |
|    whites | 9 fluid ounces | 9.5 ounces | 270 grams |
| powdered sugar | 1¼ cups (lightly spooned into the cup and leveled off) | 5 ounces | 144 grams |
| salt | ½ teaspoon | | |
| pure vanilla extract | 2 teaspoons | | |
| sifted cake flour | 1¼ cups (sifted into the cup and leveled off) | 4.5 ounces | 125 grams |
| cream of tartar | 1⅛ teaspoons | | |

## CARAMEL GLAZE

| | | | |
|---|---|---|---|
| sugar | 1 cup | 7 ounces | 200 grams |
| water | ⅓ liquid cup | | |
| cream of tartar | ⅛ teaspoon | | |

## CHOCOLATE FILLING AND FROSTING

| | (about 3¼ cups) | (28 ounces) | (800 grams) |
|---|---|---|---|
| bittersweet chocolate (preferably Lindt Excellence) | 4 3-ounce bars | 12 ounces | 340 grams |
| 3 large eggs | scant ⅔ liquid cup | 5.25 ounces | 150 grams |
| powdered sugar | 1½ cups | 6 ounces | 172 grams |
| unsalted butter | 16 tablespoons | 8 ounces | 227 grams |
| pure vanilla extract | 1 teaspoon | | |

PREHEAT THE OVEN: 375°F.
BAKING TIME FOR LAYERS: 6 to 8 minutes
SERVES: 12

EQUIPMENT: 2 to 3 9-inch round cake pans (measuring about 8½ inches at the bottom—use the inexpensive hardware store variety), greased, bottoms lined with parchment and sprayed with Baker's Joy (which contains flour and shortening) or greased and floured; small offset spatula

## CAKE

_Preheat the oven to 375°F._

In a large mixing bowl, preferably with the whisk beater, beat the yolks, sugar and salt on high speed for 5 minutes or until the mixture is very thick and ribbons when dropped from the beater. Lower the speed and beat in the vanilla. Sift the flour over the yolk mixture without mixing it in and set aside.

In another large mixing bowl, beat the whites until foamy. Add the cream of tartar and beat until stiff peaks form when the beater is raised slowly. Add about one third of

_(continued)_

the whites to the yolk mixture and, with a large wire whisk or rubber spatula, fold until incorporated. (If using the wire whisk, periodically shake out the batter that accumulates in the center.) Gently fold in the remaining whites.

Pour 1 cup (2.25 ounces/64 grams) of the batter into each of the prepared pans and spread evenly with a small angled spatula or rubber spatula. The batter will be just under ¼ inch thick. Bake for 6 to 8 minutes or until the cake is springy to the touch. It should not begin to brown.

Unmold each layer at once onto a flat surface lined with a sheet of plastic wrap, lightly sprayed with nonstick vegetable spray, that is large enough to wrap over the top of the layer to keep it from drying and shrinking. Remove the parchment immediately, while the layers are still hot. If the parchment sticks, brush it lightly with water to loosen it. As soon as each layer is cool, cover it with the plastic wrap to keep it from drying.

Continue with the remaining batter. You should have 8 to 9 layers. (There will be enough buttercream to fill 9 layers but 7 are enough to make a nice size cake.)

Choose the most attractive layer and invert it onto a piece of heavy-duty foil. Trim the foil to the size of the layer and place it near the range on a cake rack set on top of another piece of foil.

CARAMEL GLAZE

Have ready a 1-cup heat-proof glass measure, long metal spatula and long sharp knife, all either sprayed with nonstick vegetable shortening or oiled.

In a small heavy saucepan, combine the sugar, water and cream of tartar and stir until the sugar is completely moistened and no dry crystals are left on the sides of the pan. Cook over medium-low heat, stirring constantly to dissolve the sugar. Then increase the heat and boil *without stirring* until deep amber, the color of dark corn syrup (365°F.). Pour it immediately into the glass measure and stir for about 20 seconds or until the bubbles disappear.

Then pour the caramel quickly onto the cake layer, immediately spreading it evenly with the oiled spatula. Allow it to stand for a few seconds, just until it is firm but not brittle.

Score the caramel quickly with the sharp knife into 12 wedges. (The easiest way to do this evenly is to first cut it into quarters, then cut each quarter into thirds.) If the caramel is too soft and tacky, wait a few more minutes. Slip a pancake turner between the foil and the rack and transfer the caramel-covered cake to the counter. As the caramel hardens, continue to deepen the score marks until you have cut through to the foil. When completely cool, use a scissors to cut through the foil and separate the caramel-covered wedges. Set them aside, uncovered, at room temperature.

CHOCOLATE BUTTERCREAM FILLING AND FROSTING

Break the chocolate into pieces and place it in the upper container of a double boiler set over an inch of very hot, not simmering, water. Stir often, until melted.

Meanwhile, whisk together the eggs and sugar.

Whisk the eggs and sugar into the melted chocolate. Raise the heat and continue cooking, stirring often, until thick enough to pool slightly when dropped back into the mixture from the stirring spoon (an accurate thermometer* should read 160°F.), about 10 minutes. Pour the mixture into a bowl and allow to cool completely, stirring occasionally with the whisk.

In an electric mixer bowl, preferably with the whisk attachment, cream the butter on medium speed until it is soft and creamy. Beat in the cooled chocolate mixture until uniformly incorporated. On low speed, beat in the vanilla extract.

*The Cordon Rose candy thermometer is available through Dean & DeLuca (800-227-7714) and La Cuisine (800-521-1176).

(continued)

## ASSEMBLING THE TORTE

Spread a small amount of the buttercream on a cardboard round cut to 8¼ inches or a serving plate. Fold back the plastic wrap from the top of one of the cake layers. Grasping the plastic wrap on either side of the layer, invert the cake layer over the buttercream (it will adhere to the plastic) and when it is positioned evenly, lower it onto the buttercream-covered surface, pressing lightly on top of the plastic wrap to cause it to adhere. Carefully peel back the plastic wrap.

Spread ⅓ cup (2.75 ounces/80 grams) of the buttercream evenly on top of the cake layer. Continue until you have used all the layers. Peel away the foil from the bottoms of the caramel-glazed cake wedges and arrange them on top. Frost the sides of the cake with the remaining buttercream. Place an oiled sheet of foil, wax paper or plastic wrap on top of the caramel.

To serve, cut with a sharp thin knife that has been dipped in hot water and wiped dry. If the cake has been refrigerated, cut it while still cold for the most attractive slices, but allow it to sit at room temperature for at least 20 minutes before serving to soften the buttercream to its most luxurious texture and flavor.

KEEPS: 2 days at room temperature, 3 days refrigerated. (If there is humidity in the air, the caramel will soften and get sticky. The cake freezes well for several weeks without the caramel. If desired, freeze the top layer separately and apply the caramel the day of serving.)

POINTERS
FOR SUCCESS

- If you wish, you can start by making the buttercream. It will then not be necessary to cover the cake layers with plastic wrap to keep from drying out and shrinking, as long as you frost them as soon as they are room temperature.
- It is very hard to remove the parchment when the layers cool, and they cool very fast. What works best is to stagger the baking: As soon as 1 layer is ready, put it in the oven so it can start baking while you spread the batter into the second pan. Brushing water on the parchment also helps to loosen it.

*(continued)*

DESSERTS

- To prevent crystallization when making the caramel, do not allow any sugar crystals to get on the sides of the pan and be sure to moisten all the sugar with the water. Stop stirring entirely as soon as it comes to a boil.
- If you do not have an accurate thermometer for making the caramel, use a white porcelain spoon to stir or place a drop of the caramel on a white plate to gauge the color. You must be sure to rinse off any utensil that has caramel or sugar syrup on it before reinserting it into the caramel or it will crystallize.

UNDERSTANDING   The powdered sugar in the cake makes it more dense and keeps its moisture longer.

The cream of tartar is added to the sugar when making the caramel as an "interfering agent" to minimize the possibility of crystallization.

# THE BAR MITZVAH CAKE

In *The Cake Bible*, I described a cake that I considered to be one of the most beautiful I had ever designed, although "the bar mitzvah mother" had thought it "not quite beautiful enough." In response to the many requests of curious readers I have re-created the cake design here.

This cake can be the grand finale to a lavish bar mitzvah dinner: Perfect Crisp Roast Duck (page 140), Kasha Varnishkes (page 177), Rhubarb Compote (page 188) and Fruit Jewel Tarts (page 294).

| INGREDIENTS<br>*room temperature* | MEASURE<br>*volume* | WEIGHT<br>*ounces/pounds* | *grams/kilograms* |
|---|---|---|---|
| PASTILLAGE | (1¾ cups) | (1¼ pounds) | (600 grams) |
| water | scant ⅓ liquid cup | | |
| gelatin | 1 tablespoon | 0.35 ounce | 10 grams |
| powdered sugar | 4 cups (lightly spooned into the cup and leveled off) | 1 pound | 454 grams |
| cornstarch | ½ cup (lightly spooned into the cup) | 2.25 ounces | 64 grams |
| OPTIONAL: cream of tartar | a pinch | | |
| ROYAL ICING | (2¼ cups) | | |
| meringue powder* | 3 tablespoons | 0.85 ounce | 25 grams |
| water | 3 fluid ounces (6 tablespoons) | | |
| powdered sugar | 4 cups (lightly spooned into the cup and leveled off) | 15.75 ounces | 450 grams |
| gold powder or petal dust† | 1 tiny container | | |
| vodka or other high-proof clear drinking alcohol | a few drops | | |

*Three large egg whites (3 fluid ounces, 3 ounces/90 grams) can be used in place of the meringue powder and water. This icing can be rebeaten but not as many times as the meringue powder variety.
†The Chocolate Gallery (212-675-2253) carries an excellent variety of gold powder from England.

*(continued)*

ROLLED FONDANT

| | | | |
|---|---|---|---|
| water | 3 fluid ounces (6 tablespoons) | | |
| gelatin | 2 tablespoons | 0.7 ounce | 20 grams |
| corn syrup | 1 liquid cup | 11.50 ounces | 328 grams |
| glycerine* | 2 tablespoons | 1.25 ounces | 36 grams |
| solid white shortening | ¼ cup | 1.5 ounces | 48 grams |
| powdered sugar | 16 cups (lightly spooned into the cup and leveled off) | 4 pounds | 1 kilogram 840 grams |

CHOCOLATE CAKE

| | | | |
|---|---|---|---|
| unsweetened cocoa (Dutch-processed) | 1¾ cups (measured by dip and sweep method) | 6 ounces | 168 grams |
| boiling water | 2⅔ liquid cups | | |
| 8 large eggs | scant 1⅔ liquid cups (13 fluid ounces) | 14 ounces (weighed without shells) | 400 grams |
| pure vanilla extract | 2 tablespoons | | |
| sifted cake flour | 7 cups | 1 pound 6 ounces | 158 grams |
| sugar | 4 cups | 1¾ pounds | 400 grams |
| baking powder | 3 tablespoons + 1¾ teaspoons | 1.8 ounces | 52.7 grams |
| salt | 2 teaspoons | 0.5 ounce | 13 grams |
| unsalted butter (must be softened) | 2⅔ cups (5¼ sticks) | 1 pound 5 ounces | 595 grams |

DARK GANACHE

| | | | |
|---|---|---|---|
| | (6 cups) | ( 3.5 pounds) | (1 kilogram 588 grams) |
| bittersweet chocolate | 9 3-ounce bars | 1 pound 11 ounces | 765 grams |
| heavy cream | 3¾ liquid cups | | |

APRICOT JEWEL GLAZE

| | | | |
|---|---|---|---|
| | (2 cups) | (24 ounces) | (680 grams) |
| apricot preserves | 3 cups | 36 ounces | 1020 grams |

*Available at cake decorating supply stores such as Wilton Enterprises (312–963-7100), Maid of Scandinavia (800-328-6722) and The Chocolate Gallery (212-675-2253). Note: Drugstore glycerine (not the variety in rose water) can be substituted.

ADVANCE PREPARATION:

The pastillage tablets, royal icing and gold calligraphy and scroll-work can all be done months ahead if desired. It is best to make the cake and ganache 2 days before serving. Make the rolled fondant the day before serving; fill and frost the cake and then cover it with the fondant. Allow it to sit for at least 2 hours before placing the decorations.

SERVES: 40

EQUIPMENT: 18-inch by 12-inch by 2-inch cake pan, greased, bottom lined with parchment or wax paper and sprayed with Baker's Joy or greased and floured; 2 large wire racks; rigid serving board (22 inches by 16 inches by ⅜-inch-thick plywood is perfect), covered with decorative laminated paper; long serrated knife; sturdy cardboard 18 inches by 12 inches to move the cake layers; sturdy cardboard 21 inches by 16 inches to transfer the fondant; long heavy rolling pin; K5 KitchenAid mixer; pastry bag, coupler, and plain decorating tubes: #7, #4, #3, #2 and #1; small artist's paintbrush; miniature Torah*, small bottle of gold paint and artist's brush for the posts

PASTILLAGE

Place the water in a small heat-proof glass cup. Sprinkle the gelatin over the top and let the gelatin soften for at least 3 minutes. Place the glass measuring cup in a small saucepan of simmering water and stir the mixture for 2 to 3 minutes, until the gelatin is completely dissolved. (This can also be done in a few seconds in a microwave on high power, stirring once or twice.) Remove it from the heat.

Combine the sugar, cornstarch and optional cream of tartar in a large bowl and make a well in the center. Add the gelatin mixture and stir with a wooden spoon until blended. Mix with lightly greased hands and knead vigorously in the bowl until most of the sugar is incorporated. Turn out onto a lightly greased smooth surface such as Formica or marble and knead until smooth and satiny. If the pastillage seems very dry, add several drops of water and knead well. If it seems too sticky, knead in more powdered sugar. The pastillage will resemble a smooth, well-shaped stone. When dropped, it should not spread.

Pastillage is easiest to work with if it has rested for at least 1 hour. It dries very quickly so it is important to cover it to prevent drying. I wrap it first in a cloth rubbed with a bit of solid white shortening, then tightly in plastic wrap (preferably Saran brand), and place it in an airtight container.

To roll out, dust the work surface heavily with cornstarch and spray the rolling pin with nonstick vegetable spray.

Divide the pastillage in half, keeping one part well covered. Roll the other into an 11-inch by 9-inch rectangle, ³⁄₁₆ inch thick. Repeat with the second half. Lay the template on top of one piece and, with a sharp knife, cut around it. Repeat with the second piece. Make sure that there is enough cornstarch underneath the pieces so that they do not stick and can still slide freely on the countertop. Allow the pastillage to dry until very hard. If it is a rainy day, it may take as long as 24 hours. (If you will need to move the pastillage, line 2 baking sheets with plastic wrap and transfer the rectangles to them *before* cutting them so as not to distort the shape.

*Available from J. Levine's, 5 West 30th, New York, New York 10001 (212-695-6888).

*(continued)*

ROYAL ICING

In a large grease-free bowl, using a hand-held electric mixer set at low speed, beat the meringue powder and water until mixed. Add the powdered sugar and beat for 30 seconds or until the sugar is moistened. Increase the speed to medium high and continue beating for 5 to 8 minutes, until the icing forms stiff, glossy peaks when the beaters are lifted slowly. (The tips of the peaks should curve slightly.)

Trace or photocopy the templates onto paper with dark ink. Tape the tracings securely to rigid pieces of cardboard or a baking sheet and lay parchment on top. Use a few pieces of tape to hold the parchment in place.

PIPE THE HEBREW LETTERS: Following the template, use a Number 1 tube to outline the letters first and then to fill in the center. Use a small clean artist's brush dipped in water to smooth the surface.

APPLY THE GOLD: Sprinkle a little gold powder or petal dust into a small cup and add a few droplets of the vodka to dilute it and produce a thick "paint." Use a small clean artist's brush to apply the silver.

PIPE THE SCROLLWORK: Use a Number 2 tube for the scrollwork. Then use a Number 3 tube and slightly soft-ened icing (stir in a small amount of water) to overpipe areas of the scroll with a feathering technique (make small closed ees).

ROLLED FONDANT

Place the water in a 2-cup heat-proof glass measuring cup. Sprinkle the gelatin over the top and let the gelatin soften for at least 3 minutes. Place the glass measuring cup in a small saucepan of simmering water and stir the mixture well for 2 to 3 minutes, until the gelatin is completely dissolved. (This can also be done in a few seconds in a microwave on high power, stirring once or twice.) Blend in the corn syrup and glycerine, then add the shortening and stir until almost com-pletely melted. Remove from the heat.

Place the powdered sugar in a large bowl and make a well in the center. Add the gelatin mixture and stir with a lightly greased wooden spoon until blended. Mix with lightly greased hands and knead vigorously in the bowl until most of the sugar is incorporated. Turn out onto a lightly greased smooth surface such as Formica or marble and knead until smooth and satiny. If the fondant seems dry, add several drops of water and knead well. If it seems too sticky, knead in more powdered sugar. The fondant will resemble a smooth, well-shaped stone. When dropped, it should spread very slightly but retain its shape. It should be malleable like clay, soft but not sticky.

Wrap the fondant tightly with plastic wrap and place in an airtight container. It will firm slightly on standing.

## CHOCOLATE CAKE

*Preheat the oven to 350°F.*

In a medium bowl, whisk together the cocoa and boiling water until smooth. Cover and cool to room temperature.

In another medium bowl, lightly combine the eggs, 1 cup of the cocoa/water mixture and the vanilla.

In a large mixing bowl, preferably with the paddle beater, combine the remaining dry ingredients and mix on low speed for 30 seconds to blend. Add the remaining cocoa/water mixture. Mix on low speed until the dry ingredients are moistened. Increase to medium speed and beat in the softened butter 2 tablespoons at a time. Raise the speed to high and beat for 1 minute to aerate and develop the cake's structure. Scrape down the sides of the bowl. Gradually add the egg mixture in 3 batches, beating for 20 seconds after each addition to incorporate the ingredients and strengthen the structure. Scrape down the sides.

Scrape the batter into the prepared pan and smooth the surface with a spatula. The pan will be about half-full. Bake 35 to 45 minutes or until a tester inserted near the center comes out clean and the cake springs back when pressed lightly in the center. *The cake should not start to shrink from the sides of the pan until it has been removed from the oven.* For even baking, turn the cake around after the first 20 minutes of baking, leaving the oven door open as briefly as possible.                                  *(continued)*

4 sides                    4 tops and bottoms

אנכי יי

לא יהיה

לא תשא

זכור את

כבד את

לא תרצח

לא תנאף

לא תגנב

לא תענה

לא תחמד

4 corners

Let the cake cool in the pan on a rack for 20 minutes. Loosen the sides with a small metal spatula and invert onto a greased wire rack. Invert the cake onto the covered serving board. Cool completely before wrapping airtight with Saran brand plastic wrap.

### DARK GANACHE

NOTE: If your food processor is smaller than the Cuisinart DLC7 (7-inch diameter, 5-inch-high work bowl), make the ganache in 2 batches.

Break the chocolate into pieces and process in the food processor until very fine. Heat the cream to the boiling point and, with the motor running, pour it through the feed tube in a steady stream. Process a few seconds until smooth. Transfer to a bowl and cool completely.* Allow to cool for several hours until of frosting consistency. Or cover tightly and store overnight at room temperature.

### APRICOT JEWEL GLAZE

In a food processor, process the preserves for a few seconds to break up the large pieces of fruit. Scrape the preserves into a small saucepan (or glass bowl if using the microwave). Over medium heat, bring the preserves to a boil, stirring often. (Or microwave on high power about 3 minutes.) Place a strainer over a small bowl and pour the hot preserves into the strainer. Using the back of a metal spoon, press as much as possible through the strainer. Return this purée to the saucepan (or bowl) and reduce to 2½ cups, about 5 minutes (about 10 minutes in the microwave). Set aside to cool to room temperature.

### ASSEMBLING THE CAKE

Use a long serrated knife to scrape off the top crust and to cut the cake in half horizontally. Use the 18-inch by 12-inch cardboard to slide between the layers and lift off the top layer. Brush half the strained apricot preserves (if too thick to spread easily, heat or add a little water) on

*Alternatively, you can grate or chop the chocolate fine, place it in a bowl and add the hot cream all at once. Cover for 3 minutes, then stir until smooth.

ROSE'S MELTING POT

the bottom layer and spread with 4 cups of the ganache. If the cake is slightly higher in the center, spread a little extra ganache around the periphery. Brush the remaining preserves on top of the ganache. Place the reserved layer carefully on top, using the cardboard to support it until you have the edges of the 2 layers lined up. Keeping the cardboard tilted up so that it doesn't touch the preserves-covered ganache, slip the top layer onto the bottom layer. Use a small serrated knife to bevel the sharp edges of the cake all around the border. Frost the cake with the remaining ganache. Don't be concerned if some of the cake crumbs lift up and get into the frosting, but try as much as possible to press the ganache down onto the cake, sliding the spatula away rather than lifting it off. Scrape off any excess ganache; you want only the thinnest possible layer to hold the fondant in place.

Clean the countertop very thoroughly and dust it heavily with cornstarch. Spray a large heavy rolling pin with non-stick vegetable shortening or rub it with white vegetable shortening.

Knead the fondant until it has softened enough to roll. Roll it into a 21-inch by 16-inch rectangle or a little larger if necessary so it can be trimmed to that size. It will be ¼ inch thick. Roll from the center out as it tends to be thicker than at the sides. Add more cornstarch as necessary to keep it from sticking to the counter. Run a long thin spatula between the fondant and the counter to make sure it has not stuck.

Dust the 21-inch by 16-inch cardboard with cornstarch and slip it under the fondant. It is helpful to have another person watch that you are lining up the fondant evenly with the cake but it is possible to do alone despite the size using this cardboard-transferring technique (thank you, Kevin Pavlina). Lower the fondant onto the cake, using the same method as for the second cake layer. Don't panic if the fondant has been placed incorrectly and a little of the cake shows. It can be stretched at least 1 inch by smoothing it into place using pressure from the palm of

*(continued)*

your hand, but, *above all, do not yield to the temptation of pulling it—it will always tear.* Smooth the fondant with the palm of your hand until it feels satiny smooth.

Place the tablets and scrollwork on the surface, leaving room for the torah in the center. When you are sure of the placement, secure with dots of royal icing. Use about 4 dots underneath the thickest area of the scrollwork. Pipe a pearl border around the tablets using a Number 4 tube. Pipe a pearl border around the base of the cake using a Number 7 tube. Hold the pastry bag at a 90-degree angle (upright to the surface), tube slightly above the surface. Squeeze with steady, even pressure. As the icing begins to build up, raise the tube with it, keeping the tip buried in the icing. When a well-rounded shape is achieved, stop the pressure as you bring the tip to the surface. Use the edge of the tip to shave off any point, moving the tip in a clockwise direction. Points can also be removed by waiting until the icing crusts slightly and pressing gently with a fingertip. If the icing is still soft, dip the fingertip in water first.

To serve, using a long sharp knife and wiping the blade between slices, cut the cake into quarters the long way (3¼-inch-wide strips) and tenths the short way (about 1¾ inches wide) to make 40 pieces.

UNDERSTANDING PASTILLAGE

The acidity of cream of tartar whitens the pastillage. Because there is no corn syrup or shortening, the pastillage does not have the pearlized quality of rolled fondant.

APRICOT JEWEL GLAZE

The apricot preserves serve two purposes: They add depth of flavor and they enable the ganache to adhere to the soft tender crumb of the cake. Without them, the ganache would lift away when you cut and serve the cake.

Reducing the apricot preserves in the microwave results in a purer flavor than does the stove-top method, which slightly caramelizes the sugar in the preserves.

# TIRAMISÙ

My neighbor Heidi, who has lived in Italy, once asked me if I had ever heard of tiramisù. "Is it a mountain peak?" I asked, captivated by the exotic and lofty sound, which made me think of Katmandu. She laughed and explained that in a way it was because it was an Italian dessert so delicious its title means "pick me up." It consists of savoiardi biscuits dipped in strong espresso, topped with a gloriously rich custard of egg yolks, mascarpone and marsala and sprinkled with cocoa. It sounded like a recipe I would want to include in *The Cake Bible*, which I was working on at the time, so I immediately called my friend and colleague Anna Teresa Callen. "Ah, Rosa," she sighed and went on in her marvelous singing Abruzzi accent, rolling every *r* that came her way, "you don't want a recipe for that; you are the Michelangelo of cakes and that is such a simple, ordinary dessert." Flattered and intimidated by the certainty of her tone, I sheepishly agreed and put it out of my mind.

It was only a matter of a few years before tiramisù became the most popular dessert in America. It even reached Japan where it was so loved they turned it into a beverage! And everywhere I went around the country, someone was sure to come up and tell me that Anna Teresa had been teaching a cooking class and told the story about my request and how she was sure I must hate her. I even read the story in a food column generating from Miami. Finally we ran into each other in a bus in New York City, and she immediately introduced me to her two nieces from Italy as "Rose Levy Beranbaum, the one I was telling you who hates me because of that tiramisù." "Anna Teresa, I could never hate you—it really doesn't matter," I tried to convince her but I knew she wouldn't believe me. Now I know that she will. I developed my own version, but because of the recent scare about salmonella in uncooked eggs I cook the egg yolks, making a zabaglione. It has never been more voluptuous and more delicious. Not only that, it is firm enough to cut into attractive portions and freezes beautifully. In fact, it's even delicious as a frozen dessert. I'm so glad I waited. Anna Teresa, I love you.

*(continued)*

| INGREDIENTS | MEASURE | WEIGHT | |
| --- | --- | --- | --- |
| | *volume* | *ounces* | *grams* |
| 8 large egg yolks | 4.5 fluid ounces | 5.25 ounces | 149 grams |
| sugar | ¾ cup + 2 tablespoons, divided | 6 ounces | 175 grams |
| sweet Marsala | ¼ liquid cup, divided | | |
| Medaglio d'Oro instant espresso powder* | ¼ cup | 0.5 ounce | 15 grams |
| water | 2 liquid cups, divided | | |
| pure vanilla extract | 2 teaspoons, divided | | |
| mascarpone, preferably imported, softened | about 2 cups | 17.5 ounces | 500 grams |
| heavy cream, cold | 1 liquid cup | | |
| savoiardi (Italian ladyfingers)† | 36 | 10.5 ounces | 300 grams |
| unsweetened cocoa | 1 tablespoon | | |

MAKE AHEAD: at least 6 hours or up to 3 months
SERVES: 12

EQUIPMENT: 13-inch by 9-inch by 2-inch 3-quart baking dish

Place a medium mixing bowl in the refrigerator to chill for the whipped cream. Have ready near the range a rubber scraper and medium bowl.

In a large unlined copper bowl or the upper container of a double boiler, whisk together the egg yolks, ¼ cup plus 2 tablespoons of the sugar and 3 tablespoons of the Marsala. If using the copper bowl, set it directly on the burner over low heat. If using the double boiler, place the upper container over the lower one, filled with simmering water that does not touch the bottom of the upper container. Whisk constantly until the mixture approximately triples in volume and begins to thicken, 3 to 5 minutes. Be careful not too overcook the yolks or they will scramble!

Immediately scrape the mixture into the bowl by the range. Cover with plastic wrap (preferably Saran brand) and refrigerate for at least 30 minutes or until completely cool.

*Meanwhile, prepare the espresso syrup:* In a small saucepan, stir together the espresso, ¼ cup plus 2 tablespoons of the

*Available in many supermarkets; most will place a special order if it is not regularly stocked.
†Homemade ladyfingers can be used if desired but are too fragile to dip and should instead be brushed with the espresso syrup.

ROSE'S MELTING POT

sugar and 1 cup of the water. Bring to a boil, stirring constantly to dissolve the espresso and sugar. Remove it from the heat and add the remaining 1 cup water, 1 teaspoon of the vanilla and the remaining 1 tablespoon of Marsala. Transfer the syrup to a shallow pan and set it aside.

In a large mixer bowl, preferably with the whisk beater, beat the mascarpone on low speed for about 10 seconds or until creamy. Raise the speed slightly and gradually beat in the cooled egg yolk mixture until completely incorporated, scraping the sides of the bowl once or twice with a rubber spatula. Set aside.

In the chilled mixing bowl, combine the heavy cream and the remaining 2 tablespoons of sugar. Beat until the cream begins to thicken. Add the remaining 1 teaspoon of vanilla extract and beat just until stiff peaks form when the beater is raised slowly.

With a large rubber spatula, fold the whipped cream into the mascarpone mixture.

Dip each ladyfinger very quickly in the espresso syrup, dipping first one side, then the other, taking no longer than a second a side. After each ladyfinger is dipped, set it in the large rectangular serving pan, forming 3 rows of 6 fingers for the first layer. If necessary, press the biscuits slightly to get them to fit into the pan. Spread half (3 cups) of the mascarpone mixture evenly over the fingers. Arrange a second layer of dipped ladyfingers on top. (You will have ½ to ¾ cup of leftover espresso syrup, which can be discarded.) Pour the remaining mascarpone mixture over the top and use a spatula to spread it evenly.

Place the cocoa in a fine strainer, held over the tiramisu, and sprinkle it lightly over the surface, using a small spoon to stir the cocoa in the strainer. I prefer a light sprinkle but more cocoa can be added if a thicker coat is desired.

Cover tightly with plastic wrap and refrigerate for at least 6 hours or up to 3 days.

To serve, use a large serving spoon or pancake turner to scoop out portions. For 12 servings, use a knife to score it in thirds the long way and quarters the short way.

(continued)

KEEPS: At least 3 days refrigerated, 3 months frozen.

VARIATION: *Chocolate Snowflake Topping*

Bittersweet chocolate is a lovely and sweeter alternative to the bitter cocoa dusting but it must be grated so finely it melts on the tongue to maintain the harmonious creaminess of the dessert. You will need to grate 1 ounce (28 grams) chocolate, for about ⅓ cup grated. The chocolate needs to be as hard as possible to grate finely so it must not be at all warm. If you have a large block of chocolate, use a melon baller to scrape the chocolate, making short, light strokes that do not cut too deeply into the chocolate. Alternatively, use the coarse holes on a cheese grater to grate the edge of a chocolate bar. Hold the chocolate with a paper towel so that your fingers don't melt the chocolate. Allow the flakes to fall onto a small cool baking sheet. Place the sheet inside a large plastic bag and shake the flakes into the bag. Avoid touching them because they melt very easily. Use a large spoon to lift the chocolate flakes and sprinkle them on the surface of the tiramisù.

UNDERSTANDING

This filling is actually very similar to Bavarian cream. The essential difference is that about two thirds the volume of thick, slightly tangy mascarpone, which is a triple cream cheese, replaces the usual milk so no gelatin is required to thicken it.

I like to flavor each component so that it would be delicious on its own and also blend perfectly with the others. For example, I sweetened the espresso syrup to the point that the coffee is just bitter enough to temper the sweetness of the savoiardi. The dusting of bitter cocoa, however, is so fine that it absorbs immediately into the whole.

# SPANISH CREAMY CARAMEL FLAN (Crème Caramel)

*Spanish Paella Party*
Raspberry Peach Sangria
Party Paella
Lettuce and Tomato Salad
    with California Heirloom
    Salad Dressing
Spanish Creamy Caramel
    Flan

Flan, with its creamy, custardy, comforting texture and burnt sugar flavor is, for Elliott and me, the perfect finale for a grand paella dinner (page 89). When we order it in restaurants, we always hold our breath until it comes. We don't have it often, so when we do, we want it to be just right. The waiter probably wonders why we are staring at this simple dessert with such desperate hopefulness. It's because we can tell its texture as it is being brought to the table. If it doesn't jiggle provocatively, it will be rubbery, bounce-off-the-wall in texture and our hearts fall. Also, we want the caramel to be deeply flavored but not burnt.

Flan could be the one dish on which Elliott and I are in total agreement. Unfortunately, I worked so long and hard on perfecting this recipe, making at least two flans a day during our week-long vacation last summer, that Elliott may just never want to taste flan again—even though I have at last come up with this final winner. The main breakthrough occurred when my dear friend Helen Schull came to visit in the middle of the flan marathon. It was she who suggested the evaporated milk, which gives the perfectly firm yet creamy texture characteristic of the Spanish flan.

CARAMEL

In the small heavy saucepan, stir together the sugar and water until the sugar is completely moistened. Heat, stirring constantly, until the sugar dissolves and the syrup is

*(continued)*

---

*Spanish Flan.* The Spanish very rarely drink milk as a beverage, except occasionally in rural areas. However, they consume milk in its other forms such as cheeses and dairy desserts. One of the most common of these sweets is flan, which can be made with either evaporated or fresh milk. This custard delight is so popular that it is invariably part of the dessert course in Spain even when other pastries and fruits are served. "Flan" comes from the Old French "flaon," itself a derivative of the Latin "flado" or "flat cake." The Spanish usually make flan in molds. After setting, the flan is removed, chilled and served cold, often with a caramel or fruit topping. In Spain, the center of social activity is not the home. Guests and friends are invited to eat out at restaurants, congregate at local coffeehouses for "tertulia" (leisurely conversation) or spend an evening "chateo" (strolling from bar to bar and enjoying the local company). Obviously, pastries like flan are an important part of such a culture where leisure and entertainment revolve around food and drink.

---

| INGREDIENTS | MEASURE | WEIGHT | |
| --- | --- | --- | --- |
| | *volume* | *ounces* | *grams* |

**CARAMEL**

| INGREDIENTS | MEASURE | WEIGHT | |
| --- | --- | --- | --- |
| sugar | ¾ cup | 5.25 ounces | 150 grams |
| water | ¼ liquid cup | | |

| | | | |
| --- | --- | --- | --- |
| evaporated milk | (1 ½ liquid cups/ 1 12-ounce can) | 13.3 ounces | 377 grams |
| milk | 2 liquid cups | | |
| ¼ Tahitian vanilla bean,* split lengthwise | | | |
| ½ Madagascar vanilla bean, split lengthwise | | | |
| 10 large egg yolks | ¾ liquid cup | 6.5 ounces | 186 grams |
| sugar | ½ cup | 3.5 ounces | 100 grams |
| salt | ¼ teaspoon | | |
| pure vanilla extract | 1 teaspoon | | |

MAKE AHEAD: at least 4 hours
PREHEAT THE OVEN TO: 325°F.
BAKING TIME: 45 to 55 minutes
SERVES: 8

EQUIPMENT: eight 6-ounce custard cups, preferably ceramic, lightly sprayed with nonstick vegetable shortening or greased; roasting pan or baking pan large enough to hold the cups and at least 2 inches deep, lined with a piece of parchment; small heavy saucepan, ideally with a nonstick lining; heat-proof glass measure, sprayed with nonstick vegetable spray or greased; metal measuring tablespoon, sprayed with nonstick vegetable spray or greased

bubbling. Stop stirring completely and allow it to boil undisturbed until it turns a deep amber (350°F. to 370°F. on a candy thermometer). Immediately remove the pan from the heat and pour the caramel into the glass measure to stop the cooking. Quickly pour scant tablespoons of caramel into each custard cup and roll the caramel around the sides to coat them. If the caramel should become to thick to pour, you can place it in the microwave on high power for a few seconds to reliquify it.

*Preheat the oven to 325°F. 15 minutes before baking.*

Place the custard cups on top of the parchment in the roasting pan.

In a medium saucepan (or a 4-cup heat-proof glass measure if using a microwave on high power), heat the evaporated and whole milk with the vanilla beans just until very hot. Do not boil. Remove from the heat.

*Available in specialty food stores such as Dean & DeLuca (800-227-7714). Or use a total of 1 Madagascar vanilla bean. If vanilla beans are unavailable, increase the vanilla extract to 1½ teaspoons.

In a medium bowl, with a wooden spoon, stir together the yolks, sugar and salt until blended. Remove the vanilla beans from the milk, reserving them, and gradually stir the milk into the egg mixture, stirring slowly to prevent bubbles. Strain the mixture through a fine strainer into a bowl, preferably with a pouring spout.

With a sharp knife, scrape the vanilla seeds into the mixture. Stir gently until the seeds separate. Rinse the strainer and strain the mixture again, pressing well with the back of a spoon to break up any clumps of vanilla seeds and to press them through. Stir in the vanilla extract. (You will have 4⅓ cups.)

Pour a full ½ cup of the custard into each custard cup, on top of the caramel. Pour enough hot tap water around the cups to come halfway up their sides.

Bake for 45 to 55 minutes or until a knife inserted into the center comes out clean. (A thermometer will read 160°F.)

Remove the custard cups from the hot water bath and place them on a rack to cool. When *completely* cool, cover each tightly with plastic wrap (preferably Saran brand). Refrigerate for at least 4 hours or up to 5 days. The longer the flan sits, the more the caramel dissolves. If liquid should form on the surface, blot it gently with paper towels.

To unmold, run a small metal spatula around the sides of each custard. Place a flat serving plate on top and invert the custard onto the serving plate. Lift off the custard cup. The caramel will flow down the sides of the custard.

POINTERS
FOR SUCCESS

• To prevent crystallization, do not allow any sugar crystals to get on the sides of the pan and be sure to moisten all the sugar with the water. Stop stirring entirely as soon as it comes to a boil.
• If using a thermometer, be sure to rinse it and dry it if removing and reinserting in the syrup. If any sugar remains on the thermometer, it will cause crystallization.

*(continued)*

- Allow the custards to cool completely before covering or they might become slightly watery. Cover tightly to prevent absorption of other aromas.
- If making only half the recipe, start checking for doneness after 35 minutes.

UNDERSTANDING

The higher the temperature of the caramel, the darker the color and the deeper the flavor. Too high, however, and there will be a burned flavor. If you do not have an accurate thermometer,* or it is not immersed adequately, it may read 370°F. when the temperature of the caramel is actually much higher and it will begin to burn. I usually bring my caramel up to 380°F. but then have to work quickly to get it out of the pan before it begins to burn. Alternatively, you can gauge the color by sight. Use a white porcelain spoon to stir or place a drop of the caramel on a white plate. You must be sure to rinse off any utensil that has caramel or sugar syrup on it before reinserting it into the caramel or it will crystallize.

The parchment in the water bath keeps the bottoms of the custard cups from coming into direct contact with the hot pan. The water surrounding them equalizes the temperature and creates a moist environment.

The milk is heated to extract the maximum flavor from the vanilla beans. If not using the vanilla beans, you can add the milk without heating it, but strain the mixture for the smoothest texture and bake the custards for an extra 10 to 15 minutes.

Egg yolks make a more flavorful and more tender, yet firmer, custard than do whole eggs.

Fresh farm eggs produce a softer custard, probably due to their higher water content.

When the knife comes out clean, the custard has reached 160°F., the point at which the amylase (an enzyme) in the yolks will not water out on standing.

*The Cordon Rose candy thermometer is available through Dean & DeLuca (800-227-7714) and La Cuisine (800-521-1176).

ROSE'S MELTING POT

# HOT FUDGE SUNDAE

There is probably no dessert in the world more delicious than the classic American hot fudge sundae, so just imagine raising it to its well-deserved heights by making your own heavenly vanilla ice cream, hot fudge using the best-quality chocolate, and home-brandied cherries. Desserts get fancier, but never ever better!

| INGREDIENTS | MEASURE<br>*volume* | WEIGHT<br>*ounces/pounds* | *grams/kilograms* |
|---|---|---|---|
| TRIPLE VANILLA LOVER'S ICE CREAM | (5 to 6 cups, depending on the ice cream maker) | (2¾ pounds) | (1 kilogram 247 grams) |
| 8 large egg yolks | 4.5 fluid ounces | 5.25 ounces | 150 grams |
| sugar | ¾ cup | 5.25 ounces | 150 grams |
| salt | a pinch | | |
| heavy cream | 3 liquid cups | | |
| milk | 1 liquid cup | | |
| 1 Tahitian vanilla bean,* split lengthwise | | | |
| 1 Madagascar vanilla bean, split lengthwise | | | |
| pure vanilla extract | 2 teaspoons | | |
| OPTIONAL: vodka | 2 tablespoons | | |

*Available in specialty food stores such as Dean & DeLuca (800-227-7714). If Tahitian vanilla beans are unavailable, use a total of 3 ordinary vanilla beans.

(*continued*)

---

*Hot Fudge Sundae.* While the Venetians are credited with the development of sorbets and ice cream, America is the undisputed home of the Ice Cream Sundae. Invented in the 1890s in Evanston, Illinois, it was all the rage by the turn of the century. However, its discovery was something of an accident. Regional laws used to prohibit the sale of soda water—the central ingredient in ice cream sodas—on Sundays. Rather than give up ice cream altogether, local folks simply went without soda, christening this new refreshing delight the "Sunday" or the "Soda-less Soda." The rather peculiar "ae" ending was probably a substitution encouraged by community religious leaders who felt that naming a dessert after the Sabbath was slightly disrespectful. By 1900, soda fountain supply salesmen carried samplers of tulip-shaped "Sundae Specials" from town to town throughout America's heartland.

---

## Brandied Cherries*

| | | | |
|---|---|---|---|
| frozen dark sweet cherries, without sugar | 4 cups (2 12-ounce bags) | 24 ounces | 681 grams |
| sugar | ½ cup | 3.5 ounces | 100 grams |
| cognac | ¼ liquid cup, or more as necessary | | |

## Hot Fudge

| | | | |
|---|---|---|---|
| | (2 cups) | (23 ounces) | (652 grams) |
| chocolate, preferably Lindt Excellence or Valrhona extra bittersweet† | 1½ 3-ounce bars | 4.5 ounces | 129 grams |
| unsweetened cocoa (Dutch-processed) | ¼ cup + 2 tablespoons | 1.5 ounces | 36 grams |
| water | 1 liquid cup | | |
| unsalted butter | 9 tablespoons | 4.5 ounces | 129 grams |
| sugar | 1 cup | 7 ounces | 200 grams |
| corn syrup | 3 fluid ounces (6 tablespoons) | 4.5 ounces | 129 grams |
| salt | ⅛ teaspoon | | |
| pure vanilla extract | 1½ teaspoons | | |

## Whipped Cream (optional)

| | | | |
|---|---|---|---|
| heavy cream | 1 liquid cup | | |
| sugar | 1 tablespoon | 0.5 ounce | 13 grams |
| pure vanilla extract | ¼ teaspoon | | |

Make ahead: ice cream, at least 8 hours; brandied cherries, at least 14 hours
Serves: 8

## Triple Vanilla Lover's Ice Cream

Have a fine strainer suspended over a medium mixing bowl ready near the range.

In a medium heavy noncorrodible saucepan, stir together the yolks, sugar and salt until well blended, using a wooden spoon.

In a small saucepan (or a heat-proof glass measure if using a microwave on high power), scald the cream and milk with the vanilla beans.‡ Stir a few tablespoons into the yolk mixture; then gradually add the remainder, stirring constantly.

*Or substitute 2 cups griottines in brandy, which are available from La Cuisine (800-521-1176).
†Available at Williams-Sonoma (800-541-2233).
‡Heat just to the point when small bubbles appear around the edges.

Heat the mixture to just below the boiling point (170°F. to 180°F.). Steam will begin to appear and the mixture will be slightly thicker than heavy cream. A finger run across the back of a spoon dipped in the mixture will leave a well-defined track. Immediately remove it from the heat and pour the custard into the strainer, scraping up the thickened cream that has settled on the bottom of the pan. Cool slightly, then remove the vanilla beans and scrape the seeds into the custard. Stir until the seeds separate. Return the pods to the custard until ready to freeze.

Cool the custard in an ice-water bath or the refrigerator until cold, at least 2 hours or overnight.

Stir in the vanilla and the optional vodka. Freeze in an ice cream maker. Allow the ice cream to ripen for at least 4 hours in the freezer, or until firm, before serving. (If serving without the hot fudge, and if it has been held longer and is very hard, allow it to sit refrigerated or at room temperature until softened and creamy.)

STORE: Ice cream has the best texture within 3 days of freezing but with the vodka will maintain its texture for up to a week.

BRANDIED CHERRIES

Empty the frozen cherries into a large colander suspended over a bowl, and allow them to defrost. (This will take several hours.)

Add enough water to the drained cherry juice to equal 1 cup. Empty it into a medium saucepan and add the sugar. Bring the mixture to a boil, stirring constantly. Add the cherries and simmer, covered, 1 minute. Remove the pan from the heat and transfer the cherries with a slotted spoon to a pint jar. Add the cognac.

Boil the syrup until reduced to ¼ cup and pour it over the cherries. Cover tightly and swirl to mix. (If you are planning to store the cherries for longer than 3 months, add enough cognac to reach almost to the top of the jar.) Cool on a rack. Let sit for 14 hours before serving. Refrigerate if not serving within 3 days.

(continued)

## Hot Fudge

In a medium-size heavy saucepan (ideally with a nonstick lining) melt the chocolate and cocoa with the water, stirring constantly. Add the butter, sugar, corn syrup and salt. Simmer, stirring, until the sugar has completely dissolved. Stop stirring and cook at a moderate boil for about 8 minutes or until the mixture thickens and reduces to 2 cups. (Use a greased heat-proof glass measuring cup to measure the mixture.) Swirl the mixture in the pan occasionally but do not stir.

Cool slightly and add the vanilla. Keep warm or reheat in a water bath or microwave, stirring gently.

## Optional Whipped Cream

In a large mixing bowl, combine the heavy cream, sugar and vanilla and refrigerate for at least 15 minutes. (Chill the beater alongside the bowl.)

Beat only until soft peaks form or the cream mounds softly when dropped from a spoon.

To serve, scoop the ice cream into sundae glasses or serving bowls. Pass the griottines or brandied cherries in a decorative bowl, along with their syrup. Pass the hot fudge in a pitcher and the whipped cream, if desired, in a bowl. Alternatively, scoop ¾ cup ice cream into each bowl, top with ¼ cup of cherries, including some of the brandy, and ¼ cup of the fudge. Spoon on a dollop of whipped cream if desired.

POINTERS FOR SUCCESS

## Triple Vanilla Lover's Ice Cream

- Don't use a whisk to stir if not using an accurate thermometer because the foam makes it difficult to see when the mixture is getting close to boiling. Do not heat above 180°F. or the custard will curdle. If it is overheated and *slight* curdling does take place, pour instantly into a blender and blend until smooth before straining.
- Do not add more than the recommended amount of vodka or ice cream will not freeze.

286

- Do not soften the ice cream before serving as the hot fudge will accomplish this!

BRANDIED CHERRIES

- To brandy fresh cherries, simmer 1 cup of pitted cherries in ¾ cup of water in a covered saucepan for 10 minutes or until easily pierced with a cake tester. Remove the cherries with a slotted spoon to a pint jar and add the ¼ cup of cognac. Add the ½ cup of sugar to the liquid in the pan and bring to a boil, stirring constantly. Reduce to between ¼ and ⅓ cup. Pour it over the cherries. Cover tightly and swirl to mix. Add enough cognac to reach almost to the top of the jar. (The recipe can be increased as desired.)

HOT FUDGE

- Avoid stirring as it will cause the sugar to crystallize.
- A microwave is great for making the hot fudge but an 8-cup microwave-safe bowl is needed as the fudge bubbles up while cooking.

UNDERSTANDING TRIPLE VANILLA LOVER'S ICE CREAM

The custard mixture must be heated adequately (to at least 160°F.) to thicken and prevent thinning out on setting, but for a silky smooth sauce that does not curdle, the mixture must not be allowed to boil.

The boiling point of water is 212°F. but the ingredients in the custard lower the boiling point.

The vodka acts as antifreeze, preventing the formation of large ice crystals.

# CHOCOLATE POTS DE CRÈME (poh duh krehm)

This classic French dessert is one of the most satisfying and glorious ways to enjoy chocolate in the world while being one of the simplest recipes to prepare. Despite its charms, it is not nearly as well known as its fluffier cousin, chocolate mousse. So my offering to my friend Marcel Desaulniers's delightful collection of chocolate recipes, *Death by Chocolate*, was this perfectly bittersweet, dense, silken chocolate bliss. He, in return, perfected it by using a special technique that cooks the egg, making it safe to eat, and at the same time smoothens the texture, making it more luxurious.

This dessert is so perfect for the chocolate lover it would be appropriate as part of any dinner from casual to ultraformal. To dress it up to its ultimate, start a collection of pots de crème pots.

| INGREDIENTS | MEASURE | WEIGHT | |
| --- | --- | --- | --- |
| | *volume* | *ounces* | *grams* |
| heavy cream | 1 liquid cup | | |
| milk | ¾ liquid cup | | |
| bittersweet or semisweet chocolate, preferably Lindt | 4 3-ounce bars | 12 ounces | 340 grams |
| 6 large egg yolks | 7 tablespoons | 4 ounces | 112 grams |
| OPTIONAL: Kahlúa | 1 tablespoon | | |
| OPTIONAL: candied violets, for decoration | 8 small candied violets or broken pieces | | |

MAKE AHEAD: at least 6 hours or up to 2 days
SERVES: 8

EQUIPMENT: 8 pots de crème cups or custard cups

In a small saucepan, scald* the cream and milk.

While the cream mixture is heating, break the chocolate into pieces and place it in the upper container of a large double boiler set over an inch of very hot, not simmering, water. Stir often until melted. Whisk in the yolks. The mixture will thicken.

Gradually pour the hot cream mixture into the chocolate mixture, whisking constantly. Increase the heat so that the

*Heat just to the point when small bubbles form around the edge.

water in the bottom section of the double boiler simmers and, whisking constantly, cook for about 3½ to 4 minutes or until an accurate thermometer* reads 160°F. Remove at once from the heat and transfer to a metal bowl. Add the optional Kahlúa.

Set the bowl over a larger bowl containing ice water and cool, stirring constantly with a rubber spatula, for 4 to 5 minutes or until room temperature. (To prevent bubbles, do not whisk.)

Divide the mixture among the pots de crème forms or custard cups. Cover with plastic wrap and refrigerate for at least 6 hours or up to 2 days.

Just before serving, garnish if desired with small whole or bits of candied violets.

POINTERS
FOR SUCCESS

• Use my favorite (Lindt) or your favorite bittersweet or semisweet chocolate as this is the taste you will achieve in the finished recipe.
• The hot cream/milk mixture is added to the yolks and then heated to 160°F. to prevent the formation of bacteria in the yolks. It also makes the mixture more creamy. Be sure to add the hot mixture slowly at first to prevent the yolks from curdling, though the risk is not as great as usual since they are cushioned by the melted chocolate.
• Cover the completed pots de crème with Saran brand plastic wrap, which is airtight, to prevent the absorption of any off taste from other food stored in the refrigerator.

*The Cordon Rose candy thermometer is available through Dean & DeLuca (800-227-7714) and La Cuisine (800-521-1176).

# Green Tea Ice Cream

This is the perfect, much sought-after accompaniment to Oriental dinners such as Japanese Chirashi Sushi (page 101). The near-lyrical quality of the green tea harmonizes perfectly with Oriental flavors but is so pleasing it would go well as part of any dinner menu. The optional vodka is flavorless but serves to keep the ice cream velvety even after a week in the freezer.

| INGREDIENTS room temperature | MEASURE volume | WEIGHT ounces | grams |
|---|---|---|---|
| 8 large egg yolks | 4.5 fluid ounces | 5.25 ounces | 150 grams |
| sugar | ¾ cup | 5.25 ounces | 150 grams |
| salt | a pinch | | |
| heavy cream | 3 liquid cups | | |
| milk | 1 liquid cup | | |
| Japanese green tea (gold *sencha*)* | 2 tablespoons + 2 teaspoons | 0.4 ounce | 12 grams |
| OPTIONAL: liquid green food color | 4 to 5 drops | | |
| OPTIONAL: vodka | 2 tablespoons | | |

MAKES: 5 to 6 cups
(depending on ice cream maker)

Have a fine strainer ready near the range, suspended over a medium mixing bowl.

In a medium-size heavy noncorrodible saucepan, stir together the yolks, sugar and salt until well blended, using a wooden spoon.

In another small saucepan (or a heat-proof glass measure if using a microwave on high power), heat the cream and milk to the boiling point. Stir a few tablespoons into the yolk mixture; then gradually add the remainder, stirring constantly.

*Available in Eastern and Korean food stores. For a more subtle effect, Japanese powdered green tea, available by mail order from Katagiri & Company (224 East 59th Street, New York, New York 10022; 212-755-3566), can be substituted in equal volume. Stir it into the hot strained egg mixture. When cool, strain again. The little green specks will dissolve during freezing. You will need to increase the food color to 8 drops to attain the most attractive pale green hue.

*(continued)*

Heat the mixture to just before the boiling point (170°F. to 180°F.). Steam will begin to appear and the mixture will be slightly thicker than heavy cream. A finger run across the back of a spoon dipped in the mixture will leave a well-defined track. Immediately remove it from the heat and pour it into the strainer, scraping up the thickened cream that has settled on the bottom of the pan. Stir in the green tea leaves and allow the mixture to steep for 30 minutes. Strain out and discard the leaves.

Cool in an ice-water bath or the refrigerator until cold. Stir in the optional food color and vodka. Freeze in an ice cream maker. Allow the ice cream to ripen for at least 2 hours in the freezer before serving. If it has been held longer and is very hard, allow it to sit refrigerated or at room temperature until softened and creamy.

STORE: Ice cream has the best texture within 3 days of freezing but with the vodka will maintain its texture for up to a week.

POINTERS
FOR SUCCESS

• Don't use a whisk to stir if not using an accurate thermometer because the foam makes it difficult to see when the mixture is getting close to boiling.
• Do not heat above 180°F., or the custard mixture will curdle. If it is overheated and *slight* curdling does take place, pour instantly into a blender and blend until smooth before straining.
• Do not add more than the recommended amount of vodka, or the ice cream will not freeze.

ROSE'S MELTING POT

# GREEN TEA PINE NEEDLES

These green tea–scented fragile-crisp meringues are exceptionally delicate and delicious. They make a lovely accompaniment to Green Tea Ice Cream.

| INGREDIENTS | MEASURE | WEIGHT | |
| room temperature | volume | ounces | grams |
| --- | --- | --- | --- |
| superfine sugar* | ¼ cup | 1.75 ounces | 50 grams |
| powdered green tea† | 2 teaspoons | | |
| 2 large egg whites | ¼ liquid cup | 2 ounces | 60 grams |
| cream of tartar | ¼ teaspoon | | |

PREHEAT THE OVEN TO: 200°F.
BAKING TIME: 30 minutes
MAKES: about 8 dozen cookies

EQUIPMENT: baking sheet, lined with nonstick liner‡ or foil, pastry bag fitted with a Number 3 decorating tube, small clean artist's paintbrush

*Preheat the oven to 200°F.*

Process or whisk together the sugar and green tea until well combined.

In a mixing bowl, beat the whites until frothy. Add the cream of tartar and beat at medium speed while gradually adding 1 tablespoon of the sugar mixture. When soft peaks form when the beater is raised, gradually add 1 tablespoon more of the sugar and increase the speed to high. When stiff peaks form when the beater is raised slowly, gradually beat in the remaining sugar and beat until stiff and glossy.

Fill the pastry bag no more than two-thirds full with the meringue mixture. Hold the bag at a 45 degree angle with the tube slightly above the baking sheet. Each pine needle consists of 2 sticks joined at the top, but the shapes can vary. Pipe some straight in an upside-down V and others crossing 1 stick over the other, joining them at the top. Use a paintbrush dipped in water to smooth the joining.

*Superfine sugar is as fine as sand. If you have trouble finding it, make your own by processing regular granulated sugar for a few minutes in a food processor.
†Available at Eastern food stores and by mail order from Katagiri & Company, 224 East 59th Street, New York, New York 10022 (212-755-3566).
‡Nonstick liners work the best for this very fragile meringue. Liners are available through mail order from European Home Products, P.O. Box 2524, Waterbury, Connecticut 06723 (203-866-9683; outside Connecticut, 800-225-0760).

*(continued)*

Bake 30 minutes or until dry but not starting to color. Remove the meringue pine needles from the baking sheet with a small angled spatula. They are quite fragile.

For a still more realistic effect, you can dip the joined end into melted dark chocolate, but I prefer the taste when unadorned.

- All utensils and egg whites must be free of grease.
- *Avoid preparing meringues on humid days.*
- Do not use parchment or greased and floured baking sheets because the meringues may stick to them.
- To prevent cracking, do not open the oven door during the first three quarters of cooking time.

# FRUIT JEWEL TARTS

At The City Baker in New York City, these strawberry tartlets appear as jewels contained in a bittersweet dark chocolate crust which is crisp, tender and buttery— the best chocolate pastry I have ever tasted. It is complemented by a perfectly smooth, gently sweetened white chocolate cream filling. This versatile dough can be used to line any shape tart or tartlet molds. It is a delicate, slightly sticky dough, but if you follow the instructions it is all but foolproof.

Just about any fruit would be delicious in this bittersweet tartlet but the chef, Maury Rubin, crowns his with tiny perfectly shaped strawberries that have more flavor than any I can remember since many Junes ago, when I discovered with great joy, in the middle of a dark Vermont night, that my sleeping bag was resting on a bed of wild strawberries! Maury gets his berries from a company called Mt. Sweets, in Roscoe, New York, which sells produce at the Green Market at Union Square across the street from his bakery. They are called "Day Neutrals" because they were developed by a fortuitous cross between wild strawberries and June strawberries and are constantly blossom-
*(continued)*

ing despite the day's length. This makes them available from June through October. Raspberries or cherries would also be a great substitute. This is a perfect dessert for an important event such as a wedding or bar mitzvah, for those who prefer pastry to cake.

| INGREDIENTS | MEASURE<br>*volume* | WEIGHT<br>*ounces* | *grams* |
|---|---|---|---|
| **BITTERSWEET CHOCOLATE COOKIE DOUGH** | | | |
| unsalted butter | 8 tablespoons | 4 ounces | 113 grams |
| unbleached all-purpose flour | 1 cup (measured by dip and sweep method) | 5 ounces | 145 grams |
| unsweetened cocoa, preferably Dutch-processed | 2 tablespoons | 0.5 ounce | 12 grams |
| powdered sugar | ¼ cup + 2 tablespoons | 1.5 ounces | 43 grams |
| lightly beaten egg (less than 1 egg) | 2 tablespoons | | |
| **DUSTING MIXTURE** | | | |
| unbleached all-purpose flour | 3 tablespoons | 1 ounce | 27 grams |
| unsweetened cocoa, preferably Dutch-processed | 3 tablespoons | 0.66 ounce | 18 grams |
| **WHITE CHOCOLATE GANACHE** | (2⅔ cups) | | |
| white chocolate made with cocoa butter (preferably Lindt's confectionery bar), finely chopped | 1⅓ 3-ounce bars | 4 ounces | 113 grams |
| heavy cream | 2 liquid cups, divided | | |
| **FRUIT TOPPING** | | | |
| small strawberries, raspberries or other fruit of your choice | 3 to 4 cups | | |

PREHEAT THE OVEN TO: 375°F.
BAKING TIME: 10 to 13 minutes
MAKES: 8 4-inch by 1-inch deep
tartlets

EQUIPMENT: cookie sheet large
enough to hold eight 4-inch by
1-inch flan rings* with at least 1
inch of space between each

## BITTERSWEET CHOCOLATE COOKIE DOUGH

*Prepare the dough several hours or up to 1 day ahead (baked pastry will keep for 3 days at room temperature).*

Allow the butter to sit at room temperature for about 15 minutes or until it has softened slightly but is still cold. Cut the butter into 1-inch pieces.

Sift together the flour and cocoa (or process in a food processor until the cocoa has no lumps).

In an electric mixer bowl, beat the butter with the sugar until the sugar is no longer visible. The mixture will be clumpy. Add the egg and beat for about 30 seconds or until most of it is mixed in. On low speed, beat in half the flour/cocoa mixture. As soon as it is moistened, beat in the remaining flour mixture just until it is moistened but is still crumbly.

Scrape the dough onto a piece of plastic wrap and, using the plastic wrap, knead it until it holds together and is uniform in color. Press it into a flat disc and refrigerate for at least 20 minutes or overnight.

Whisk together the flour and cocoa dusting mixture. Working with half the dough at a time,[†] sprinkle it well on both sides with the flour/cocoa mixture and roll it ⅛ inch thick (about 11 inches by 7 inches) between 2 sheets of plastic wrap. Flip it over from time to time, peel off the plastic wrap and sprinkle with the flour/cocoa mixture. If the dough should stick, slip it onto a cookie sheet and refrigerate it until firm enough to peel off the plastic wrap.

Cut out four 5½-inch circles of dough. Use the plastic wrap to lift up a dough circle, invert it on to your hand and peel off the wrap. Place the dough circle evenly onto a flan ring and, without stretching it, fit the bottom into the ring. Press the sides against the sides of the ring, patching if any breaks occur. Use a small sharp knife to trim the excess level with the ring. Repeat with the remaining dough, rerolling scraps.

*Seven fluted tart molds measuring 4¾ inches across at their widest part can be substituted. Roll the dough so you can cut 6-inch circles.
†Alternatively, you can divide the dough into 8 equal pieces, (7 if using the fluted tart molds), flattening each into a thick disc and rolling each piece to the correct size.

*(continued)*

Cover the dough-filled rings with plastic wrap and refrigerate for at least 1 hour or overnight before baking.

*Preheat the oven to 375°F.*

Cut out eight 5½-inch circles of foil. Line each tartlet with a foil circle and fill each with pennies or aluminum pie weights.

Bake the tartlets shells for 10 minutes. Lift out the foil with the weights and continue baking for 2 to 3 minutes or until dough is dry but still soft to the touch and starts to come away from the sides of the rings.

Place the cookie sheet on a rack to cool. After 5 minutes, lift off the flan rings. Use a pancake turner to lift each tartlet from the cookie sheet onto a rack and cool completely.

KEEPS: In an airtight container, up to 3 days at room temperature or up to 3 months frozen.

## WHITE CHOCOLATE GANACHE

Refrigerate a mixing bowl and beater for at least 15 minutes.

In a double boiler over hot, not simmering, water (do not allow the bottom of the pan to touch the water) or microwave oven on high power, melt the chocolate with ⅓ cup of the heavy cream (stirring every 10 seconds if using the microwave). Remove from the heat before the chocolate is fully melted and stir until melted. Set aside until no longer warm. (You can also melt the chocolate by breaking it into small pieces and placing it in a small bowl. Scald* the ⅓ cup of cream and pour it on top. Cover the bowl with foil and allow it to sit for 3 minutes. Stir until smooth.)

In the chilled bowl, beat the remaining 1⅔ cups of cream until traces of beater marks just begin to show distinctly. Add the white chocolate mixture and beat just until stiff peaks form when the beater is raised slowly.

*Heat just to the point when small bubbles appear around the edge.

KEEPS: 1 day at room temperature, 3 days refrigerated, 2 months frozen.

FRUIT TOPPING

Wash the berries and hull if using strawberries. Dry on paper towels.

ASSEMBLING THE TARTLETS

Evenly spread ⅓ cup (a generous ⅓ cup if using tartlet shells) of the white chocolate filling in each tartlet shell. It will come almost to the top. Decoratively place the berries on top. Use a pancake turner to lift the tartlets onto a serving platter. If the day is cool, leave the tartlets at room temperature; otherwise refrigerate them uncovered until shortly before serving time.

NOTE: Dark chocolate ganache, drizzled on top of the berries, makes an attractive and delicious addition.

POINTERS
FOR SUCCESS

• Copper pennies make the ideal pastry weights as they are better conductors than the aluminum pie weights sold for the purpose and, oddly enough, less expensive! Dried beans can also be used.
• Don't overbake the chocolate dough or it will have a burnt flavor.

# ROSY CRAN-RASPBERRY BUTTER BARS

These buttery almond shortbread cookies, topped with a satiny layer of tart cran-raspberry curd, dissolve in the mouth as if they were lighter than air. Serve them anytime of year, but especially at holiday time—for example, after Rare Prime Ribs of Beef (page 158) for Christmas.

| INGREDIENTS | MEASURE volume | WEIGHT ounces | grams |
|---|---|---|---|
| **ALMOND SHORTBREAD** | | | |
| blanched sliced almonds | ½ cup | 1.5 ounces | 42.5 grams |
| unsalted butter, cold | 10 tablespoons | 5 ounces | 142 grams |
| powdered sugar | 2 tablespoons | 0.88 ounce | 25 grams |
| granulated sugar | 2 tablespoons | 0.5 ounce | 14 grams |
| bleached all-purpose flour | 1 cup (measured by dip and sweep method) | 5 ounces | 142 grams |
| **CRAN-RASPBERRY TOPPING** | | | |
| 4 large egg yolks | 2 full fluid ounces | 2.5 ounces | 74 grams |
| sugar | 1½ teaspoons | 0.25 ounce | 6 grams |
| frozen cran-raspberry concentrate, defrosted but not reconstituted | ½ cup (measured after defrosting) | 5 ounces | 145 grams |
| unsalted butter, softened | 4 tablespoons | 2 ounces | 56 grams |
| salt | a pinch | | |
| liquid red food color (optional) | 10 drops | | |
| **OPTIONAL** | | | |
| fresh raspberries and mint leaves, for decoration | | | |

PREHEAT THE OVEN TO: 325°F.
BAKING TIME: 30 to 35 minutes
MAKES: 1½ dozen 2⅔-inch by
  1⅓-inch bars

EQUIPMENT: 8-inch square baking pan, bottom and 2 sides lined with an 8-inch by 16-inch strip of heavy-duty aluminum foil

*Place a rack in the middle of the oven. Preheat the oven to 325°F. (If using a Pyrex pan, preheat to 300°F.).*

## ALMOND SHORTBREAD

Place the almonds on a cookie sheet and toast for 5 to 10 minutes, stirring occasionally, until lightly browned. Cool completely.

## Food Processor Method

Cut the butter into 1-inch cubes, wrap and refrigerate them.

In a food processor with the metal blade, process the almonds and both sugars until the almonds are finely ground. Add the butter and pulse in until the sugar mixture is absorbed by the butter. Add the flour and pulse in until there are a lot of little moist crumbly pieces and no dry flour particles remain.

Dump the mixture into a plastic bag and press it together. Knead it lightly until it holds together. Remove it from the bag.

## Electric Mixer Method or by Hand

Soften the butter. Grate the almonds very fine.

In a medium bowl, whisk together the almonds and both sugars.

In a large bowl, cream the butter with the sugar mixture until light and fluffy. With an electric mixer or your fingers, mix in the flour until incorporated. If using a mixer, add the flour in 2 parts.

## Both Methods

Pat the dough evenly into the prepared pan. Use a fork to prick the dough all over. Bake 30 to 35 minutes or until the edges are lightly browned and the top is pale golden. (Do not brown.)

While the shortbread is baking, prepare the topping: Have a strainer suspended over a bowl ready near the stove.

In a heavy noncorrodible saucepan, beat the yolks and sugar with a wooden spoon until well blended. Stir in the concentrate, butter and salt. Cook over medium-low heat, stirring constantly, for about 6 minutes or until thickened. (An accurate candy thermometer* will register 180°F. to 185°F.) Do not allow the mixture to boil or it will curdle.

*The Cordon Rose candy thermometer is available through Dean & DeLuca (800-227-7714) and La Cuisine (800-521-1176).

If the mixture begins to steam, remove it briefly from the heat and stir. When thickened, remove it immediately from heat and strain. Press through a fine strainer with the back of spoon until only coarse residue remains in the strainer. Discard the residue. The topping mixture will be a dark peach color. For a deep rosy hue, stir in the optional food color.

When the shortbread is baked, pour the topping on it, spreading it with a spatula until even. Then continue baking for 5 minutes. Cool completely on a wire rack.

Run a small metal spatula between the sides of the pan and the pastry on the 2 sides without foil. Use the foil to lift out the shortbread and slide it onto a cutting surface. Use a long sharp knife to cut the shortbread first in thirds, then in half the other way. Then cut each half in thirds. Wipe the blade after each cut.

Garnish each bar, if desired with a fresh raspberry and 2 small mint leaves.

KEEPS: 3 days at room temperature, 3 weeks refrigerated (individually wrapped in plastic wrap, preferably Saran brand, to prevent drying), 3 months frozen.

POINTERS
FOR SUCCESS

• Blanched almonds are almonds with the dark peel removed. If you use unblanched, there will be dark bits of the peel in the shortbread, making it less attractive and slightly bitter. To blanch the almonds yourself, it is easier to start with whole almonds (1½ ounces of whole almonds = ¼ cup, instead of ½ cup). Simply boil them for a minute or 2 until the peels slip off easily.
• If using a food processor to grind the whole almonds, be sure to grate them first with the grating disc before processing them with the blade or they will get pasty despite processing with the sugar.

UNDERSTANDING

Butter softens faster if cut into pieces so that more surface area is exposed.

ROSE'S MELTING POT

# LEMON LOVELIES

These crisp buttery cookies are tangy with bits of dried apricot and lemon zest. They are tender yet sturdy enough to pack for a picnic. These are the treats I brought along for our morning of beach plum picking (see page 194). They'd also go well with Rosy Cran-Raspberry Butter Bars (page 300) and thin slices of Lemon and White Poppy Seed Surprise Cake (page 240) for an English tea.

| INGREDIENTS | MEASURE<br>volume | WEIGHT<br>ounces | grams |
|---|---|---|---|
| powdered sugar | ⅔ cup (lightly spooned into the cup) | 2.66 ounces | 77 grams |
| blanched slivered almonds, lightly toasted* | ¾ cup, divided | 3 ounces | 85 grams |
| unsalted butter | 16 tablespoons | 8 ounces | 227 grams |
| water | 2 tablespoons | | |
| pure vanilla extract | 2 teaspoons | | |
| pure lemon extract | 1 teaspoon | | |
| bleached all-purpose flour | 2 cups minus 2 tablespoons (lightly spooned into the cup) | 8 ounces | 227 grams |
| salt | ¼ teaspoon | | |
| lemon zest, finely grated (yellow portion of peel only) | 3 tablespoons | 0.63 ounce | 18 grams |
| ½ cup dried apricot halves, chopped | ⅓ cup chopped | 1.75 ounces | 50 grams |
| 1 2.75-ounce container yellow sugar crystals | about 6 tablespoons | 2.75 ounces | 78 grams |
| sugar | ½ cup | 3.5 ounces | 100 grams |

*Or ⅔ cup sliced almonds.

*(continued)*

CHILLING TIME: at least 2 hours
PREHEAT THE OVEN TO: 375°F.
BAKING TIME: 8 to 12 minutes
MAKES: about 3 dozen 2½-inch
  cookies

EQUIPMENT: nonstick or buttered
  cookie sheets

*Place 2 oven racks in the upper and lower third of the oven. Preheat oven to 375°F. at least 15 minutes before baking.*

## FOOD PROCESSOR METHOD

In a food processor with the metal blade, process the powdered sugar with ¼ cup of the almonds until the almonds are powder-fine. Cut the butter into about 6 pieces and add it with the motor running. Process until smooth and creamy. Scrape the sides of the bowl. Add the water, vanilla extract and lemon extract and process until incorporated. Add the flour and sprinkle the salt and lemon zest evenly on top. Pulse until the dough starts to clump together.

## ELECTRIC MIXER METHOD

Soften the butter. Grate ¼ cup of the nuts so that they are powder-fine.

In a medium bowl, whisk together the flour, grated nuts, salt and lemon zest.

In a mixing bowl, cream the powdered sugar and butter until light and fluffy. Beat in the water, vanilla extract, and lemon extract until well blended. Scrape the sides of the bowl. On low speed, beat in the flour mixture until incorporated.

## BOTH METHODS

Chop the remaining almonds coarsely. Stir them, together with the chopped apricots, into the cookie dough.

Scrape the dough into a bowl and refrigerate it for at least 2 hours or overnight.

Working with a small amount of the dough at a time, briefly knead it until it is malleable but still well chilled. Measure level tablespoons of dough and roll between the palms of your hands into 1-inch balls. Stir together the yellow and plain sugars and roll the balls in this mixture. Arrange them about 2 inches apart on the cookie sheets. Using a flat-bottomed tumbler, dipped in the sugar mixture, press each ball of dough flat into a 2-inch round.

Bake the cookies for 8 to 12 minutes or just until they barely begin to brown around the edges. Remove them to cookie sheets to cool completely.

STORE: In an airtight container, refrigerated or frozen.

KEEPS: About 1 month refrigerated, 3 months frozen.

UNDERSTANDING    Butter softens faster if cut into pieces so that more surface area is exposed.

# CHOCOLATE MEXICAN WEDDING CAKES

These most delicate of all cookies have always been among my favorite. Since chocolate and cinnamon are both very popular in Mexican cooking, I was inspired to create this exceptional variation of powdery bittersweet lightness dissolving to a pool of chocolate liquid. Serve these together with the Mexican Killer Kahlúa Chiffon Cake (page 233) for a Southwestern-style dinner party.

| INGREDIENTS | MEASURE<br>*volume* | WEIGHT<br>*ounces* | *grams* |
|---|---|---|---|
| pecan halves | ½ cup | 1.75 ounces | 50 grams |
| powdered sugar | 1 cup (lightly spooned into the cup) | 4 ounces | 115 grams |
| cocoa, preferably Dutch-processed | ⅓ cup (lightly spooned into the cup) | 1 ounce | 30 grams |
| salt | a pinch | | |
| unsalted butter | 1 cup | 8 ounces | 227 grams |
| pure vanilla extract | ½ teaspoon | | |
| bleached all-purpose flour | 1½ cups (lightly spooned into the cup) | 6.3 ounces | 180 grams |
| TOPPING | | | |
| powdered sugar | 1½ cups | 6 ounces | 172 grams |
| cinnamon | about 1 teaspoon | | |

CHILLING TIME: 1 to 3 hours
PREHEAT THE OVEN TO: 350°F.
BAKING TIME: 20 minutes
MAKES: about 4 dozen 2-inch cookies

EQUIPMENT: ungreased cookie sheets

*Place 2 oven racks in the upper and lower third of the oven. Preheat the oven to 350°F. at least 15 minutes before baking.*

Place the pecans on a cookie sheet and bake them, stirring occasionally, for 10 minutes or until lightly browned. Cool completely.

## FOOD PROCESSOR METHOD

In a food processor with the metal blade, process the sugar and cocoa with the pecans and salt until the pecans are powder-fine. Cut the butter into about 6 pieces and add it with the motor running. Process until smooth and creamy. Pulse in the vanilla, then scrape the sides of the bowl. Add the flour and pulse in until the dough starts to clump together.

## ELECTRIC MIXER METHOD

Soften the butter. Grate the nuts so that they are powder-fine.

In a medium bowl, whisk together the flour, powdered sugar, salt and grated nuts. In a mixing bowl, at low speed, cream the sugar and butter until light and fluffy. Beat in the vanilla extract, and scrape the sides of the bowl. Still on low speed, gradually beat in the flour mixture just until incorporated.

## BOTH METHODS

Scrape the dough into a bowl, cover it tightly and refrigerate it for at least 1 hour and preferably no longer than 3 hours.

Measure out the dough using a 1¼-inch ice cream scoop, or 1 scant tablespoon, and roll it between the well-floured palms of your hands to form 1-inch balls.

Place the balls 1½ inches apart on the cookie sheets. Bake for 20 minutes or until set. The tops will dull slightly and a small metal spatula can be slid underneath each cookie. For even baking, rotate the cookie sheets from top to bottom and front to back halfway through the baking period.

Cool the cookies on the sheets for 2 to 3 minutes. Use a small angled metal spatula or pancake turner to lift them from the sheets. Roll them in the powdered sugar while still hot to coat them heavily. Sprinkle lightly with cinnamon. Transfer the cookies to wire racks to cool completely.

*(continued)*

STORE: In an airtight container at room temperature.

KEEPS: About 1 month.

POINTERS
FOR SUCCESS

• Using a fine wire mesh tea strainer to sprinkle the cinnamon is like having a magic wand.

UNDERSTANDING

Butter softens faster if cut into pieces so that more surface area is exposed.

# BITTERSWEET FUDGE BROWNIES

(or Dark and Dirty Brownies)

These are the moistest, chocolateyest brownies ever (a true American obsession if ever there was one!) They contain both cocoa and chocolate and a secret ingredient for creamy smooth texture: cream cheese.

| INGREDIENTS<br>*room temperature* | MEASURE<br>*volume* | WEIGHT | |
| --- | --- | --- | --- |
| | | *ounces* | *grams* |
| pecan pieces or coarsely chopped pecans | 1½ cups | 6 ounces | 213 grams |
| unsalted butter | 14 tablespoons | 7 ounces | 200 grams |
| bittersweet chocolate, preferably Lindt Excellence, broken into squares | 1 3-ounce bar | 3 ounces | 85 grams |
| unsweetened cocoa, preferably Dutch-processed | ½ cup + 2 teaspoons (lightly spooned into the cup) | 1.75 ounces | 50 grams |
| sugar | 1 cup + 3 tablespoons | 8.25 ounces | 238 grams |
| 3 large eggs | 4.5 fluid ounces | 5.25 ounces (weighed without shells) | 150 grams |
| pure vanilla extract | 2 teaspoons | | |
| cream cheese | 1 3-ounce package | 3 ounces | 85 grams |
| all-purpose flour | ½ cup | 2.5 ounces | 71 grams |
| salt | a pinch | | |

*(continued)*

*Brownies.* According to legend, the brownie came into being by accident in the nineteenth century when a Yankee American cook was baking a chocolate cake. Supposedly, the cake would not rise because of an unreliable woodburning stove or a defective leavening agent. The cake turned out flat and heavy, but because chocolate was such an expensive commodity, the cook set the botched dessert aside to cool in the hope that it could somehow be salvaged. Upon tasting, it was discovered to be moist and chewy and turned out to be a big hit with the dinner guests. So the brownie was born. The name first appeared in print in an 1897 issue of the Sears Roebuck catalogue and most likely derived from its chocolate brown coloring. Almost immediately after its discovery, the brownie created a controversy among cooks as to what its proper consistency should be. Some felt that it should be light and airy (like a cake), while others argued that it should be dense, moist and chewy (like a cookie). No matter what camp they fall in, Americans have loved the brownie for years and still eagerly compete for the status of best brownie baker at local fairs, school bake sales and other social functions.

PREHEAT THE OVEN TO: 325°F.
BAKING TIME: 30 to 35 minutes
MAKES: 16 2-inch by 1-inch-high brownies

EQUIPMENT: 8-inch by 8-inch by 2-inch baking pan, preferably metal (if using a glass pan, lower the oven temperature by 25°F.), bottom and 2 sides lined with an 8-inch by 16-inch strip of aluminum foil and lightly sprayed with nonstick vegetable shortening or greased

*Place an oven rack in the middle of the oven. Preheat the oven to 325°F.*

Place the pecans on a cookie sheet and toast them, stirring occasionally, for about 10 minutes or until lightly browned. Cool completely.

In a medium saucepan or microwave-proof bowl, melt the butter and chocolate, stirring 2 or 3 times.

Pour the butter mixture into a mixing bowl and beat in the cocoa, then the sugar, beating until it is incorporated. Beat in the eggs and vanilla until incorporated. Beat in the cream cheese until only small bits remain. Add the flour and salt and mix only until the flour is fully moistened. Stir in the nuts. Scrape the batter into the prepared pan and spread it evenly.

Bake for 30 to 40 minutes or until the batter has set around the outside but is still moist and shiny in the center. A toothpick inserted 1 inch from the side will come out clean. Place the pan on a wire rack and cool completely.

Use a small metal spatula to loosen the brownies from the sides of the pan. Use the foil overhang to lift out the brownies. Use a long serrated knife to cut 2-inch squares. (First cut the brownies into quarters in one direction, then cut into quarters the other direction.)

STORE: Wrap each brownie in plastic wrap and store in an airtight container at room temperature, or in the refrigerator or freezer.

KEEPS: 1 week at room temperature, 1 month refrigerated, several months frozen.

# BLACK FOREST MARZIPAN AND CHERRY BROWNIES

My friend Brenda McDowell came up with this terrific idea for brownies for the marzipan lover. The almond paste blends with the chocolate, giving the brownies an exceptionally moist texture. The dried cherries soaked in kirsch add a luscious tanginess. These are the ultimate grown-up brownies.

| INGREDIENTS<br>room temperature | MEASURE<br>volume | WEIGHT | |
|---|---|---|---|
| | | ounces | grams |
| dried sour cherries, coarsely chopped | 6 tablespoons | 2 ounces | 59 grams |
| kirsch (cherry eau-de-vie) | 2 tablespoons | | |
| water | 2 tablespoons | | |
| almond paste,* well crumbled | ¾ cup (1 7-ounce package) | 7 ounces | 200 grams |
| unsalted butter, softened | 8 tablespoons | 4 ounces | 113 grams |
| sugar | 1 tablespoon | | 12.5 grams |
| 2 large eggs | 3 full fluid ounces | 3.5 ounces<br>(weighed without shells) | 100 grams |
| 1 large egg yolk | 1 tablespoon plus ½ teaspoon | 0.65 ounce | 18.6 grams |
| pure vanilla extract | ½ teaspoon | | |
| bleached all-purpose flour | ⅔ cup (lightly spooned into the cup) | 2.75 ounces | 80 grams |
| salt | a pinch | | |
| bittersweet chocolate, preferably Lindt Excellence, melted and cooled to tepid | 3 3-ounce bars | 9 ounces | 255 grams |

*Do not use marzipan, as it contains a lot more sugar.

(continued)

PREHEAT THE OVEN TO: 350°F.
  BAKING TIME: 25 to 30 minutes
  MAKES: 16 2-inch by 1-inch-high
  brownies

EQUIPMENT: 8-inch by 8-inch by
  2-inch baking pan, preferably
  metal (if using a glass pan, lower
  the oven temperature by 25°F.)
  bottom and 2 sides lined with an
  8-inch by 16-inch strip of
  aluminum foil and lightly sprayed
  with nonstick vegetable
  shortening or greased

*Place an oven rack in the middle of the oven. Preheat the oven to 350°F.*

In a small nonreactive saucepan, combine the cherries, kirsch and water and heat, stirring constantly, until very hot but not boiling (or place in a microwave-proof container and microwave for 45 seconds on high, stirring twice). Remove from the heat, cover and allow to sit for at least an hour or until most of the liquid is absorbed.

In a large mixing bowl, beat the almond paste, butter and sugar until smooth (1 minute on high speed if using a hand-held electric mixer). Beat in the eggs and yolk, one at a time, until incorporated. Beat in the vanilla. Add the flour and salt and mix only until the flour is fully moistened. Scrape the sides of the bowl. Scrape in the melted chocolate and beat until incorporated. Stir in the cherries and any remaining liquid. Scrape the batter into the prepared pan and spread it evenly.

Bake for 20 to 25 minutes or until the batter has just set. It will spring back only if lightly pressed 1 inch from the edge of pan. Place the pan on a wire rack and cool completely.

Use a small metal spatula to loosen the brownies from the sides of the pan. Use the foil overhang to lift out the brownies. Use a thin-bladed sharp knife to cut 2-inch squares. (First cut the brownies into quarters in one direction, then cut into quarters the other direction.)

STORE: Wrap each brownie in plastic wrap (preferably Saran brand) and store in an airtight container at room temperature, or in the refrigerator or freezer.

KEEPS: 1 week at room temperature, 1 month refrigerated, several months frozen.

UNDERSTANDING   Butter softens faster if cut into pieces so that more surface area is exposed.

# Brazilian Quindin Sweets (keendeen)

Lenore Battles has been my escort for practically every book tour I have had in San Francisco. We have experienced many good times and adventures together, including the earthquake of '89, and love the opportunity to catch up on each other's lives each tour as we drive around the Bay Area to book signings, appearances and interviews. On my last trip to San Francisco, when Lenore, in her deeply mellow, slightly husky, altogether seductive alto, told me that she was preparing to make quindin, I was intrigued by the very delicious sound of the word.

Lenore described this North Brazilian little candy/cookie as a very rich, very yellow, creamy blend of egg yolk, sugar and butter with a macaroon-like bottom of coconut. She had discovered them on one of her trips to Brazil, where she has been an award winner at the annual exotic costume contest, for which she prepares for the entire year.

When I asked how long the quindin keep, Lenore said she had no idea because they never were around for more than a few hours—they are that delicious. I suggested that lemon zest might be a pleasant addition to temper the richness a bit but after trying one, then quickly a second one, from the batch Lenore made, decided the creamy, sticky, chewy quindin were perfect just as they were. When Lenore sent me the recipe she added a note that she had tried the lemon zest and they were great that way too. All I can say is, if ever there was an exotic erotic cookie that fully lived up to its description, this is it.

| INGREDIENTS | MEASURE | WEIGHT | |
| --- | --- | --- | --- |
| | *volume* | *ounces* | *grams* |
| unsweetened grated coconut* | 1 ½ cups | 4.5 ounces | 128 grams |
| sugar | 1 cup | 7 ounces | 200 grams |
| lemon zest, finely grated (yellow portion of peel only, from 4 lemons) | 2 tablespoons | 0.50 ounce | 12 grams |
| unsalted butter, softened | 8 tablespoons | 4 ounces | 113 grams |
| 9 large egg yolks | ⅔ liquid cup | 5.75 ounces | 167 grams |

*Available in health food stores, or use freshly grated (4.25 ounces/118 grams).

(*continued*)

PREHEAT THE OVEN TO: 350°F.
BAKING TIME: 20 to 25 minutes
MAKES: about 36 quindin

EQUIPMENT: 3 *nonstick*, mini-muffin tins, well sprayed with nonstick vegetable shortening (my favorite shape is 2 inches wide at the top and ¾ inches deep) and 3 pans large enough to serve as water baths

Place the grated coconut in a medium bowl.

## FOOD PROCESSOR METHOD

In a food processor, place the sugar and lemon zest and process for about 30 seconds or until the sugar and lemon zest are in very fine particles. Add the softened butter and pulse to combine it. With the motor running, gradually add the egg yolks. Process for about 20 seconds, scraping down the sides as necessary. The mixture will be a very pale yellow.

## MIXER METHOD

In a mixer bowl, place the sugar, lemon zest and butter and mix on medium speed until well combined. Gradually beat in the egg yolks, then raise the speed to high and beat about 3 minutes or until pale yellow, scraping the sides of the bowl partway through beating.

## BOTH METHODS

Scrape the mixture over the coconut and stir to blend evenly. Using a level measuring tablespoon, fill each muffin cup about three-quarters full. Or use a quart-size heavy duty zip-seal bag (with one corner cut) as a piping bag.

Place the muffin tins in the large pans. Stagger them in the oven so that air can circulate around the pans, and pour in hot water to come partway up the sides of the muffin tins.

Bake for about 30 minutes or until the quindin are pale golden and firm when pressed lightly on top with a finger. Cool for 5 minutes. Use a small metal spatula to run around the sides of each quindin and pop it out. Cool completely and store in an airtight container, refrigerated, if keeping longer than one day.

NOTE: If the quindin are slightly undercooked, they won't keep their shape as well, but the extra creaminess is even more delicious to my taste.

KEEPS: 2 weeks refrigerated, 3 months frozen.

- Although you can make quindin without nonstick pans, it is exceptionally tedious unmolding them because of the sticky coconut.
- If you run short and leave some of the muffin tins unfilled, be sure to add a little water to the unfilled cavities for even baking.
- If you only have 1 or 2 pans, the quindin can be baked in batches.

# CANDIED GRAPEFRUIT PEELS CHANTERELLE

I tasted these refreshingly succulent after-dinner candied grapefruit peels at David and Karen Waltuck's restaurant Chanterelle several years ago and was delighted and intrigued because most candied citrus peels are dry. The chef's secret was leaving a thin layer of pulp on each strip of skin.

These are delicious made with any grapefruit peel, but the ruby grapefruit results in a dreamy peach-orange hue.

| INGREDIENTS room temperature | MEASURE volume | WEIGHT ounces | grams |
|---|---|---|---|
| 1 large grapefruit, preferably ruby | | 12 ounces | 340 grams |
| ½ teaspoon salt | | | |
| sugar | 1 cup | 7 ounces | 200 grams |

MAKES: about 30 slices

Cut the grapefruit into 8 wedges. With a grapefruit knife or sharp paring knife, cut away the peel, leaving ⅛ inch of pulp attached. (Reserve the pulp for another use.)

Cut the wedges of peel lengthwise into ½-inch slices.

Place the slices in a saucepan and cover with cold water. Bring the water to a boil. Add the salt and continue boiling for 5 minutes.

*(continued)*

DESSERTS

315

Drain and rinse the grapefruit peels; cover again with fresh cold unsalted water and bring to a second boil. Boil for 5 minutes. Drain, rinse and repeat boiling with fresh unsalted water. Drain well.

In a large skillet, lay the grapefruit peels in a single layer and sprinkle with ½ cup of the sugar. Cook uncovered over very low heat for 30 minutes, stirring occasionally, until translucent and all of the syrup has been absorbed.

Dry the grapefruit peels on a metal rack for 1 to 1½ hours. They should be quite dry so they will absorb less sugar and retain a crunchy surface but still be succulent.

Roll each peel in the remaining ½ cup of sugar until coated on all sides. Serve at once or layer between wax paper and refrigerate.

STORE: Refrigerated

KEEPS: Up to 2 days, but the flavor is best if served the same day.

POINTERS
FOR SUCCESS

• Select grapefruits with thick rinds. The lighter the fruit, the thicker the rind. Also, fruit with pointier ends as opposed to rounded ends tends to have thicker peel.
• Oranges or lemons may be substituted for grapefruit.
• A few drops of yellow food coloring added during the third boil will enhance the color.

UNDERSTANDING

Boiling the peels in several changes of water removes the bitterness.

ROSE'S MELTING POT

# BEVERAGES

# LASSI

I adore this refreshing, slightly tangy, yogurt drink with or without spicy food. It is particularly suited to spicy food, though, because dairy products are most effective in dissolving and soothing the chili pepper's fire on the tongue. In Indian restaurants, you will find lassi in many varieties, often including mango, but the two basic lassis are plain salt or plain sweet. Here I have created a combination of the two which is my preference. I garnish it with my favorite spice, cardamom. I prefer not to mix it through so I can have the fresh dairy taste of the yogurt and then just a hint of the fragrant spice from time to time.

Lassi will be most appreciated with Tandoori Chicken (page 126) and Ethiopian Doro Wat (page 131).

| INGREDIENTS | MEASURE | WEIGHT | |
| cold | volume | ounces | grams |
| --- | --- | --- | --- |
| low-fat yogurt | 2 liquid cups | 18 ounces | 510 grams |
| very cold water | 2 liquid cups | | |
| sugar | 1 tablespoon | 0.5 ounce | 12 grams |
| salt | ¼ teaspoon | | |
| 3 ice cubes | standard size | | |
| 5 cardamom pods, husked and crushed* | ¼ teaspoon | | |
| OPTIONAL: 6 sprigs of fresh mint | | | |

MAKES: 4 tall 10-ounce drinks

Place all the ingredients except the cardamom and mint in a blender container and blend on high speed for about 30 seconds or until the ice is crushed and the liquid is very frothy. Pour it into glasses and garnish with sprinkles of cardamom and fresh mint leaves if desired.

*Use a mortar and pestle or a coffee or spice grinder.

---

*Lassi.* Indians often drink lassi, a yogurt drink, with meals because it beautifully counterbalances the zip of spicy dishes. The three most prevalent flavors are sweet, salty-mint and fruit. Before serving, it is common to pour lassi between two glasses to produce a frothy head, a large part of the appeal of this "milk shake."

---

# RASPBERRY PEACH SANGRIA

I can't remember ever having paella without its accompanying wine punch, sangria. For us it's a tradition. Of course sangria also makes a great party or cocktail hour drink and is an excellent accompaniment to cold poached fish.

The raspberries in this unusual version perfume the wine in a lush and lovely way. The Grand Marnier, which replaces the usual brandy, accentuates the fruity flavors. This sangria is hard to top.

With this glorious punch, Party Paella (page 89) and Spanish Creamy Caramel Flan (page 279), you have the makings of a fine dinner party.

| INGREDIENTS | MEASURE | WEIGHT | |
| --- | --- | --- | --- |
| | *volume* | *ounces* | *grams* |
| **SANGRIA** | | | |
| 4 large peaches, unpeeled, pitted and cut into ½-inch dice | 4 cups | 28 ounces diced | 794 grams |
| 1 pint of raspberries | 2½ cups | 12 ounces | 340 grams |
| Grand Marnier | ½ liquid cup | | |
| sugar | ¼ cup | 1.75 ounces | 50 grams |
| Rioja or other light, dry red wine, chilled | 2 750 milliliter bottles | | |

MAKES: 3 quarts (16 6-ounce servings)

In a medium bowl, toss the peaches, raspberries, Grand Marnier and sugar. Cover and refrigerate for at least 4 hours.

Place the fruit mixture in a pitcher. Pour in the red wine and stir well. Serve over ice.

KEEPS: 8 hours, covered and chilled.

NOTE: For an attractively festive presentation, serve the sangria in a punch bowl with an ice ring.

ICE RING

| | | |
| --- | --- | --- |
| 1 bottle of distilled water, cold | about 1 quart | |
| fresh raspberries, fresh mint leaves, for garnish | 1 cup total | |

MAKE AHEAD: Several hours or up to several days ahead, prepare the optional ice ring

EQUIPMENT: 4- to 6-cup ring or heart mold for optional ice ring

Several hours or up to several days ahead, pour about ½ inch of the water into the mold and freeze it. When the water is almost completely frozen, arrange the raspberries and mint leaves in the mold, pressing them gently into the ice. Add enough of the water to come about halfway up the sides of the berries but not enough to float them. Return to the freezer until the berries and mint are frozen into position. Then add the remaining water and freeze.

To unmold, dip the bottom of the mold into cold water for a few moments and invert it onto a clean plate. Slide it into the punch bowl.

UNDERSTANDING

Distilled water results in a clearer, less cloudy ice. If substituting tap water, be sure to allow it to sit in the refrigerator for at least an hour to help to prevent cloudiness.

# ELLIOTT'S INSTANT-GRATIFICATION SUMMER MARGARITAS

This classic Mexican drink is our traditional summer cocktail, alternating with an occasional gin and tonic. Elliott mixes margaritas by the half-gallon so there's always plenty on hand in the refrigerator for impromptu summer guests. We like our margaritas very limey, icy cold and on-the-rocks without salt. Elliott prefers using the lime concentrate because the flavor of fresh limes vary whereas the concentrate is more standardized. The daiquiri mix is used primarily for the dried egg whites it contains, which contribute body. And we both prefer the more orangy Triple Sec to the traditional Cointreau.

*(continued)*

| INGREDIENTS | MEASURE | WEIGHT | |
|---|---|---|---|
| | *volume* | *ounces* | *grams* |
| frozen limeade concentrate, thawed | 1½ liquid cups<br>(1 12-ounce can) | | |
| water | 3 liquid cups<br>(2 12-ounce cans) | | |
| 6 packages of dry daiquiri mix* | | 3.3 ounces | 95 grams |
| Tequila | 1¾ liquid cups | | |
| Triple Sec | 7 fluid ounces (14 tablespoons) | | |
| OPTIONAL: freshly squeezed lime juice or powdered sugar | to taste | | |
| 2 limes, cut into eighths | | | |

MAKES: 64 ounces (16 4-ounce servings)

In a 2-quart bottle or jug, combine all the ingredients, except the optional lime juice and powdered sugar and limes, in the order given. Close the container tightly and shake well to mix thoroughly. Add the optional lime juice or powdered sugar to taste, depending on whether you prefer a more limey or sweeter drink. Refrigerate.

To serve, shake well. Garnish each drink with a fresh lime wedge. I like to squeeze the lime into the drink to add extra lime flavor.

KEEPS: Refrigerated, for months.

NOTE: If you add the fresh lime juice or powdered sugar to taste, take small tastes or you will lose objectivity quickly!

*Or 2 to 3 tablespoons of Frothee or the whites from about 4 large eggs, added before the alcohol.

# SOURCES FOR SPECIALTY AND ETHNIC INGREDIENTS

Most likely your hometown has many resources for ethnic foods. Exploring these ethnic markets can be an adventure in itself. Prices for ethnic ingredients are usually lowest at the source where the people of that culture shop. Begin by checking the Yellow Pages or asking the chefs in ethnic restaurants.

Here are three excellent sources that carry a diversity of ingredients and will mail throughout the country:

Adriana's Bazaar, 2152 Broadway, New York, NY 10023 (212-877-5757). (If you send a self-addressed stamped envelope they will provide a free catalogue.)

Dean & DeLuca, 560 Broadway, New York, NY 10012 (212-431-1691; outside New York: 800-227-7714, Monday–Friday, 9A.M.–5P.M.)

Sultan's Delight, PO Box 090302, Brooklyn, NY 11209 (718-745-6844; out of Brooklyn: 800-852-5046). (If you send a self-addressed stamped envelope, they will provide a free catalogue.)

# INDEX

Chicken skin, fried (gribonyes),
26–27
Chinese dishes:
authentic zingy red shrimp,
98–100, *99*
-style honey mustard lamb
riblets, *30,* 31–32, *32*
Chinon, 43
Chipotle pasta:
fresh, 84–85
shrimp and squid, 81–83, *82–
83*
*Chirashi sushi,* Japanese, *see*
Japanese *chirashi sushi*
Chocolate:
buttercream filling and
frosting, 257, 259
cake, 264, 267, 272
cookie dough, bittersweet,
296, 297–298
Mexican wedding cakes, 306–
308
*pots de crème,* 288–289
snowflake topping, 278
"Choola" (wood- or coal-
burning stove), 126
Cinnamon ganache, dense, 250,
251–252, 255
City Baker (New York City),
294
Claiborne, Craig, 89
Clam(s):
littleneck vs. cherrystones,
93
opening, 80
sauce, spicy linguine and, *78,*
79–80, *80*
Clarified butter, 111*n,* 181*n*
spiced (*niter kebbeh*), 132, 133–
134
Classic American lemon-lime
mold, 186–187
Classic challah, 56–62, *59–62*
Classic chicken cacciatore
piccante, 135–137
Classic orange buttercream,
250–253, 255
Coconut, Brazilian *quindin*
sweets, 313–315
Coffee glaze, 236
Colaiace, Anna, 47
Colby, L. S., 131

Cold garlicky Mediterranean
mussels, 20–23, *21*
Compote, rhubarb, 188, *189*
Cookies, 300–308
Brazilian *quindin* sweets, 313–
315
chocolate Mexican wedding
cakes, 306–308
lemon lovelies, 303–305
rosy cran-raspberry butter
bars, 300–302
Cornmeal, polenta, 173–175
Corriher, Archie, 103
Corriher, Shirley, 67, 68, 103
*Coulibiac, see* Russian Rivers
salmon pie
Couscous and egg filling, 111,
115
Crab(s):
East Coast soft-shell, 94–95
salad sandwiches, 229
whipped, 246, 249, 284, 286
Cream sauce, mustard dill,
mussels in, 86, 87–88
*Crème caramel* (Spanish creamy
caramel flan), 279–282
Crêpe(s), 118
dill, 111, 114–115
noodles, egg, 104, 105–106
Cucumber *raita,* 190–191
Currant and bulgur stuffing,
mideastern, 176–177
Custard:
chocolate *pots de crème,* 288–289
Spanish creamy caramel flan
(*crème caramel*), 279–282


**D**

Dacquoise, 251, 253–254, 256
Dairy dinner crown challah, 63–
66
Dark ganache, 264, 272
Dawes, Peter, 162
*Death by Chocolate* (Desaulniers),
288
*Demi-glace,* 208
Dense cinnamon ganache, 250,
251–252, 255
Desaulniers, Marcel, 4, 288
Desserts, 231–316

bittersweet fudge brownies,
308–311, *309*
Black Forest marzipan and
cherry brownies, 311–312
Brazilian *quindin* sweets, 313–
315
candied grapefruit peels
Chanterelle, 315–316
chocolate *pots de crème,* 288–
289
fruit jewel tarts, 294–299,
*295*
green tea ice cream, *290,*
291–292
green tea pine needles, 293–
294
hot fudge sundae, 283–287
lemon lovelies, 303–305
rosy cran-raspberry butter
bars, 300–302
Spanish creamy caramel flan
(*crème caramel*), 279–282
tiramisù, 275–278
*see also* cakes
Dijon mustard, salmon steak
with black mustard grains
and, 108–109
Dill:
crêpes, 111, 114–115
mustard cream, mussels in,
*86,* 87–88
*Dolmadakia* (stuffed grape
leaves), 16–19, *18*
*Doro wat,* Ethiopian, *see*
Ethiopian *doro wat*
Dough, bittersweet chocolate
cookie, 296, 297–298
Drunken bluefish with stewed
tomatoes, 96–97
Duck, perfect crisp roast, 140–
143, *141*


**E**

East Coast soft-shell crabs, 94–
95
Egg(s):
and couscous filling, 111, 115
crêpe noodles, 104, 105–106
glaze, 111
hard-cooked, 111*n,* 133*n*

Hungarian Dobos torte, 256–
    262, *260, 262*
    assembling, 261
    cake, 257–258
    caramel glaze, 257, 258–259
    chocolate buttercream filling
        and frosting, 257, 259

## I

Ice cream:
    green tea, *290,* 291–292
    hot fudge sundae, 283–287
    triple vanilla lover's, 283–287
Icing, royal, 263, 266
Indian dishes:
    *lassi,* 319
    pistachio saffron pilaf, 181–
        183, *182*
    *raita,* 190–191
    tandoori chicken, 126–130,
        *127, 130*
*Injera,* 132
Italian dishes:
    classic chicken cacciatore
        piccante, 135–137
    fried Sicilian artichokes, 14–
        15
    late-summer pesto, 70–73, *71*
    pig-out spaghetti carbonara,
        75–77
    spicy linguine and clam
        sauce, *78,* 79–80, *80*
    tiramisù, 275–278

## J

Japanese *chirashi sushi,* 101–107,
    *102*
    egg crêpe noodles, 104–106
    marinated shiitakes, 103, 105
    seafood, 104, 106–107
    sesame seeds, 104, 107
    vinegared *sushi* rice, 103,
        104–105
Jell-O, classic American lemon-
    lime mold, 186–187
Jewish dishes:
    Bar Mitzvah cake, 263–274,
        *268–271*

classic challah, 56–62, *59–62*
dairy dinner crown challah,
    63–66
deli smoked tongue, 156–157
Friday night roast chicken
    with paprika, 123–125
no-compromise old-country
    chopped liver, 28–29
perfect *pitcha* (calf's foot
    jelly), 23–26
very best luchshon kugel,
    184–185
Justice, Elizabeth, 51

## K

Kahlúa, 236
    chiffon cake, Mexican killer,
        *232,* 233–236, *236*
Kamman, Madeleine, 43
*Kasha,* 179
    *varnishkes* (buckwheat groats
        with bowtie noodles), 177–
        180, *178*
Kashruth laws, 25, 63
Kosher salt, xiv
Kugel, 184
    very best luchshon (noodle
        pudding), 184–186

## L

*Ladies' Home Journal,* 149
Lamb:
    with prune glaze, Grandma
        Sarah's, *152,* 153–155
    riblets, barbecued, 32
    riblets, Chinese-style honey
        mustard, *30,* 31–32, *32*
*Lassi,* 319
Late-summer pesto, 70–73, *71*
Lebanese spinach, 171
Lemon(y):
    hollandaise sauce, extra-,
        204–205
    -lime mold, classic American,
        186–187
    lovelies, 303–305
    pancakes with raspberry
        butter, light, 219–220

poppy seed buttermilk
    pancakes, 221–222
and white poppy seed surprise
    cake, 240–243, *241*
Lentil salad, spicy, 172–173
Light lemon pancakes with
    raspberry butter, 219–220
Light pumpernickel bread, 55
Light whipped ganache, 250,
    252, 255
Lima beans:
    bistro-style pork chops with,
        146–147
    fresh, 146*n,* 147
    frozen, 146, 147
Lime-lemon mold, classic
    American, 186–187
Linguine and clam sauce, spicy,
    *78,* 79–80, *80*
Liver, no-compromise old-
    country chopped, 28–29
Lobster:
    cooking, 229–230
    female, 93
    salad sandwiches, 229
Lubovichers, 124
Luchshon kugel, 184

## M

McDowell, Brenda, 311
Maestro, Laura, 245
Main courses, 69–160
    capon with savory bulgur
        stuffing, 137–140
    Grandma Sarah's lamb with
        prune glaze, *152,* 153–
        155
    grilled smoky turkey, 143–
        145
    perfect crisp roast duck, 140–
        143, *141*
    *see also* Beef main dishes;
        Chicken main dishes; Pasta
        main dishes; Pork main
        dishes; Seafood main
        dishes
Margaritas, Elliott's instant-
    gratification summer, 321–
    322
Marinated shiitakes, 103, 105

Spiced clarified butter (*niter kebbeh*), 132, 133–134
Spicy lentil salad, 172–173
Spicy linguine and clam sauce, *78*, 79–80, *80*
Spicy Southern fried chicken, *120*, 121–123
Spinach:
  Lebanese, 171
  pesto, 73
Squid, shrimp and chipotle pasta, 81–83, *82–83*
Steamed asparagus, 170
Stew, Ethiopian chicken, *see* Ethiopian *doro wat*
Stock(s):
  capon, 138–139
  *glace de viande* (homemade beef essence), 205–208
  *glace de volaille* (homemade poultry essence), 209–212
Stoves, Indian cooking and, 126
Strawberries, Day Neutrals, 294, 296
Stuffed grape leaves (*dolmadakia*), 16–19, *18*
Stuffing:
  mideastern bulgur and currant, 176–177
  savory bulgur, capon with, 137–140
Sundae, *see* Hot fudge sundae
*Sushi*:
  development and description of, 103
  *see also* Japanese *chirashi sushi*
Sweet bread, Portuguese, 47–50
Swiss rösti potatoes, 165–167

T

Tandoori chicken, 126–130, *127*, *130*
Tandoori stove, 126
Tarts, fruit jewel, 294–299, *295*
Tcheng, Chingwan, 98
Tea, green:
  ice cream, *290*, 291–292
  pine needles, 293–294

Tequila, in Elliott's instant-gratification summer margaritas, 321–322
Tiramisù, 275–278
  chocolate snowflake topping for, 278
Tomato(es):
  peeling of, 75
  stewed, drunken bluefish with, 96–97
Tomato sauce, summer garden fresh spaghetti with, 73–75
Tongue, Jewish deli smoked, 156–157
Topping:
  chocolate snowflake, 278
  cran-raspberry, 300, 302
Torte, *see* Hungarian Dobos torte
Touraine, 43
Trellis, French roasted garlic soup, 4–6
Trellis Restaurant, The, (Williamsburg, Va.), 4
Triple vanilla lover's ice cream, 283–287
Turkey, grilled smoky, 143–145

U

Ultimate BLT (on black pepper brioche), 223–230, *224–225*

V

Vanilla lover's ice cream, triple, 283–287
Vegetable side dishes, 162–171
  *gratin de pommes de terre* (scalloped potatoes), 168–169
  Lebanese spinach, 171
  mashed potatoes with caramelized pears, 162–164, *163*
  steamed asparagus, 170
  Swiss rösti potatoes, 165–167
Velouté, 110, 114
Very best luchshon kugel (noodle pudding), 184–186

Viazzi, Alfredo, 70
Vinaigrette, raspberry walnut, endive and walnut salad with, 196–197
Vincent's (Scottsdale, Ariz.), 81
Vinegar, raspberry, 197, 201
Vinegared *sushi* rice, 103, 104–105
*Voyage to Russia, A* (Justice), 51

W

Walnut:
  and endive salad with raspberry walnut vinaigrette, 196–197
  *fougasse*, 43–46, *44*
  raspberry vinaigrette, endive and walnut salad with, 196–197
Walnut oil, 46
Waltuck, David and Karen, 315
Wasabi, soy, avocado with, 7–9, *8*
Waters, Alice, 43
Weber grill, 143–144
Weights and measures, xiii–xiv
Whipped cream, 246, 249, 284, 286
White chocolate ganache, 296, 298–299
Wild rice, 155
Willinger, Faith, 77
Wine, red, in raspberry peach sangria, 320–321
Wonder Bread, 215, 216

Y

Yeast:
  potato (potato water) and, 50
  proofing, 117
Yiddish, 184
Yogurt
  *lassi*, 319
  *raita*, 190–191
Yorkshire popovers, 66–68
  herbed, 68

## A Sampling of Other Ethnic Books of Interest

Anderson, Jean. *The Food of Portugal.* New York: William Morrow and Company, 1989.

Barer-Stein. *You Are What You Eat: A Study of Ethnic Food Traditions.* Toronto: McClelland and Stewart, 1979.

Bayless, Rick and Deann. *Authentic Mexican.* New York: William Morrow and Company, 1986.

Bugialli, Giuliano. *The Fine Art of Italian Cooking.* New York: Random House, 1990.

Casas, Penelope. *The Foods of Spain.* New York: Alfred A. Knopf, 1982.

Darby, William J. et al. *Food: The Gift of Osiris.* Vols. 1 & 2. London: Academic Books, 1976.

Derecskey, Susan. *The Hungarian Cookbook.* New York: HarperCollins, 1987.

Devi, Yamuna. *The Art of Indian Vegetarian Cooking.* New York: E. P. Dutton, 1987.

Egerton, John. *Southern Food: At Home, On the Road, In History.* New York: Alfred A. Knopf, 1987.

Fussell, Betty. *The Story of Corn.* New York: Alfred A. Knopf, 1992.

Goldstein, Joyce. *Back to Square One.* New York: William Morrow and Company, 1992.

Grier, Anne Lindsey. *Foods of the Sun.* New York: Harper & Row, 1988.

Harris, Jessica B. *Tasting Brazil.* New York: Macmillan, 1992.

Harris, Lloyd J. *The Book of Garlic.* Berkeley, California: Aris Books, 1971.

Hazan, Marcella. *Essentials of Classic Italian Cooking.* New York: Alfred A. Knopf, 1992.

Jaffrey, Madhur. *An Invitation to Indian Cooking.* New York: Alfred A. Knopf, 1973.

Jones, Judith and Evan. *The L. L. Bean Book of New New England Cookery.* New York: Random House, 1987.

Kamman, Madeleine. *When French Women Cook.* New York: Atheneum, 1982.

Kasper, Lynne Rossetto. *The Splendid Table.* New York: William Morrow and Company, 1992.

Kirchner, Bharti. *The Healthy Cuisine of India.* Los Angeles: Lowell House, 1992.

Kochilas, Diane. *The Food and Wine of Greece.* New York: E. P. Dutton, 1987.

Lang, George. *The Cuisine of Hungary.* New York: Outlet Book Co., 1990.

Lang, Jenifer Harvey, ed. *Larousse Gastronomique.* New York: Crown Publishers, 1988.

Leonard, Leah H. *Jewish Cookery.* New York: Crown Publishers, 1949.

Levy, Faye. *Faye Levy's International Jewish Cookbook.* New York: Warner Books, 1991.

Lin, Florence. *Florence Lin's Complete Book of Chinese Noodles, Dumplings, and Breads.* New York: William Morrow and Company, 1986.

London, Anne, and Bishov, Bertha K. *The Complete American-Jewish Cookbook.* New York: Harper-Collins, 1971.

Martinez, Zarela. *Food from My Heart.* New York: Macmillan, 1992.

McGee, Harold. *On Food and Cooking: The Science and Lore of the Kitchen.* New York: Charles Scribner's Sons, 1984.

Middione, Carlo. *The Food of Southern Italy.* New York: William Morrow and Company, 1987.

Molokhovets, Elena. *Classic Russian Cooking.* Bloomington: Indiana University Press, 1992.

Nathan, Joan. *The Jewish Holiday Kitchen.* New York: Schocken Books, 1988.

Richie, Donald. *A Taste of Japan.* New York: Kodansha International, 1985.

Sahni, Julie. *Classic Indian Cooking.* New York: William Morrow and Company, 1980.

Style, Sue. *A Taste of Switzerland.* New York: Hearst Books, 1992.

Toussant-Samat, Maguelonne. *A History of Food.* Cambridge: Blackwell, 1992.

Tropp, Barbara. *The Modern Art of Chinese Cooking*. New York: William Morrow and Company, 1982.

Volokh, Anne. *The Art of Russian Cooking*. New York: Collier Books, 1987.

Von Bremzen, Anya, and Welchman, John. *Please to the Table*. New York: Workman Publishing Co., 1990.

Wheaton, Barbara K. *Savoring the Past: The French Kitchen and Table from 1300 to 1789*. Philadelphia: University of Pennsylvania Press, 1983.

Wolfert, Paula. *World of Food*. New York: Harper & Row, 1988.

Zeidler, Judy. *The Gourmet Jewish Cook*. New York: William Morrow and Company, 1988.

# ABOUT THE AUTHOR

Rose Levy Beranbaum has her B.S. and M.A. cum laude in food science and culinary arts. In addition to continuing her studies at many of the world's leading cooking schools, she has also studied art and design at the Fashion Institute of Technology in New York City. Rose has received accreditation from the International Association of Culinary Professionals as a food writer and a teacher.

A frequent contributor to all the major food magazines and *The New York Times*, she also writes a syndicated food column for the Los Angeles Times Syndicate and is a consultant to the baking and chocolate industries. In 1992 and 1993 Rose was national spokesperson for the United Dairy Industries Association. For ten years she was owner and director of the Cordon Rose Cooking School in New York City.

Rose is the author of the best-selling *The Cake Bible*, 1988, winner of the IACP/Seagram Book of the Year and the National Association for the Specialty Food Trade Showcase Award for the cookbook that has contributed most toward the education of the consumer of specialty foods. An Anglicized version of *The Cake Bible* was published in the United Kingdom in early 1992.

Rose translated from the French and adapted *A Passion for Chocolate*, 1989, winner of the IACP/Seagram Best Book of the Year in the Dessert and Baking Category. In 1990, she published *Rose's Christmas Cookies*, winner of the James Beard Best Book in the Dessert and Baking Category. *Rose's Celebrations*, her first book to include favorite home cooking as well as baking, was published in the fall of 1992.

Rose is currently working on *The Pastry Bible*.